SELF-FULFILLMENT

SELF-FULFILLMENT

Alan Gewirth

PRINCETON UNIVERSITY PRESS   PRINCETON, NEW JERSEY

Library of Congress Cataloging-in-Publication Data
Gewirth, Alan.
Self-fulfillment / Alan Gewirth.
p. cm.
Includes index.
ISBN 0-691-05976-4 (alk. paper)
1. Self-realization.   I. Title.
BJ1470.G48   1998
171′.3—dc21   98-5127   CIP

This book has been composed in Galliard

Princeton University Press books are printed
on acid-free paper and meet the guidelines for
permanence and durability of the Committee on
Production Guidelines for Book Longevity
of the Council on Library Resources

http://pup.princeton.edu

Printed in the United States of America

1   3   5   7   9   10   8   6   4   2

For Jeanie

Contents

IF I WERE TO SAY that I have tried to fulfill myself by writing this book, I could be accused of contradicting one of my main theses: that self-fulfillment, like happiness, is attained not by being directly aimed at but rather as a by-product of one's dedicated pursuit of other purposes. But just as I have suggested qualifications of that thesis at various points in this book, so I also express my hope that the reader will share with me the awareness I have acquired of the great importance, complexity, and fascination of the ideal of self-fulfillment. The ideal's prominence has waxed and waned at various periods of human history; but the present age has taken it up anew as a prime object of human striving, as a value that gives zest and meaning to the lives of the persons who adopt it as a central aim of their activities and aspirations. If this aim is to be success-ful, it must be conceived as an accompaniment or consequence of spe-cific projects, such as, in my own case, the writing of this book.

My purpose in this book is to give a detailed analysis of the ideal of self-fulfillment. The analysis is not only conceptual but also normative: I have tried to assess the value of what I have taken to be the main modes of self-fulfillment. The assessment has involved an appeal to rational cri-teria whose contents and relevance I have sought to elucidate in a sys-tematic way. In each of the two modes of self-fulfillment that I discuss, which I call "aspiration-fulfillment" and "capacity-fulfillment," I have presented their strong points but also their problematic features. Espe-cially in connection with capacity-fulfillment I have invoked moral prin-ciples whose rational justification I have worked out more fully else-where, especially in *Reason and Morality* (1978). The present book can, however, be understood independently of the earlier one.

In recent years many philosophers have written books on well-being, perfectionism, the examined life, the good life, and related topics. Amid the many merits of these books, my present one differs from them in several ways. I draw and elaborate much more explicitly the above-mentioned distinction between aspiration-fulfillment and capacity-ful-fillment. And I work out the process and contents of capacity-fulfillment through its relations to three kinds of morality, which I call "universal-ist," "personalist," and "particularist." In contrast to some recent philo-sophical attempts to downgrade morality as an essential value of human life, I have argued that self-fulfillment in its various phases is indissolubly bound up with one or another of these kinds of morality. I have tried through these distinctions to give a somewhat fuller and more critical elaboration of the many forms that self-fulfillment can take.

One of my main emphases in this book is that self-fulfillment has not only an individual but also an important social dimension. The kind of society in which one lives affects strongly the character of the self-fulfillment that persons can achieve. In my previous book, *The Community of Rights* (1996), I have discussed in some detail the economic and social rights that should undergird a society that provides equal opportunities for self-fulfillment. The present book incorporates the essential part of the argument for these rights. But I also try to show how the freedom and well-being that constitute the generic objects of the rights provide the bases for some of the main kinds of self-fulfillment. The ideal is thereby shown to have a quite specific foundation in the principle of universalist morality.

I gratefully acknowledge the help I have received in my work on this book. My fellowship from the National Endowment for the Humanities gave valuable support, as did another research grant made available to me by Dean Philip Gossett of the Division of the Humanities at the University of Chicago. Faculty seminars and workshops at the University of Chicago on practical reason, contemporary political philosophy, law and philosophy, and related subjects have enriched my background knowledge. My early mentor, Richard McKeon, provided an eminent model for understanding the rich diversities of historical philosophical traditions. Three of my contemporary Chicago colleagues have generously shared some of their ideas with me: Don S. Browning, Mihaly Csikszentmihalyi, and Richard A. Shweder. David Heyd and an anonymous reader for Princeton University Press gave me valuable comments on my manuscript. Kathy Cochran provided her usual fine competence in word-processing the manuscript, and Joanne Grencius graciously gave me excellent assistance. Specific helps were also given by my daughter, Letitia Naigles, and my brother, Nathaniel L. Gage. From my wife, Jean Laves, I have received love and other valuable support, for which I am most grateful. In addition, I want to associate Jim, Susela, and Dan with this book, as well as Beverly, Gregory, Carmen, and Simone.

SELF-FULFILLMENT

CHAPTER 1

The Ideal of Self-Fulfillment

1.1. SELF-FULFILLMENT: PRO AND CON

Self-fulfillment is a traditional ideal that has been exalted in both Western and non-Western cultures. While it continues to exert fascination for philosophers, psychologists, theologians, and ordinary people, it has been construed and evaluated in many different ways, each of which incurs difficulties of explication and justification. But there is a general conception of it which can give an initial idea of why self-fulfillment has so often been highly valued as a primary constituent, or indeed as the inclusive content, of a good, happy human life. According to this conception, self-fulfillment consists in carrying to fruition one's deepest desires or one's worthiest capacities. It is a bringing of oneself to flourishing completion, an unfolding of what is strongest or best in oneself, so that it represents the successful culmination of one's aspirations or potentialities. In this way self-fulfillment betokens a life well lived, a life that is deeply satisfying, fruitful, and worthwhile. It is diametrically opposed not only to such other reflexive relations as self-defeat, self-frustration, self-alienation, and self-destruction, but also to invasions whereby such injuries are inflicted by forces external to the self. The struggle for self-fulfillment has figured centrally in our literary heritage as well as in much of the actual history of human beings.

According to this general conception, other ideals or norms have value only insofar as they serve, directly or indirectly, to further personal self-fulfillment. Morality, religion, aesthetics, and other realms of value may focus on actions and institutions, on artifacts, on nature with its living beings and environmental ecology, and on many other kinds of objects. But insofar as these are values for human beings they come down finally to impacts on the development or fruition of the human self. It is how the human self experiences these objects or relates to them regarding its fulfillment that determines, in the final analysis, whether and how they are good or bad, right or wrong. Because of its concern for what is deepest or best in oneself, self-fulfillment is a maximizing conception; it consists in superlatives of desire and achievement; it subsumes all other values of human life and is the ultimate goal of human striving. So to seek for a good human life is to seek for self-fulfillment.

These strong claims on behalf of self-fulfillment will receive intensive critical scrutiny in various parts of this book. But already at this beginning stage it is important to note that, despite its purported superlativeness and its widespread internalization as a personal ideal, self-fulfillment has suffered a diminution of concern in much of modern moral and political philosophy. Partly as a reaction to the seemingly elitist focus of many ideals of the good life, the dominant concern of modern moral philosophers has been not with the nature and attainment of the good life for individual persons but rather with the interpersonal relations whereby one owes duties to other persons. Many of those duties have implications for the good lives of individuals, but even these have emphasized moderate or even minimal but indispensable needs rather than the superlative fulfillment of aspirations and capacities.

A similar shift has occurred in political philosophy. In ancient times self-fulfillment was a social ideal as well as a personal one. For Plato and Aristotle the ultimate goal of the polis was not only to provide the means whereby persons could fulfill themselves but also to exemplify such fulfillment in its central institutions. The development of the human virtues was to be embodied in the polis's educational system, its arts, and its provisions for social and political comity, all with a view to promoting and exalting self-fulfillment. In the modern era, in contrast, with the vast difference between the nation-state and the polis, the focus of political philosophy has been far less on personal self-fulfillment and far more on guaranteeing the stability of civic order and political liberty, with special attention to minimal needs and rights and to justice as providing for their equal protection. The idea of the state as an educational institution concerned with its members' self-fulfillment and maximal development has largely been given up, although some concern with it can be found in Rousseau, Hegel, and Marx, and more recently in Hegelians like T. H. Green, F. H. Bradley, and John Dewey. The focus on self-fulfillment has been greatly dimmed not only because the poverty, disorder, and violence of modern life have made concern with it appear less pressing but also because the ideal itself raises serious conceptual and moral problems. To put it bluntly, to many moderns self-fulfillment has seemed a murky and confused concept that should not be invoked by serious-minded analytic philosophers.

Let us look briefly at some of the main conceptual and moral doubts that have been raised concerning both the value and the very feasibility of the ideal of self-fulfillment. The most familiar of these bears on the egoism, the self-absorption and self-aggrandizement which the quest for self-fulfillment is thought to engender. As a superlative object of aspiration, self-fulfillment is considered to focus so exclusively on the self that it leaves no space for other values, including the goods and rights of other persons.[1] It is also held that the ideal of self-fulfillment is elitist because the maximizing perfectionism it embodies is beyond the reach of most persons, and because they reject the exertions required for achieving it: the *homme moyen sensuel* is contented with secure mediocrity rather than with achievement.

Further objections adduce quantitative and qualitative features of the self that are held to render the ideal of self-fulfillment impractical or obscure. According to thinkers from Hobbes to Freud, the ideal is impractical because, as the realization of aspirations, it can have no finite attainment since aspirations are limitless: as soon as one is realized another is put in its place, so that there are no final ends or desires; rather, there is an unending continuum of aspirations and fulfillments. Hence, the desire for self-fulfillment is ultimately ineffectual. Qualitative features of the self are said to have the same outcome: the human self is multiple; it has parts that are distinguished from one another not only by varying external historical and geographic circumstances but also within itself. As psychologists from Plato to Freud have emphasized, the self's diverse components may conflict with one another, so that there is a problem of which of these divergent selves is to be fulfilled and how the conflicts are to be resolved. It is also maintained that many human aspirations and capacities are evil or otherwise unworthy, so that what is required is not their fulfillment or actualization but rather their frustration or negation. More generally, self-fulfillment is held to be so value-neutral that it can characterize sinners as well as saints.[2] If, on the other hand, self-fulfillment is defined as the actualization of one's "highest" or "best" capacities, this definition is confounded by inveterate conflicts over the criteria of "highest" or "best," so that the exaltation of self-fulfillment is bound to reflect the author's prejudices rather than values on which all rational persons can, let alone must, agree.

I shall try in this book to develop an interpretation of self-fulfillment that can help to overcome these doubts and can serve to justify the high place it has been accorded in conceptions of the human good. To be successful, the interpretation must satisfy two main requirements. First, it must take adequate account of the difficulties that self-fulfillment is held to incur. Second, it must analyze the justified contents of self-fulfillment, show why it is a worthy ideal to aim at, and explain the conditions of its attainment.

In pursuit of this aim my primary focus will not be historical but

[1] See Daniel Yankelovich, *New Rules: Searching for Self-Fulfillment in a World Turned Upside Down* (New York: Random House, 1981).

[2] See Henry Sidgwick, *The Ethics of T. H. Green, Herbert Spencer, and J. Martineau* (London: Macmillan, 1902), p. 64; Sidgwick, *The Methods of Ethics*, 7th ed. (London: Macmillan, 1907), pp. 91, 95.

rather dialectical, analytical, and systematic.[3] I shall not for the most part discuss the many different interpretations that self-fulfillment has received from Plato to the contemporary world. Instead, I shall begin from our present informal understandings of the concept and try to clarify them in light of various considerations I regard as cogent. In pursuit of this aim, I shall proceed dialectically: I shall present various familiar hypotheses about what self-fulfillment consists in; I shall indicate difficulties incurred by these hypotheses; and I shall then try to move on to further hypotheses that overcome the previous difficulties. Two main conceptions of self-fulfillment will emerge from this dialectical process, and each in turn will be scrutinized on the basis of relevant criteria. The upshot I shall try to establish is that while each conception incurs difficulties, they can be largely resolved and the high esteem accorded self-fulfillment as a worthy ideal of the good human life can be vindicated.

The general conception of self-fulfillment to which I referred at the outset remains an enduring and exalted ideal that is relevant to moral philosophy concerned with the goodness of human life as well as to political philosophy concerned with the justice of a society that reflects and fosters that goodness. Despite the instabilities and even terrors that plague modern societies, the ideal continues to be of central importance for moral and political philosophy.

1.2. SOME TERMINOLOGICAL DISTINCTIONS

Let us begin with some terminological considerations. "Self-fulfillment" has two near synonyms: "self-realization" and "self-actualization." While these are mainly used, respectively, by philosophers and by humanistic psychologists, "self-fulfillment" occurs much more frequently among ordinary people;[4] and this is one of the reasons favoring its use in the present context. All three of these terms signify not only a kind of reflexive relation but also a favorable development wherein persons achieve goods that are somehow inherent in their "natures," by unfolding certain of their latent powers. In this way each development is both a process of valuable growth and the outcome of that process.

Certain tentative distinctions can, however, be drawn between these terms. In listing them here I shall be using concepts whose fuller import will appear only subsequently; they are intended more as suggestive and provisional than as definitive characterizations of the respective processes.

[3] For an excellent historical analysis, which focuses mainly on varying conceptions of the self rather than on self-fulfillment, see Charles Taylor, *Sources of the Self: The Making of the Modern Identity* (Cambridge, Mass.: Harvard University Press, 1989).

[4] See, e.g., Yankelovich, *New Rules.*

To begin with, we may note four differences between self-fulfillment and self-realization.[5] First, self-realization may suggest that the self is somehow not fully "real" before the process of realizing it is completed.[6] But the capacities that are developed in self-fulfillment are themselves also real in that they exist as powers inherent in the self. Second, where self-realization seems to pertain primarily to capacity-fulfillment, self-fulfillment also comprises the distinct process of aspiration-fulfillment. In this regard self-fulfillment has a strong desire side as well as a capacity side. Third, where self-realization can be construed as consisting solely in activities that have purposes beyond themselves,[7] self-fulfillment consists at least in part in states or activities that are valued for themselves. This is especially true of self-fulfillment conceived in terms of aspiration. Self-fulfillment is thus a maximalist value, focused on persons' attainment of their strongest and deepest desires. Self-realization, on the other hand, is more moderate in its value status because of its tie to means as against ends. This difference cannot be pressed too far, however, because self-realization may also be viewed as the end for which various activities are undertaken as means. Fourth, some persons may not desire self-realization because its activities may be deemed too arduous. On the other hand, self-fulfillment, at least as fulfillment of aspirations, is desired by all persons even though the means toward attaining it may not themselves be desired.

Turning now to "self-actualization," we may note three differences from self-fulfillment.[8] First, "self-actualization" suggests that the self to begin with is already present as a set of determinate potentialities that await actualization: the potentialities are determinate even if the actuality is not. In self-fulfillment, on the other hand, there may be indeterminacy on both sides: the self is indeterminate in its potentialities as well as in its actuality. The potentialities are indeed real powers, but their contents are diffuse and indeterminate. Thus self-fulfillment leaves more room for creativity than does self-actualization: in fulfilling oneself one creates oneself in that one creates both one's powers (by giving them determinate form) and one's developed states or activities. This development is shaped by one's aspirations, which help to mould one's implicit powers as well as the ends toward which they are directed.

[5] The characterizations of self-realization that I present here are based in part on writings of such British Idealist philosophers as T. H. Green, F. H. Bradley, and Bernard Bosanquet.

[6] See David L. Norton, *Personal Destinies* (Princeton: Princeton University Press, 1976), p. 15.

[7] See Jon Elster, "Self-Realization in Work and Politics: The Marxist Conception of the Good Life," *Social Philosophy and Policy* 3, no. 2 (spring 1986), pp. 99–100.

[8] The characterizations of self-actualization that I present here are based largely on the writings of such humanistic psychologists as Abraham H. Maslow, Carl Rogers, and Erich Fromm.

A second distinction bears in a related way on the respective processes. In self-actualization, at least as conceived on a certain "Aristotelian" model (to be further discussed below), the actualization may be automatic, in a way not too different from the natural processes whereby plants grow to fruition. In self-fulfillment, on the other hand, the process is marked by choices made by the self-fulfilling person: she freely chooses which of her indeterminate potentialities she will undertake to develop, in the light of her strongest aspirations. Thus freedom is an important component of self-fulfillment as against self-actualization. Third, in self-actualization the aspect of the self that is held to be actualized or to require actualization consists in various "needs" based largely on desires that stem from problems of adjustment encountered by persons in various of their social relations. In self-fulfillment a similar place is occupied by "aspirations," construed as persons' strongest desires for self-gratification; but there is also a largely independent role for capacities as the objects of self-fulfillment.

Thus while self-fulfillment, like self-realization and self-actualization, is both a process and a product, the process consisting in an unfolding of certain implicit or inherent powers, self-fulfillment differs from the others in that it is an intrinsic value desired for itself, and is marked by choice, creativity, and capacity-development. In what follows, however, when I quote writers who use one of the other expressions, I shall usually not take the trouble to remind the reader of these distinctions. Also, in important respects the features that unite self-fulfillment with self-realization and self-actualization are more significant than the differences.

1.3. SELF-FULFILLMENT AS ACTUALIZATION
OF POTENTIALITIES

To come to fuller grips with the ideal of self-fulfillment it will be helpful to develop further a distinction mentioned in the previous section. This distinction reflects one of the most traditional and influential formulations of self-fulfillment: that it consists in the "actualization of one's potentialities."[9] The self is here viewed as a locus of powers or capacities that are primed for growth or development toward an inherent end, which is the good of the self; and self-fulfillment is the process of attaining this development. The good life or the good functioning of a person is held to consist in such actualization of her potentialities.

---

[9] See Elster, "Self-Realization," who attributes to "the Marxist tradition" the formula that "self-realization is the full and free actualization and externalization of the powers and the attributes of the individual."

A crucially important issue concerns the nature of this development. As it is often interpreted, the human actualization of potentialities is conceived on the same model as the growth of plants and animals, as a kind of semiautomatic process in which latent primitive capacities are unfolded and the organism is brought to maturity and its "natural end," its perfected functioning. It was this model that Marx followed when he wrote that "Milton produced *Paradise Lost* as a silkworm produces silk, as the activation of his own nature."[10] This is also the model upheld by humanistic psychologists when they write that "self-actualization" is "a fundamental characteristic, inherent in human nature, a potentiality given to all or most human beings at birth," so that it "must ultimately be defined as the coming to pass of the fullest humanness, or as the 'Being' of the person."[11] "Self-actualization" is "the tendency of the organism to move in the direction of maturation.). . . It moves in the direction of greater independence or self-responsibility."[12] A person's "natural self relentlessly pushes toward health and growth. Their potentials for self-fulfillment are never lost or destroyed."[13] "Under favorable conditions man's energies are put into the realization of his own potentialities . . . inherent in man are evolutionary constructive forces, which urge him to realize his given potentialities . . . man, by his very nature and of his own accord, strives toward self-realization. . . . You need not, and in fact cannot, teach an acorn to grow into an oak tree, but when given a chance, its intrinsic potentialities will develop. Similarly, the human individual, given a chance, tends to develop his particular human potentialities. He will develop then the unique alive forces of his real self."[14]

---

[10] Karl Marx, "Results of the Immediate Process of Production," in Marx, *Capital*, vol. 1, trans. Ben Fowkes (New York: Vintage Books, 1977), p. 1044.

[11] Abraham H. Maslow, *Toward a Psychology of Being*, 2nd ed. (New York: Van Nostrand Reinhold, 1962), pp. 138, 145.

[12] Carl R. Rogers, *Client-Centered Therapy* (Boston: Houghton Mifflin, 1951), p. 488. See also Rogers, *On Becoming a Person* (Boston: Houghton Mifflin, 1961), p. 35.

[13] Jerry Greenwald, *Be the Person You Were Meant to Be* (New York: Dell Publishing Co., 1973), p. 12. See also Erich Fromm, *Man for Himself* (New York: Rinehart and Co., 1947), p. 20: "All organisms have an inherent tendency to actualize their specific potentialities. The aim of man's life, therefore, is to be understood as the unfolding of his powers according to the laws of his nature."

[14] Karen Horney, *Neurosis and Human Growth: The Struggle Toward Self-Realization* (London: Routledge and Kegan Paul, 1951), pp. 15, 17. Horney also says that man "can grow, in the true sense, only if he assumes responsibility for himself" (p. 15). See also Anthony Storr, *The Integrity of the Personality* (Harmondsworth: Penguin, 1963), p. 27: "I propose to call this final achievement self-realization, by which I mean the fullest possible expression in life of the innate potentialities of the individual, the realization of his own uniqueness as a personality: and I also put forward the hypothesis that, consciously or unconsciously, every man is seeking this goal." For a good critical discussion of the humanistic psychologists, see Don S. Browning, *Religious Thought and the Modern Psychologies*

Among the many issues raised by this conception of self-fulfillment or self-actualization as an internally driven development toward optimal human functioning, two are especially important in the present context. First, unless human potentialities are defined in a question-begging way, they include capacities for evil or malfunctioning as well as for good; hence, the actualization of potentialities cannot be used as a general formula for the human good, whether "good" is given either a moral or a nonmoral interpretation. Second, the conception does not, as such, provide a place for ethically important processes like choice, deliberation, and decision, so that its relevance for human ethical development is left obscure.

In this connection it may be helpful to look briefly at Aristotle, who first gave a technical philosophical elucidation of the concepts of potentiality and actuality. It is significant that Aristotle defined *all* motion as "the actualization of the potential as such."[15] For in all motion, including not only locomotion but also qualitative, quantitative, and substantial change, specific potentialities or capacities are in process of being actualized or fulfilled; for example, when a physical body's potentiality for rolling is actualized or exercised, this constitutes its actual motion of rolling.

But Aristotle did not apply this simple formula of the actualization of potentialities to the ethical sphere of the development of the virtues or excellence of character. He drew a sharp distinction between the objects or subject matters of the theoretical sciences of physics and biology, where the formula applies, and the objects or subject matters of the practical sciences of ethics, economics, and politics, where it does not.[16] The subject matters of the theoretical sciences consist in essences or natures that exist and have their basic characteristics quite independent of human control or contrivance.[17] On the other hand, the subject matters of the practical sciences consist in human actions, characters, and institutions that depend upon and vary with the choices, deliberations, and actions of human beings. Accordingly, the theoretical natural sciences trace a sequence of natural movement or development from potentiality to actuality. Each natural species of thing has certain distinctive potenti-

---

(Philadelphia: Fortress Press, 1987), ch. 4. For discussion of some further bearings of Freudian psychoanalysis on ethics, see Alan Gewirth, "Psychoanalysis and Ethics: Mental or Moral Health?," *Christian Register* 135 (1956), pp. 12–13, 30–31.

[15] *Physics* 3. 1. 201a10. See also *Metaphysics* 11. 9. 1065b16.

[16] See *Metaphysics* 6. 1; 9. 1–9; *Nicomachean Ethics* 6. 3–7.

[17] In view of the immense technological constructs that are applied in modern scientific research it is necessary to note here the distinction between the artificial means used, for example, to bombard electrons and the objective physical realities that such technological contrivances are designed to disclose or discover.

alities or powers of movement or development deriving from its essence or nature and, unless there are impediments, these potentialities are actualized in correspondingly distinctive ways which, for biological entities, constitute their respective goods or ends. Thus, for example, acorns become oak trees, and embryos grow to adulthood.

In the case of the practical sciences, on the other hand, Aristotle held that the movement or development of their subject matters cannot be accounted for by this simple scheme of the actualization of inherent potentialities. Rather, an intermediate concept must be invoked: habit or habituation (*hexis* or *ēthos*), which reflects human choices and conditionings. This is intermediate between potentiality and actuality in that, while the practical subject matters are indeed *based upon* inherent natural potentialities or capacities, as their material causes or necessary conditions, these potentialities can be turned in many different directions so far as concerns the various virtues, vices, and other psychological states that may be developed on the basis of them. For example, humans, like other animals, have natural potentialities to feel various emotions or passions. But these potentialities in humans can be developed in different ways, through varying human choices, so that some persons become cowards, others reckless daredevils, still others heroes, saints, and martyrs, and others still courageous in an intermediate way. Thus Aristotle emphasized that the process of development of the various states of character cannot be accounted for by nature (*physis*), where nature is the efficient and formal cause that drives natural entities along the path from potentiality to actuality. As he put it, if man's moral virtues were generated by nature, then, since "nothing that exists by nature can form a habit contrary to its nature,"[18] it would follow that there are no moral vices. But of course there are. Hence, moral virtues must have a different source or efficient cause than nature or natural potentialities, including human nature, and this source consists in the way in which human passions or emotions are conditioned through choices in one direction rather than in others. Thus it is by habituation that the various states of character are developed, in that there must be a certain kind of training of the emotions, which proceeds not only or mainly by intellectual instruction but rather by discipline, force of example, legislation, and other ways that depend upon human desires and choices. Hence the human goods, including the moral virtues, cannot be derived from or accounted for by man's nature alone; this nature is not the sufficient condition of man's good.[19] From this it follows that self-fulfillment,

---

[18] *Nicomachean Ethics*, 2. 1. 1103a20.

[19] This distinction is overlooked in Thomas Hurka's discussion of Aristotle; see Hurka, *Perfectionism* (New York: Oxford University Press, 1993), pp. 19–20.

construed as at least part of the human good, is not constituted by or derived from the natural actualization of human potentialities.

This point also bears on the idea that self-fulfillment consists in an unfolding of one's "nature," either generic or individual.[20] The difficulty here is that insofar as your nature is something with which you are born, your self-fulfillment would not be under your control so far as concerns the content that gets fulfilled or is actualized. While if it is under your control, then it is not your "nature" that gets fulfilled. Here again the reply is that our nature gives us diffuse, indeterminate potentialities or tendencies, and we can choose among them which will be fulfilled by the kinds of actions we voluntarily perform. This, of course, raises the question of the criteria for choice, which I will address in detail later.

Despite the immense differences between Aristotelian and modern conceptions of the physical sciences, the distinction he drew between natural and practical modes of development is still sound. It is true that in the *Politics* Aristotle said that "the state exists by nature" and "man is by nature a political animal."[21] But here he used "nature" in a normative sense, not as efficient cause but as final cause: "the nature of a thing is its end," and "the final cause and end of a thing is the best."[22] So the "natural" here signifies a normative selection from among the many potentialities or potential habituations that bear on human development. Being a civilized or "political" animal is not merely the actualization of human potentialities as such; it is their best actualization or development. There remains, then, the contrast between nature and choice or habituation as different kinds of sources or efficient causes of human movement and development. It is thus a mistake to interpret Aristotle's doctrine of the human good along the lines of his "metaphysical biology," as if that good were a "natural end" or telos consisting in the actualization of human potentialities.[23] There is also a parallel contrast between choice and the idea upheld by some Marxists according to which human history is controlled by inexorable social forces in which choice or desire has little or no place.

[20] See Joel Feinberg, *Freedom and Fulfillment* (Princeton: Princeton University Press, 1992), pp. 318–19.

[21] *Politics*, 1. 2. 1253a2.

[22] Ibid., 1. 2. 1252b32ff.

[23] For this mistaken interpretation, see Alasdair MacIntyre, *After Virtue* (Notre Dame, Ind.: University of Notre Dame Press, 1981), p. 139: "Human beings, like the members of all other species, have a specific nature, and that nature is such that they have certain aims and goals, such that they move by nature towards a specific telos. The good is defined in terms of their specific characteristics. Hence, Aristotle's ethics, expounded as he expounds it, presupposes his metaphysical biology." For a much more extensive and sophisticated interpretation of "natural ends" in Aristotle, see Henry B. Veatch, *Human Rights: Fact or Fancy?* (Baton Rouge: Louisiana State University Press, 1985), ch. 2.

What emerges from these considerations is not that human powers or potentialities do not figure at all in self-fulfillment, but rather that they must be guided or controlled through deliberation and choice, which are functions of desire. Our nature gives us diffuse powers or potentialities; and while some of these may be stronger than others, we can, by the voluntary actions we perform, choose which among them we want to fulfill. So the fulfillment of desires—or, rather, of aspirations as one's deepest or strongest desires—will emerge as at least one kind of self-fulfillment. But their objects cannot be read off from some static "end" of human nature. In what follows, especially as regards what I shall call "capacity-fulfillment," I shall sometimes use the formula of the actualization of potentialities, but this will always be with the understanding of the difference from the non-Aristotelian interpretation of it sketched above.

1.4. TWO MODES OF SELF-FULFILLMENT

On the basis of the distinctions we have just examined, self-fulfillment can be considered in two main ways. One derives from the element of choice, or more generally desire, that figures in the development of character. Because of the superlativeness that pertains to self-fulfillment, it can be referred to as aspiration-fulfillment, where "aspiration" signifies one's deepest or supreme desires. A second construal derives from the element of potentiality or power to which the formula of the actualization of potentialities was addressed. With due recognition for the selectivity and deliberation that are required for the development of character, self-fulfillment can here be referred to as capacity-fulfillment. These construals provide an initial answer to the question of which "self" is intended when we speak of self-fulfillment. As I noted above, philosophers and psychologists from Plato to Freud have distinguished many different "selves" as constituting the human person. But in the present context the self that figures in self-fulfillment may be defined in terms of certain aspirations or capacities. The self is fulfilled when its deepest desires or its best capacities are brought to fruition. These features also indicate in a preliminary way the bases for the superlativeness of self-fulfillment as a supremely valuable condition of the self.

Certain general features of the self cut across the distinction between aspirations and capacities. The self that enters into self-fulfillment is a continuing or enduring embodied entity that is aware of itself as a distinct person, that can anticipate a future for itself, and that has desires on which it can reflect. It can evaluate these desires on the basis of second-order desires that take account of its relevant abilities or capacities. This taking account may vary in degree from one self to another and from one time to another, and it includes some reference to the desires of other persons. These features of the self will be more fully developed in what follows.

Amid these general features, we can distinguish more specifically between aspiration-fulfillment and capacity-fulfillment by reference to the different basic questions each is designed to answer. The question for aspiration-fulfillment is: What will satisfy my deepest desires? The question for capacity-fulfillment is: How can I make the best of myself? To fulfill oneself by reference to one's aspirations involves that the self is viewed as a center of desiderative force which strives to achieve intended outcomes. To fulfill oneself is to achieve these outcomes and thereby to bring oneself, as thus centered in one's aspirations, to fruition, although, as we shall see, the objects of the aspirations may be things other than oneself. To fulfill oneself by reference to one's capacities involves that the self is viewed as a more or less ordered set of powers, abilities, or potentialities. To fulfill oneself is to bring the best of those powers to as full development as possible, so it involves a normative selection among a person's capacities. The selection aims to single out excellences, virtues, or perfections, and self-fulfillment consists in attaining these. This attainment is a self-fulfillment for the double reason that it is a good, indeed a (or the) highest good, for the person in question, and that it is this person's own capacities that are developed or exercised in attaining and possessing this good. But neither aspiration-fulfillment nor capacity-fulfillment is an automatic process; it involves second-order choices and controls on the part of the self.

The aspirations and capacities on which these two modes of self-fulfillment rest are directly related to two distinct factors or features of the self: its appetitive-conative side on the one hand, and its rational side on the other.[24] As modes of a person's self-fulfillment, both aspirations and capacities serve to define who the person is, but in different ways. The difference is that aspirations and their fulfillment are tied more closely to persons' actual desires, while capacity-fulfillment bears more on making the best of oneself and thus serves as a normative guide to what desires one ought to have, where this 'ought' may (but need not) go beyond persons' actual desires. The two modes of self-fulfillment, accordingly, are associated with, or even equivalent to, two different conceptions of happiness. If happiness is the fulfillment of one's desires or one's deepest

[24] These two kinds of self-fulfillment and features of the self are present but not clearly distinguished in Aristotle, *Nicomachean Ethics*, book 1, in the sequence from his discussion of happiness as what "we desire for its own sake, everything else being desired for the sake of this" (1. 2. 1094a18) to his discussion of it in terms of "the function of man" as "an activity of soul which follows or implies reason" (1. 7. 1098a7).

desires, then it is equivalent to aspiration-fulfillment. If, on the other hand, happiness consists in the highest development of one's best capacities, then it is equivalent to capacity-fulfillment.[25] In the following chapters we shall examine various qualifications that must be imposed on each of these equivalences; but their putative connection with happiness brings out further why self-fulfillment is so highly valued as a superlative condition of the self.

Aspiration-fulfillment is both a process and a product or outcome. It is a process of development whose outcome or culmination is the successful attainment of the objects of one's deepest desires. These objects may vary from person to person, from one cultural milieu to another, and between different historical epochs. But in all cases they reflect the inherent purposiveness of human action and the freedom or autonomy that is a generic feature of such action. Because of this purposiveness, aspiration-fulfillment, at least as envisaged outcome, is regarded as a great good by all the persons who are able to achieve it or who strive for it.

Where such self-fulfillment is relative to persons' aspirations, in capacity-fulfillment the criterion of self-fulfillment is located rather in the objective goods or values that persons can achieve by developing certain of their inherent capacities. These goods or values have an objective status independent of whether they are aspired to or desired by the persons who are capable of achieving them. Thus, for example, persons like Hitler or Stalin might be held to have achieved aspiration-fulfillment at least on the occasions of their greatest triumphs; but they would not have achieved capacity-fulfillment because the objects of their aspirations, far from being genuine goods, were execrable evils. The criteria for such evaluations in less extreme and obvious cases will be dealt with in detail below.

The two modes of self-fulfillment have had varying relations to the history of thought. We may to some extent tie the distinction to two different traditions of Western philosophy. Aspiration-fulfillment reflects the liberal and individualist tradition of John Stuart Mill's insistence that "free scope" should be given to "different experiments of living,"[26] as well as corresponding emphases in Rousseau and the German Romantics of the nineteenth century. Capacity-fulfillment reflects the perfectionist exaltations of reason found in Plato and Aristotle as well as, variously, in Kant and Hegel and such of their nineteenth-century continuators as T. H. Green and F. H. Bradley.

---

[25] For a related but not identical distinction, see Richard Kraut, "Two Conceptions of Happiness," *Philosophical Review* 88 (April 1979), pp. 167–97; John Kekes, *The Examined Life* (Lewisburg, Pa.: Bucknell University Press, 1988), chs. 10–11.

[26] *On Liberty*, ch. 3, para. 1.

From these considerations it follows that self-fulfillment in the aspirational and in the capacitative senses, at least in their initial bearings, may be independent of one another. This independence may be further marked by calling them, respectively, "subjective" and "objective" or, again respectively, "relative" and "absolute." But these characterizations should not be pressed too far. Self-fulfillment in the aspirational sense has to take account of objective facts about personal desires and their contents, including facts about the abilities or capacities of the person who seeks to achieve his aspirations and about their envisaged objects. And self-fulfillment in the capacitative sense must take account of persons' choices, both those they actually make and those they ought to make, where this 'ought' has among its criteria persons' deepest desires and strivings. Questions about the motivations for persons' seeking to fulfill their capacities also arise here.

If the questions of aspiration-fulfillment and capacity-fulfillment are indeed distinct, their distinctness may be exemplified in at least two ways. First, one may have capacity-fulfillment without aspiration-fulfillment: one may fulfill one's highest capacities and yet not fulfill one's aspirations because, for example, one feels that one has not measured up to the high standards one upholds for oneself, or because one's aspirations are for something other than high achievement. This does not mean that capacity-fulfillment can dispense entirely with the element of desire or choice; but this may be moderated in the light of what one discovers about the capacities that are within one's reach. Second, one may have aspiration-fulfillment without capacity-fulfillment because one's aspirations are far lower than the high achievements of which one is capable. In this case one may be satisfied with a surpassable level of mediocrity. Persons who are risk-averse or unduly modest may aspire only to be lost in the crowd, with no desire to achieve excellence. A further basis for upholding the distinction between the two modes of self-fulfillment derives from the kinds of criteria that enter into them. The criteria for aspiration-fulfillment are directly personal; they derive from the aspiring person herself; they consist in what she most deeply wants. The criteria for capacity-fulfillment, on the other hand, are in important respects impersonal. For to ascertain what is the best in oneself requires that one select from among one's aspirations or other desires on the basis of appropriate tests for goodness; and these tests (which will be more fully discussed below) may involve looking beyond one's aspirations to more objective considerations both about oneself and about kinds of value. Again, this does not mean that desires or choices are completely overlooked, but they are subjected to relevant critical scrutiny. Moreover, whereas aspirations may vary from person to person, what is best in oneself may reflect standards that apply more generally.

Nevertheless, the separation of aspiration-fulfillment from capacity-fulfillment raises difficulties and dangers. If what is best in you does not correspond to what you most deeply want, then the way may be opened for authoritarian or paternalistic imposition of standards of perfection that take no account of your own desires or wishes. And, conversely, if what you most deeply desire takes no account of what is best in you, of what can bring your best capacities to fruition, then aspiration-fulfillment may result in disappointment and even disaster for you.

Despite these considerations, we might try to equate the two modes of self-fulfillment by the following line of argument. Aspirations are a kind of desire, and when desires get translated into action they become the purposes for which one acts. Now every agent regards his purposes as good—not necessarily as morally good but at least as having sufficient value for him to merit his trying to attain them. Hence one's deepest desires have as their objects what one regards as superlatively good, or best, not only because they have been chosen from among the alternatives that are available to one, but also because they reflect one's deepest desires. So aspirations are for what, from the agent's point of view, is best. And insofar as this best represents a conative development of the agent herself, as what she aims to be, become, or achieve by her own striving, the object of her aspiration is what is best in herself. So, according to this argument, aspiration-fulfillment is the same as capacity-fulfillment.

This conclusion would be warranted only if there were no criteria for what is best in oneself independent of one's deepest desires. But that there are such criteria is suggested by the fact that there are desires that are mistaken, misguided, or self-frustrating. This means that desires, as such, do not necessarily fulfill criteria of adequacy, especially as bearing on capacity-fulfillment. We might, however, try to obtain such criteria by invoking higher-order desires as bases of both aspiration-fulfillment and capacity-fulfillment. For a particular desire to be mistaken would mean that it in some way is opposed to a higher-order desire. Thus it might be said, for example, that everyone supremely desires the good or the best, but some persons are mistaken about the particular desires they seize upon as means to fulfill their higher-order desire for the good. So in this way higher-order desires could be appealed to for providing, from among desires themselves, appropriate criteria for the adequacy or soundness of desires, so that the proposed identification of aspiration-fulfillment with capacity-fulfillment could still be maintained.

This attempt to base capacity-fulfillment on the fulfillment of one's higher-order desires incurs at least three difficulties. First, there is the question of the sense in which one "has" the higher-order desire. If persons are not aware that they have this desire, then in what way can it be truly attributed to them? Second, even if there are higher-order desires, must they be for the good of the person who has them? It will be recalled that capacity-fulfillment bears on making the best of oneself. But higher-order desires may have other objects, such as the happiness of strangers, the beautification of some city, the discovery of scientific laws, the domination of other persons, and so forth. Hence, this could still leave aspiration-fulfillment and capacity-fulfillment independent of one another, since the former, unlike the latter, could have an impersonal object distinct from making the best of oneself. Third, it makes sense to say that even higher-order desires may be mistaken, unless one puts them at such a high level of generality—such as being for the good or the true—that they seem to be beyond criticism. But such a procedure would be question-begging, and it would still leave open the question of the adequacy of the more specific desires one pursues as means of attaining these highest-level objects. Thus if the "deepest desires" in which aspirations consist are to be practically relevant, they must be given more specific contents that enable them to be motivational as objects of pursuit and that hence go beyond the alleged higher-order desires. So this argument in support of the identity of capacity-fulfillment with aspiration-fulfillment does not succeed. Capacity-fulfillment, while taking sufficient account of desires and aspirations, will have to be explicated in ways that go beyond aspiration-fulfillment.

In the remainder of this book I shall discuss first aspiration-fulfillment and then capacity-fulfillment. While the discussions will be distinct, I shall also be concerned to bring out their main relations both to one another and to the various goods that make each of them especially worthy objects of human striving.

CHAPTER 2

Self-Fulfillment as Aspiration-Fulfillment

2.1. WHAT ARE ASPIRATIONS?

We may distinguish four questions about aspiration-fulfillment. The first concerns aspirations themselves: what are they? The next two concern the process of aspiration-fulfillment: how does one get aspirations, and how does one fulfill them? The fourth question bears on the product of the process: what are the objects at which aspirations aim and should aim? While it will be difficult to keep these four questions entirely separate, I shall try to do so in the interests of clarity.

In general, we know what aspirations are. A dictionary defines "aspiration" as "a strong desire for high achievement,"[1] and we can take this as a starting point, although, as we shall see, certain qualifications are needed. The "high achievement" in question may take various forms, including not only outstanding success in one's profession but also winning someone's love, having a happy family milieu, good health and longevity, a strong sense of personal autonomy and identity, interesting and engrossing plans of life, promoting ideals of social betterment, and so forth. But such familiar aspirations are beset by various complexities, many of which stem from the fact that the aspiring self and what it aspires to are intermingled in different ways. A central issue here is whether what one aspires to is to be a certain kind of person or to achieve certain results or values. Obviously these may be closely related; but as the emphasis falls on the one or the other the outcome may be more self-oriented or more object-oriented. If the focus is on certain values, one may lose sight of the self that aspires to them; while if the focus is on the aspiring self, the values that give it justificatory worth may be obscured or lost. So at the extreme, aspirations may lead either to self-abnegation or to self-aggrandizement. This alternative bears closely on the features of egoism and elitism that are held to characterize all endeavors toward self-fulfillment.

One of the forms that such conflicts may take involves what may be called "domination" by one or the other pole. On the one hand, aspirations toward certain values may be so strong that they dominate the self,

---

[1] *The American Heritage Dictionary of the English Language* (Boston: American Heritage Publishing Co., 1969), p. 78.

in that they ride roughshod over others of the self's interests or values, including its physical health, its family attachments, and so forth. On the other hand, aspirations (despite the above definition's reference to "strong desire") may be so weak that they are dominated by other interests or desires of the self. A husband who aspires to have a happy family life may browbeat his wife or children; a man who aspires toward professional success may waste his talents in alcohol or philandering. In such cases the question may arise of whether the persons do in fact have the aspirations they think they have; questions about weakness of will or the vectorial nature of desires may arise here. But in any case the relations of the self to its aspirations must take account of such possibly self-defeating behaviors.

What especially contributes to such problems is the fact that in having aspirations the self strives toward being what it is presently not. Even if it aspires simply to continue in its present state, this continuation may not itself be assured, so that the aspiring self is dynamic rather than static. So there arises the question of whether the present self has the resources to become the future self it aspires to be. But since it is the present self that copes with this question, a certain extrapolation—which is often risky—is required from present to future. And this in turn involves an at least implicit comparison of its envisaged future values with the values it presently has. So again the emphasis may fall either on the values one aspires to achieve or on the self that may emerge from such achievement.

Despite these complexities, one of my main emphases in what follows will be unitary: I shall try to seek out the ways in which the aspiration to be a certain kind of person cannot be separated from the aspirations toward values that are reflected in such personhood. So I shall be working toward a normative selection from among the various complexities. This will still leave open the further normative question of the moral status of the respective persons and values.

The unitary conception must take account of other complexities of aspirations. Especially in view of the alleged connection of self-fulfillment with egoism and elitism, we must note at least four further alternatives about the questions listed above. First, are the objects of aspirations—what they aim to achieve—subjective or objective: do they consist in one's having certain kinds of feeling or in certain states of affairs? The former alternative would especially buttress the egoistic interpretation of self-fulfillment. Second, if what aspirations aim at are certain states of affairs, and if aspirations are one's deepest desires, does this still include some essential normative reference to the aspiring self, not as having certain feelings but as wanting to be a certain worthy kind of a certain kind of person, such as an eminent scientist or physician, is not a desire to succeed in having certain mental contents; it is rather to be an appreciator and pursuer of what one takes to be values one most wants to attain and indeed exemplify. It is in this attainment with its higher-order background that self-fulfillment as aspiration-fulfillment consists; and it is because of its connection with such depth of desire in relation to one's self-conception that aspiration-fulfillment is regarded as a great good by the persons who have the aspirations. On this ground aspirations may also be termed supreme desires, in that their objects are what one most wants to have. But, as we shall see, certain qualifications are required here.

The distinction of orders or levels of desire may raise a problem of infinite regress. You want object O (e.g., love) because you want to be a certain kind of person P (e.g., someone who is worthy of being loved). But then the question arises, why do you want to be P? Is it because you want to be Q (e.g., to contribute to the development of a benevolent society or a kingdom of ends)? If the initial aspiration, as the pursuit of a certain value, involves such self-reference, then why doesn't this self also require further validation in other values or objects of desire? Why aren't we condemned to what may be called a "bottomless pit of reflection"?

The most direct answer to this question is that the object of aspirations is not separated from the aspiring self as if the latter were a distinct entity. On the contrary, what one aspires to includes, as an indissoluble part, the self as envisaged attainer of the object. But the focus of the aspiration is on the object aspired to, not on the aspiring self; the desire about the latter is dependent upon the desire for the object (see 2.4). So there is no need for an infinite array of aspirations; the aspiring self is not needed to validate the aspiration but to anchor it in an inclusive whole. This distinction between self and object is not absolute; I shall return to it in other contexts, where it will be seen to deflect certain charges of egoism regarding aspiration-fulfillment.

The fact that aspirations are one's deepest desires, with the implicit ordering this entails, can contribute in a further way to the self's effectiveness in aspiration-fulfillment. This involves that one has a sense of centrality and perspective in one's strivings or desires. These are not all on a par: the person who has aspirations can differentiate what she wants into greater and lesser orders of importance. She is not buffeted about by each desire in turn in an unending cycle of frenetic activities; instead, she can sort out and coordinate her desires so that some are seen to be means to others, and she can maintain some sense of an organizing principle that enables her to pursue her main goals while putting her subor-

person? This would involve that aspirations are structured according to different levels or lower and higher orders of desire, with accompanying diversities of evaluative status. Questions of the elitism of self-fulfillment arise here. Third, if aspirations are supreme desires, how does this enable us to distinguish between ordinary desires that on one account are "supreme" and the extraordinary desires that figure more directly in aspiration-fulfillment as achieving certain highly valued states of affairs? Fourth, how are aspirations related to basic needs and the lacks that are often held to characterize all desires as such? Are aspirations independent of basic needs, or do they build on them, or do they stand in some other relation? How are the felt impacts of aspirations related to the felt impacts of basic needs and of strong emotions? The elitism attributed to efforts toward self-fulfillment is partly bound up with these questions, and so too is the more general psychology of aspirations.

From these introductory remarks it can be seen that the question "what are aspirations" involves basic considerations about the objects, the structure, and the value status of the aspiring self. Let us now examine how far these questions can be given cogent answers.

To begin with, we must note that while all aspirations are desires, not all desires are aspirations. A desire is a pro-attitude, but again not all pro-attitudes are desires. One may have a pro-attitude toward something in that one likes it or approves of it, but these need not be desires. To have a desire for something, one must not merely like it but must also aim to have or get it. Thus desiring is vectorial, and this raises issues of effectiveness in attaining what one desires. One may not go about getting or even trying to get what one desires; one may, for instance, think the cost is greater than the benefit. But one must at least have a tendency to go about getting it, such that the tendency will be actualized if obstacles such as cost are removed or diminished. So desires have, among their other relevant features, that they are implicit tendencies to action and that their objects are regarded, by the persons who have the desires, as worth trying to get. An element of evaluativeness or normativeness thus enters into desires.

Already at this early stage, however, there arises a question about desires that has an important bearing on the value status of self-fulfillment as aspiration-fulfillment and on the relation between the self and its values. The question reflects a pervasive tendency in modern thought: a tendency to subjectivize or internalize what would normally be regarded as objective or external. This tendency figures especially prominently in modern epistemology. Beginning with Descartes, it is held that what one directly perceives by one's senses is not a physical object, such as a tree; rather, what one directly perceives is the idea or image of a tree, i.e., a certain mental content. A reason for this thesis is that since the physical world is held to consist solely in material particles moving according to natural laws, it follows that colors, sounds, and other "secondary qualities" that one directly perceives cannot directly be parts of that world; hence, they must be regarded solely as mental contents or "ideas." Their relation to the physical world thus becomes the celebrated "problem of the external world": how can one validly infer from these directly perceived mental contents to the material particles that presumably caused them to appear to the mind? How, beginning from contents that are purely mental, "inside" the mind, can we know that there is an "external" world?

In a closely parallel way the objects of desires are sometimes, especially by utilitarians, held to be certain mental contents, especially feelings of pleasure. Underlying this view is a philosophical drive for both generality and measurability: amid the large variety of desired objects, they have it in common that they aim at certain mental satisfactions, which can be weighed and measured and hence be treated "scientifically." On this view, when I desire to have a certain book, what I really desire to have are the positive sensations or pleasant feelings that are aroused in me by my having the book. Since aspirations are certain kinds of desires, this view amounts to a subjectivizing and even trivializing of aspiration-fulfillment. If all the efforts one puts into fulfilling one's aspirations aim only at one's having certain pleasurable feelings, then the great value and importance that attach to many objects of aspirations are reduced to subjective feelings of pleasure or contentment. This would reduce to a low common denominator the rich qualitative variety of what persons aspire to. The view would also help to buttress the thesis that all aspiration-fulfillment is egoistic because it aims only at acquiring certain inner feelings of oneself, and at the extreme it would amount to a kind of narcissism. So this way of unifying the self with the values it aspires to achieve is unacceptable.

The unsoundness of an important part of this view was pointed out as far back as Aristotle, when he noted that happiness as an object of desire or choice cannot consist simply in feelings of pleasure because the having of such feelings cannot of itself account for the value of important objects of choice and desire. For example, "no one would choose to live with the intellect of a child throughout his life, however much he were to take pleasure in the things that children take pleasure in, nor to get pleasure by doing some most disgraceful deed, though he were never to feel any pain in consequence. And there are many things we should be keen about even if they brought no pleasure, e.g. seeing, remembering, knowing, possessing the virtues. If pleasures necessarily do accompany these, that makes no odds; we should choose these even if no pleasure

resulted."[2] So the objects of desires in general, including aspirat cannot be reduced to the simple common denominator of having tain pleasurable self-centered feelings; they are far more varied than The aspiration to be a certain kind of person must encompass aspec the self that go beyond such feelings, and the values it seeks to a must be correspondingly broadened.

Two qualifications should be noted here. First, there may be as tions whose direct objects, what one aspires to, are certain feeling oneself. In such cases the subjective aspect of felt satisfaction is p mount among the aspirant's aims. But this is far from being the case all aspirations. Second, the nonsubjectivity of objects of aspiration d not mean that aspirations and aspiration-fulfillment do not have an sential relation to the self that has them.

We must now note that aspirations are not merely desires; they one's deepest desires. The term "deepest" suggests the idea of a str ture or layers of desire, some of which derive more closely from the in core of the self than others; and they can be unconscious or conscio In the former case there arises the problem, to which I shall return, how well one can know one's aspirations, including their genesis. But either case desires that are deepest are usually not only stronger th others in their motivational force; they express the most intimate yea ings of the self, and they reflect most directly the values and indeed t very definition of the self as an enduring conative entity. What one a pires to is rooted in one's conception of oneself as the kind of pers one most wants to be as having a certain identity, living a certain kind life, and attaining certain kinds of experiences and values. In this regar aspirations are higher-order desires; they are desires to have not only th objects of one's desires but also to be a person who is characterized bot as having those desires and as being successful in attaining them.[3] A important element of self-evaluation, and also possibly of elitism, thu enters into all aspirations. In this way aspirations toward certain object or values are unified with aspirations about oneself. This reflexivity is no the same as the mental-content view discussed above. The desire to be

[2] Aristotle, *Nicomachean Ethics* (trans. W. D. Ross), 10. 3. 1174a. See also the discussion of the "experience machine" in Robert Nozick, *Anarchy, State, and Utopia* (New York: Basic Books, 1974), pp. 42–45. On "mental state" accounts of utility see the valuable discussion in James Griffin, *Well-Being* (Oxford: Clarendon Press, 1986), chap. 1. See also Sigmund Freud, "On Narcissism: An Introduction," in Freud, *Collected Papers* (New York: Basic Books, 1959), vol. 4, pp. 30–59.

[3] For the distinction of orders of desire, see especially Harry G. Frankfurt, "Freedom of the Will and the Concept of a Person," *Journal of Philosophy* 68 (January 1971): 5–20. For critical discussion of the distinction, see the essays collected in Gary Watson, ed., *Free Will* (Oxford: Oxford University Press, 1982). My discussion in the text is indebted to Watson's introduction to this anthology.

dinate ones into their proper place. This need not involve a rigid fixation on a single goal without regard to experiential factors that call for modifying one's initial aims. One can and should learn from experience (see below, 2.3). But the aspiring person can try to have some perspective in becoming aware of what are her deepest desires in relation to her overall strivings.

Such ordering of desires toward one's aspirations is an important step toward maturity and having a secure sense of self. At its best it involves not only that one knows what one wants and that one can order one's life toward attaining it; it involves also that one knows who one is, what one's prime values are, and how one stands both toward fulfilling them and hence also toward fulfilling oneself. To recognize certain of one's desires as "deepest" entails a corresponding recognition of who "at bottom" one is or wants to be. This latter recognition may sometimes be terrifying because it calls for a firm commitment about one's values and goals of life. But such an attitude toward one's aspiration-fulfillment can also engender a kind of serenity that stands in marked contrast to the person who is bewildered by his life because he doesn't know what he wants or because he wants too many things without reflecting on how he came to have those wants and how they bear on what he wants to get out of life. As we shall see (2.2), a certain kind of desire-autonomy is vitally important here.

Three aspects may be distinguished in aspirations: the self, its deepest desires, and the desired objects. As I noted above, the human self, whatever else it may be, is an embodied entity that can think in general and systematic terms, can have desires of varying degrees of complexity, and can reflect on its desires (1.4). In aspirations the self tends to identify itself in part with the other two aspects; far from taking a detached view of its desires and their objects, its attitude toward them is evaluative, conative, and proactive. But at the same time the self turns its desires on itself, in that, by a higher-order desire, it aspires to be a certain kind of person. The elitism sometimes attributed to self-fulfillment arises from this loftiness of self-conception. So aspiration-fulfillment does not consist simply in bringing certain objects into existence; there must also be the relation of those objects to the aspirations for them and to the evaluating self that has these aspirations.

The idea of aspirations as one's deepest and second-order desires raises the question of the structure or organization of the "self" that has these desires. As we saw above in criticizing the pseudo-Aristotelian conception of the actualization of potentialities (1.3), the self's aspirations do not flow from the self as reflecting its "nature" or its "natural end." But are there distinct selves, including unconscious ones, that have, or correspond to the distinctions of, more and less deep desires and second-order and first-order desires? Such a possibility would have a serious impact on the attainability of aspiration-fulfillment, for it would disrupt the continuities between these several sets of desires, including the ways in which higher-order desires can influence lower-order desires by, among other things, coming to have greater knowledge of the causes and consequences of the lower-order desires. More generally, the idea of self-fulfillment as aspiration-fulfillment does not require positing two distinct selves, one that gets fulfilled and one that does the fulfilling. To understand the notion of self-fulfillment it is sufficient to posit a single enduring self which can gradually acquire greater knowledge of itself and use this knowledge to guide its lower-order desires. In this way the self can fulfill itself through fulfilling its aspirations while remaining the same self. But this exclusive centrality of the self may also buttress the charge that self-fulfillment is egoistic.

It will help to further clarify the notion of aspirations as deepest desires if they are contrasted with "supreme desires," which I characterized above as consisting in what one most wants to have. What does it mean for someone to "most want" something? On a certain view of human action it might seem that in every action, or at least in every successful action, the agent fulfills herself in that she gets what she most wants to have. For all action is purposive in that the agent intends to achieve some end or goal that she regards as good, as having sufficient value to merit her trying to attain it, on whatever criterion of goodness and value figures in her purpose in acting. Now if, from among the alternative actions open to her, the agent unforcedly chooses one and performs it, then it is plausible to hold that this is the action which on that occasion she most wants to perform. So it would follow that, on the model of aspirations as strongest desires, self-fulfillment as aspiration-fulfillment is a feature of *every* action. A thesis of this sort has been attributed to T. H. Green: "In every act of willing a man's aim is . . . some realization of himself in a state of affairs projected as his own good . . . in all voluntary action a man seeks to realize himself in what he takes to be his own good." F. H. Bradley said something similar: "for morality the end implies the act, and the act implies self-realization."[4]

We may call such a view of self-fulfillment an *occurrent* view. Its implausibility stems from the fact that it overlooks the aspect of aspiration as one's deepest higher-order desire that involves a person's general conception of himself as embodying certain wished-for values. Not

---

[4] The paraphrase of Green is from J. B. Schneewind, *Sidgwick's Ethics and Victorian Moral Philosophy* (Oxford: Clarendon Press, 1977), p. 406. See also F. H. Bradley, *Ethical Studies*, 2nd edition (Oxford: Clarendon Press, 1927), pp. 65–66.

every particular action has such a general involvement; many are trivial and transitory in relation to the depth and intimacy of desire that characterize aspirations.

It is also important, however, to avoid the opposite extreme of assuming that generality of self-conception is incompatible with occurrent conceptions of the objects of aspiration. The dictionary definition of "aspiration" as "a strong desire for high achievement" that I quoted above might suggest that only "high achievement" can figure as the object aimed at by aspiration-fulfillment. But while such height may indeed characterize many attempts at self-fulfillment, more modest goals may also be envisaged, so that a blanket association of self-fulfillment with an exclusivist elitism is to be rejected. Some persons may aspire only to a life of simple pleasures or even of ascetic self-denial, as in Omar Khayyam's wish to have only "a jug of wine, a loaf of bread—and thou" or in Tolstoy's renunciation of worldly goods for the life of a religious ascetic. Such goals may indeed by interpreted as "high achievement" by the persons who pursue them; but this brings out the variability and relativity of the objects of aspiration-fulfillment. So the depth of desire that constitutes aspiration does not, as such, entail any specific or absolute supremacy or heights of the objects of aspiration. But it does reflect the general conception of who one wants to be that is central to aspirations as higher-order desires.

Even if the occurrent view is maintained whereby for some person a certain momentary experience or action may constitute his aspiration-fulfillment, the aspects of depth and centrality of conception may still figure vitally in the accompanying aspiration. Consider, for example, the culminating action in the film *Claire's Knee*, where the protagonist's height of satisfaction comes when he touches the knee of the beautiful Claire. Jérôme's desire to touch her knee was not simply an episodic aim; it was an end he had long cultivated, guiding many of his other motives and actions and representing his higher-order conception of himself as a profound appreciator of feminine beauty. His fulfillment of his aspiration in touching Claire's knee, while it may have been momentary in its actual duration, was not on a par with all his other particular purposive actions; it represented the carefully thought out climax of a whole sequence of actions controlled by his conception of himself as aiming at a certain profound satisfaction. In such ways aspirations are pervasive desires that affect major phases of one's life. They may be identified in part with whole "plans of life,"[5] but as such they are directly not so much inclusive but rather culminative of other desires.

[5] See John Rawls, *A Theory of Justice* (Cambridge, Mass.: Harvard University Press, 1971), pp. 407–16.

A tradition going back to Plato holds that desires are always for something that one does not have; and although Aristotle presented some well-founded criticisms of this thesis, it can be used here to bring out an important further point about aspirations in their relation to elitism. Many persons who have aspirations to fame, beauty, or other values proceed on the comfortable, realistic assumption that they already have the necessities of life, and so can afford to concentrate on such "luxuries." Other persons may maintain such high aspirations even at the expense of their not having the basic necessities: the starving artist in the garret is a traditional example. But even for those who have the necessities and recognize that they are indeed indispensable preconditions of their attaining the heights to which they aspire, it would be incorrect to say that they aspire to have the necessities, since desires are for what one does not have. One may instead want to say that they aspire to *continue* to have the necessities. But even if such continuation is not something they already have, insofar as they do not have to worry about the continuation it does not figure among their aspirations. As deepest desires, aspirations involve keen, purposeful awareness, even if at some level it may not be entirely conscious, and the awareness is conative, aiming at something not yet (fully) possessed.

Nevertheless, aspirations may have contents that are negative as well as positive: they may involve the removal of deficiencies as well as the achievement of new heights, and can thus be had among many different, non-elitist levels of society. When slaves have as their deepest desires to get rid of their shackles as central parts of their conceptions of themselves as rightfully free persons, the motivational force of their aspiration is at least as potent as that of the artist whose deepest desire is to create a new form of beauty. The attainment of new heights may indeed be construed as the removal of deficiencies: the artist's motivation may be described as the overcoming of a felt lack of beautiful objects, just as choice in general, because it requires surrendering one favored alternative for the sake of another, may be construed as essentially negative.[6] Such relativity can be avoided, however, if we take further note of a certain plausible baseline: the needs of human action. There is a difference between situations where these needs are threatened or not satisfied, and situations where one proceeds on the basis of already satisfied needs of action. The starving person aspires to have food, and the well-fed person aspires to write a novel. But even if the latter's aspiration is characterized as the desire to overcome the lack of a personal achievement, the fact that his need for food and other necessities of life and action has

---

[6] Cf. Lionel Robbins, *An Essay on the Nature and Significance of Economic Science* (London: Macmillan, 1952), pp. 15, 30.

already been satisfied differentiates his positive aspiration from the negative aspiration of the removal of hunger. The latter is below the baseline, while the former is above it. So each aspiration is marked by depth
and centrality but in different ways, relative to different levels of need or
affluence.

There is, nevertheless, an important similarity between aspirations
and basic needs. In each case they obtrude upon the self; their insistent
demands make themselves strongly felt. So it would seem pointless to
ask whether one can know what one's aspirations are. But the 'what'
here is ambiguous; it may mean at least three different things: first, a
vivid desiderative mental state; second, the directly perceived object of
this mental state, its direct content, what it is directly a deep desire for;
third, the envisaged outcome of having this direct object. The first two
of these are at least partly known by direct second-order awareness, although some of their contents as well as their causes may be unconscious. The third, the envisaged outcome, is more conjectural. But all
three figure as aspects of aspiration; and, as was noted above, the second, the direct object, cannot as such be reduced to the first. What one
desires in aspirations is a certain object, not an extended mental state of
oneself, so that a certain kind of egoism or self-centeredness may be
avoided. But there may be complications that sometimes render these
distinctions doubtful.

Consider, for example, love as a deep desire to possess and/or benefit
someone. First, there is the feeling or emotion itself which one recognizes as love and as characterizing oneself as having or wanting love;
second, there is the person who is the direct object of this emotion,
whom one recognizes as the beloved; and third, there is the joy that one
anticipates experiencing as a consequence of having the beloved. The
anticipation may be disappointed while the first two may be securely
known. And the joy is consequential upon the having of the beloved;
but while it may be distinct from the having in some cases, in others it
may not be.

These features of aspiration may be illustrated by some passages from
eminent works of modern fiction. Consider, for example, Emma Bovary
as described by Flaubert: "Love, she believed, should come with the
suddenness of thunder and lightning, should burst like a storm upon her
life, sweeping her away, scattering her resolutions like leaves before
a wind, driving her whole heart to the abyss." She experienced "overmastering desire." "She was realizing the long dream of her youth, seeing herself as one of those great lovers whom she had so much envied."[7]

---

[7] Gustave Flaubert, *Madame Bovary*, trans. Gerard Hopkins (Oxford: Oxford University
Press, 1981), pp. 94, 142, 154.

Or consider Anna Karenina as described by Tolstoy: Vronsky's love of her "constituted the whole interest of her life." "She knew beforehand that religion could help her only on condition that she renounce what constituted the whole meaning of her life." "God made me so that I needed love and life."[8] For a further example, from Dreiser's *Sister Carrie*, George Hurstwood said to Carrie, "I want you to love me. You don't know how much I need someone to waste a little affection on me." "I could be content if I had you to love me." Hurstwood "dreamed a new dream of pleasure which concerned his present fixed condition not at all."[9]

These quotations raise questions about the meaning of the "love" they invoke. But each protagonist is saying, in effect, that she will be fulfilled if she gets the love she so deeply desires. The passages depict love as an aspiration, an "overmastering desire," as constituting "the whole meaning of life," as a deep "want" that derives from the most intimate part of oneself and, as a higher-order desire, reflects the love-seeker's central conception of herself. There can hardly be any mistaking of either the feeling or its direct object, quite apart from its underlying unconscious causes or the tragic outcome of suicide that befell each of the love-seekers. Besides the depth of the desires brought out in the quotations, there is also the strong "subjectivation" and possible narcissism of the objects of aspiration: did the love-seekers desire to have a certain person or to experience a certain feeling? The two were vitally intermingled, and this may help to account for some of their love's pathological features. But, as I have argued above, such interminglings are not true of all aspirations, so that there is a corresponding diversity in the relation of aspiration-fulfillment to an egoism of desires.

2.2. HOW DOES ONE GET ASPIRATIONS?

If aspirations are one's deepest and higher-order desires, the question arises of how one comes to have them and, more generally, how they figure in persons' biographies. As desires, aspirations are vectorial; but do the vectors derive from within or from without? Are they generated solely by the personal or social circumstances in which one finds oneself, or are they to some extent controlled (or controllable) by oneself? Are they products of one's autonomous choice, or is there little or no autonomy here, their causes being unconscious forces beyond one's control?

---

[8] Leo Tolstoy, *Anna Karenina*, trans. Joel Carmichael (New York: Bantam Books, 1981), pp. 134, 308, 312.

[9] Theodore Dreiser, *Sister Carrie* (Oxford: Oxford University Press, 1991), pp. 119, 121, 136–37.

What motivates persons to have aspirations? And, in connection with the preceding section, do the aspirations reflect more the kind of person one wants to be or the values one wants to attain? These questions bear on the feasibility of aspiration-fulfillment as a practical goal or ideal of human striving. And in their invocation of concepts of freedom or autonomy they raise issues about the value of self-fulfillment not only as a product of human activity but also as a process of engagement in that activity.

The formation of aspirations may be strongly influenced by one's awareness of the obstacles to their fulfillment. Both internal and external circumstances may limit one's formation of aspirations. A youth who feels himself to be deficient in mathematical or literary ability is unlikely to aspire to be a mathematical physicist or a novelist. Circumstances of poverty, race, and gender may also limit persons' formation of aspirations because of the obstacles they set to success in fulfilling them. On such grounds, even the having of aspirations may seem to be elitist: one may feel that only the fortunate few who are likely to succeed will have aspirations in the first place.

Nevertheless, it seems clear that having aspirations comes naturally to many persons. This naturalness should not be construed on the model of the "natural ends" discussed above (1.3). There are, indeed, desires for food, drink, and so forth that derive from our natures as biological beings, and these set important limits to aspirations. But, beyond these necessities, aspirations may arise in many ways that reflect personal choices and the varieties of the human condition, including even the lacks and deficiencies that may serve to stimulate aspirations. In these ways, aspirations tell us a great deal about the aspiring self, the self that has, gets, and fulfills its aspirations. In this process the self reveals much about itself: as you aspire, so you are. The process may also confront obstacles that prevent the self from fulfilling its aspirations and even from having them. But the self may also develop strategies for dealing with these obstacles.

If, for example, one is dissatisfied with one's life or one's world, one may form a conception of something better: an ideal of personal or social development that remedies the deficiencies of one's present existence and moves on to a better phase of one's life. This new phase may be viewed as a fulfillment both of aspirations and of tendencies or potentialities that are latent in oneself; the fulfillment also creates new potentialities that are improvements of what one was before. The idea of improvement is central here: one moves on to something that one regards as definitely better than what one was or had before. The desire for this something better may become a ruling passion, one's deepest desire, and one may invest central parts of oneself in developing it and trying to achieve its object. Sometimes this object is modeled on some past master—Moses, Socrates, Jesus, Marx, Gandhi, Freud, Martin Luther King, Jr.—but at other times one may dream of being a great scientist, a great lover, a great artist or athlete, and so forth. But these ideals may be viewed not as alien to one's present self but as developments of it that bring to fruition its most vital and valuable inherent abilities. One is here pregnant with possibilities whose procreation and development become one's dearest wish. The question for aspiration-fulfillment thus is: How can I make my dearest wishes come true?

From this it follows that the having of aspirations is, as such, a good. The person who has aspirations has something to live for that is especially significant for him, something that gives meaning, zest, and focus to his life. It is true that aspirations imply lacks, unsatisfied desires. But this very dissatisfaction may be a stimulus toward activity that holds one's interest and provides goals for action. A person without aspirations is likely to be mired in conditions from which he does not seek to escape—perhaps because he sees no way of escape. So the formation of aspirations is affected by environing social conditions that set limits to what one regards as attainable.

But what if someone is fully satisfied or at least not dissatisfied with his life? Such a person would have no desire, let alone a deep, higher-order desire, to go beyond (or to rise above) the present condition either of himself or of other parts of the world. There are at least three different possibilities here. One is that he is simply not aware of any changes that might make his life better. A second is that he is aware of possible improvements in his life, but sees no way to achieve them; his life, for him, is hopeless. A third is that he is aware of possible changes in his life, but he does not want to pursue them either because of slothfulness or because he is perfectly satisfied with what he has. An example of the latter case would be the man who has what is sometimes called a fulfilling career and also a loving and happy wife whom he deeply loves and is committed to, as well as fine children. But aspirations may be found even in such a case—not only for his children but for further successes in his career, as well as for continued long life with his wife.

As for persons whose lack of aspirations is due to ignorance or inability, these conditions are pathological because they signify the thwarting of capacities that could be within the persons' reach and that, if fulfilled, would enable the persons to be more in control of their lives or at least to get more out of their lives. It might turn out that even if they achieved such control they would still resist having aspirations because of slothfulness or fear. It might be said of such a person that he does not know what he is missing, and he doesn't care. But a deep desire to maintain his status quo may still be attributed to him.

In all such cases, however, it is important to take note of environing social circumstances that condition both the presence and the absence of aspirations, and if the presence, that affect what their objects are. These circumstances add another important variable to the self, its desires, and their objects to which we have thus far confined the consideration of aspiration-fulfillment. For example, what one aspires to if one lives in a theocratic society or a totalitarian state may well be different from the aspirations found in secular liberal democracies. The reason for this is a matter both of conditioning and of feasibility. In theocratic and totalitarian societies persons' conceptions of themselves may be so shaped that aspirations take the form of abiding by what is proclaimed as the will of God or of the ruling party, while in liberal societies the objects of aspirations may be matters of personal choice. Even in the latter cases, however, there are many obstacles to aspiration-fulfillment, and these may strongly influence the aspirations one has. One's aspirations may be shaped by one's beliefs about their feasibility both consciously and unconsciously. A woman living in a strongly patriarchal society may suppress her aspirations to be a lawyer either because she is explicitly aware that the society will not tolerate her fulfilling her ambition or because, without being explicitly aware of this, she simply accepts the society's limitations. She "has" the aspiration in that it is her deepest desire reflecting her wished-for conception of herself, while at the same time she suppresses her desire because of her recognition of the obstacles. In such a case she may come to have a different aspiration, such as being a dutiful housewife; this represents her "adaptive preference." In such preferences "people tend to adjust their aspirations to their possibilities," where the possibilities themselves are set by external circumstances[10] (see also below, 5.4).

Besides the broader social context, familial circumstances may also strongly influence the presence, kind, and absence of aspirations, especially in their impact on persons' self-esteem. A child who is constantly belittled by his parents may grow up having a poor self-image; so what aspirations he has may be colored by his conviction that he doesn't and cannot amount to much. The expectations in many families that girls are inherently inferior to boys also serve to color girls' conceptions of themselves and to engender self-fulfilling prophecies about their being doomed to failure if they have any but the most modest aspirations.

---

[10] See Jon Elster, *Sour Grapes* (Cambridge: Cambridge University Press, 1983), chap. 3, including p. 109.

More generally, the nurturing or lack thereof that one receives from one's parents can have a powerful effect on the development of children's aspirations.[11]

Such variations raise at least two questions. First, if one's aspirations are influenced by one's social or familial context, doesn't this suggest that one's deepest desire is to conform to that context? A partial answer is that causal or other influences on desires should not be confused with the conscious desires themselves so far as concerns their objects. One may be influenced by situation S to desire some X, but this does not entail that one desires S or that one is even conscious of S.

Second, may one not have unconscious desires: to sleep with one's mother, to murder one's father, to imitate Moses or Jesus, and so forth? In such cases aspirations may involve conflicts between deep conscious and unconscious desires which lead to frustration and unhappiness.

These considerations raise moral issues that will be dealt with more fully below (3.4). As I shall argue, persons have a moral right to be free from the aforementioned social obstacles to their effective formation of aspirations. In this connection the vital importance of personal autonomy must be stressed, because this affects the extent to which persons can control their having of aspirations.

We may begin from the familiar etymological idea of autonomy as setting one's law for oneself, by "law" meaning rules of conduct. But we must distinguish two kinds of autonomy: desire-autonomy and behavior-autonomy. Desire-autonomy bears on the process whereby the rules are formed; it involves that one controls the process in that one has chosen the rules in a self-critical way, such that one has brought one's second-order reflective choices to bear on one's first-order choices.[12] In this way desire-autonomy enables a person to move closer to self-understanding; he not only has certain desires but he also knows why he has them. The self that has such understanding is the person in a fuller sense than the passive undergoer of powerful forces, for she now can understand and control the forces that impinge on her—where 'her' signifies the narrower sense of the person viewed apart from the self-knowledge that she can attain.

Nevertheless, as Freud and others have emphasized, unconscious forces within the self may have a powerful impact on its formation of

---

[11] See Everett Waters *et al.*, eds., *Caregiving, Cultural and Cognitive Perspectives on Secure-Base Behavior and Working Models: New Growing Points of Attachment Theory and Research*, in *Monographs of the Society for Research in Child Development*, 60, nos. 2–3 (1995).

[12] See Gerald Dworkin, *The Theory and Practice of Autonomy* (Cambridge: Cambridge University Press, 1988), p. 20. See also John Christman, ed., *The Inner Citadel* (New York: Oxford University Press, 1989), pp. 6, 13.

aspirations. These forces, stemming in part from one's familial environment, may operate to shape one's self-conception as well as one's deepest wants. One may find oneself returning to certain kinds of desires through an unconscious "repetition compulsion," even though one has previously experienced the harmfulness of the desires. Such conditions, antithetical to desire-autonomy, may severely limit the possibility of aspiration-fulfillment as something that is good for the self, and psychotherapy may be needed. I shall return to this matter below in dealing with love as a part of particularist morality (4.7).

Desire-autonomy, in contrast, enables you to control your aspirations rather than having them shaped either from without or from unconscious forces within the self. So desire-autonomy adds, to the components of aspiration-fulfillment previously considered, the further elements of knowledge of, or at least critical reflection on, the genesis of one's aspirations and the control of that genesis. Such autonomy carries forward the general idea of self-fulfillment as bringing to fruition parts or phases of oneself that bear on one's attainment of a good or satisfying life, and this without positing a multiplicity of selves.

In its fullest extent, aspiration-fulfillment requires that one's aspirations be formed by desire-autonomy on the part of the aspirant. This derives from the idea that aspirations include reference not only to desired objects but also to the person's conception of himself as reflected in his higher-order desire. By desire-autonomy the person brings this conception of himself to bear on his deepest desires. So the aspiration to be a certain kind of person goes together with the aspiration to achieve certain values. In this regard, then, aspirations are themselves chosen, not merely undergone. Even if what you aspire to reflects your upbringing, including your cultural milieu, you can take effective cognizance of your aspirations and decide whether to maintain them or to seek others. This is parallel to the way in which, according to Aristotle, while the learning of ethical norms requires a good initial upbringing, what one does with that upbringing, the actions one performs, depends upon oneself through one's own informed efforts.[13]

In these ways, autonomy comes to figure not only in the formation of aspirations but also as itself an object of aspiration. One wants to be in control of one's formation of aspirations not only because this will help one to achieve other objects but also because one identifies oneself with one's aspirations. So autonomy is itself regarded as a good worthy of being sought after and attained. This may reflect in part the "subjectivism" of desires considered above. But the desired autonomy is not simply a feeling or a mental state but an objective condition of one's con-

---

[13] See *Nicomachean Ethics*, 1. 4. 1095b4; 3. 5. 1113b3 ff.

duct, and, far from subsuming the whole of objects of aspirations, it leaves a distinct place for them. You desire not only autonomy but also the various other goods that your desire-autonomy makes possible for you as objects of your aspirations.

Is desire-autonomy possible? In a general sense this question concerns the ancient problem of freedom of the will. But more specifically the question bears on the constraints that operate to restrict the range of effective desires, including not only unconscious forces but also poverty, illness, ignorance, and various forms of coercion. Persons who are subject to such constraints may be debarred from controlling even which desires will figure in the aspirations they may adopt. Both their self-conceptions and their envisaged values may thereby be severely diminished. Moreover, the desire for autonomy may be counteracted by various fears and other influences. You may fear the lack of external guidance and control that comes with autonomy; and your outlook may be so dominated by external environmental influences that you reject, or do not even think of, your autonomy as itself a good worthy of support (see below, 4.2). As we have seen, one's upbringing, including disparagement by one's parents or peers, may cause one to doubt one's abilities and to take the easy way out, as against "sticking one's neck out." The social environment, including discrimination, suppression, poverty, or lack of opportunities may make it difficult even to aspire to levels of excellence that may match one's inherent potentialities, so that there is little or no desire-autonomy in relation to such aspirations.

These negative considerations do not counteract the relevance or importance of the connection of aspiration-fulfillment with autonomy. For the considerations themselves stem from or reflect a lack of autonomy. Hence, the value or requiredness of autonomy is not disproved by pointing to conditions whose efficacy stems from a violation of autonomy. The solution to this problem is to maintain or restore autonomy, not acquiesce in its violation. As we shall see, this aim requires an effective system of human rights as a way of avoiding elitist restrictions of desire-autonomy in relation to aspiration-fulfillment. Moreover, persons can themselves control to an important extent whether they can achieve or approach desire-autonomy.

Thus far I have been discussing desire-autonomy. Let us briefly look at a second kind of autonomy: behavior-autonomy. This goes beyond desire-autonomy in that it bears on one's actions following upon one's desires or choices. It is not enough for the self to control its desires, for such control taken by itself is compatible with control of one's behavior by external forces. For aspiration-fulfillment the self must also be able to control its actions in accord with those desires. In this way autonomy now concerns not the desires that enter into the formation of rules but rather the actions that one undertakes in accordance with the rules. This brings us to our next topic: what serves to bring about aspiration-fulfillment.

2.3. HOW DOES ONE FULFILL ONE'S ASPIRATIONS?

In dealing with this question, two essential preliminaries must be considered, each hearkening back to the preceding two sections. As we have seen, aspirations are one's deepest desires, and desires are vectorial, such that one tries to get what one desires. But this requirement of trying raises the question of whether what one has is a genuine desire or is instead a kind of wishful thinking. It is not enough for you to think how nice it would be for you to get something, such as outstanding success as a novelist or athlete or entrepreneur. Such thoughts amount to little more than daydreaming unless you are willing to invest the energy, time, hard work, and careful planning that are required for you to get what you want, with due regard for the organizing principles referred to above (2.1). This does not call for a kind of fanaticism in which the ordinary needs of daily living are ignored, nor does it overlook the obstacles to desire-autonomy noted above. Moreover, there may be important advantages of spontaneity both in forming and in fulfilling one's aspirations. Aspiration-fulfillment at its best can be, and is, enjoyable. But the enjoyment is much deeper and more stable and meaningful than what one gets by watching a television show. The drive toward aspiration-fulfillment, when one does the hard work it requires, can lift one's spirits and confirm one's second-order view of oneself as the kind of person one wants to be.

Another preliminary carries further the notion of effective desire. The obstacles to desire-autonomy noted above may lead persons to think that the fulfillment of their aspirations depends not on themselves but on external circumstances for which they are not responsible (see also 5.4). As we shall see, there may be a genuine alternative here. Nevertheless, to achieve aspiration-fulfillment it is vitally important to accept responsibility for one's actions. It is all too easy to blame others for one's failings—one's parents, one's associates, one's society. Such blame may often have a factual basis. But to remain mired in such blaming is a sure recipe for failure. One must be ready and eager to seize ways of overcoming the obstacles one finds in one's way. One must regard oneself not as a passive recipient (let alone victim) of the agency of others but rather as an autonomous agent on one's own behalf.

The charge of elitism may be raised against these attributions of desire- and behavior-autonomy. It may be noted that too many of the world's peoples are so sunk in poverty, ignorance, illness, and oppression that they cannot achieve the kinds of aspiration-fulfillment just sketched. There is much truth in this, and it shows again how the human rights to be discussed below are crucially relevant to the universal availability of aspiration-fulfillment. Nevertheless, the requirements here indicated have their own independent justification.

To carry on this analysis, we must note again that there is a direct connection between the formation of aspirations considered above and the question of their fulfillment. To base one's aspirations on "false consciousness" or on unconscious drives incurs the danger either that the aspirations will not be fulfilled or—what is partly the same thing—that they will turn out not to be what one "really" wanted, where the "really" signifies that the desires have been brought to conscious awareness and have survived critical evaluation in the light of one's other relevant higher-order desires, including the facts that bear on them.

Such awareness and scrutiny show again the importance of distinguishing levels of desire. The second-order desires of desire-autonomy that one has on the basis of reflective evaluation—what one desires to desire as a result of such evaluation—can be considered to be one's desires in a more stable and authentic sense than the desires one has and pursues without subjecting them to critical scrutiny. In this way, too, the depth of desire that characterizes aspirations is brought more fully into line with the person's autonomy because he is more fully in control of his desires.

Let us now consider this issue by connecting it more explicitly with behavior-autonomy. In self-fulfillment, is it the person himself who brings about his own fulfillment? In the reflexive phrase "fulfillment of oneself," is the "of" not only an objective genitive—it is oneself that gets fulfilled—but also a subjective genitive—it is oneself that does the fulfilling? This view has been implied by Jon Elster: "The reason why the choice of a vehicle for self-realization must be freely made by the individual is that otherwise it would not be *self*-realization. The individual is both the designer and the raw material of the process."[14] This view would make the self's own desire- and behavior-autonomy essential to self-fulfillment, since it would require that the self be in control of the process. But this has also been denied: "Nor is autonomy a precondition of self-realization, for one can stumble into a life of self-realization or be manipulated into it or reach it in some other way which is inconsistent with autonomy . . . [it] can be developed by simulation and deceit."[15]

[14] See Jon Elster, "Self-Realization in Work and Politics: The Marxist Conception of the Good Life," *Social Philosophy and Policy* 3, no. 2 (spring 1986): 101 (emphasis in original).

[15] Joseph Raz, *The Morality of Freedom* (Oxford: Clarendon Press, 1986), pp. 375–76. See also S. I. Benn, *A Theory of Freedom* (Cambridge: Cambridge University Press, 1988), p. 199.

For an example of such nonautonomous self-fulfillment, suppose that A's aspiration is to become a millionaire by controlling his own investments, and B arranges for A to get a million dollars but misleads A into thinking he has done it by himself. Here A attains self-fulfillment without any control on his part, so that his own autonomy does not figure in the attainment.

Each of these views is partly correct, but they overlook certain salient points. The pro-autonomy view may not take sufficient account of conditions external to the self that affect both the formation and the fulfillment of aspirations. Even in the relatively benign case of liberal democracies with their protection of individual rights to desire- and behavior-autonomy, it must be recognized that these protections themselves make an important contribution to persons' ability to fulfill their aspirations. Aspiration-fulfillment requires a social context that at least does not prevent either the formation or the fulfillment of aspirations. But this context provides only a general causal background, at most a necessary condition for aspiration-fulfillment. Given this background, a person can have autonomous control of his aspiration-fulfillment.

The anti-autonomy position may incorporate a realistic view of the role of luck in human affairs, but it takes too mechanical a view of self-fulfillment and may entirely disregard the role of aspirations. Even if it is confined to capacity-fulfillment, the position overlooks that when a person is subjected to such operations as simulation and deceit, his own rational capacities may be frustrated, so that he is prevented from developing and using them at their best. With regard to aspiration-fulfillment, the anti-autonomy position overlooks that such fulfillment consists not only in attaining certain desired objects but also in fulfilling one's higher-order desires that reflect one's conception of the self one wants to be. It is the central presence of this self-conception in aspiration-fulfillment that makes the person's autonomy an essential part of such fulfillment. He exercises both desire-autonomy and behavior-autonomy in forming his aspirations in accordance with his conception of himself and in acting to fulfill them.

There are at least three reasons for tying aspiration-fulfillment to autonomy, if not logically then at least practically. First, if one does not control the process whereby one fulfills one's aspirations, there is a danger that the process will not be successful. To rely solely on others for such achievement is to render it precarious. The help of other persons may indeed be sought and obtained, but the would-be successful aspirant should also be realistically aware of the contingencies of this help and be prepared to marshal his own efforts as effectively as possible toward this end. Second, an important kind of self-esteem is lost if one's achievement of one's aspirations is the result of manipulations by other persons.

Third, for aspiration-fulfillment to be more than temporary or transitory, for it to have the depth that characterizes genuine aspirations, it cannot be something that one "stumbles" into; instead, it must be based on relevant knowledge of oneself and of what, at bottom, one wants for oneself. So for all these reasons the process of aspiration-fulfillment, if it is to be effective, should be under the aspirant's control, so that it is tied to her own autonomy.

To attain such control, the depth of desire that directly constitutes aspirations needs to be modified by the knowledge that enters into the autonomous person's conception of himself. This knowledge can be spelled out in certain familiar ways as having two kinds of objects: the process of aspiration-fulfillment and the envisaged product. With regard to the process, one realistically needs to know, first, whether one is capable of attaining the aspired-to object. This involves not only one's physical, intellectual, and technical capacities but also one's emotional and conative abilities. As thinkers like Spinoza and Freud have emphasized, one must know how to limit one's desires in the light of one's capacities. If you aspire to become a famous novelist, do you have the required equipment of linguistic facility and imagination? And do you have the temperament to go through the arduous exertions and inevitable disappointments that may confront a literary career? It is often exceedingly difficult to attain such knowledge amid the strength of the desires that enter into aspirations. And often one is in a position to approach answers to these questions only after one has actually tried to act in the required ways. Self-deception frequently occurs here. This apparently paradoxical reflexive relation involves, among other things, that the self, while knowing certain facts that enter into its higher-order desires, suppresses that knowledge in pursuing its first-order desires.

Another important factor that may affect the process of aspiration-fulfillment is the phenomenon of conscious or unconscious self-defeat. Because of adverse childhood conditioning, one may seek to frustrate one's aspirations while thinking one wants to fulfill them. Such self-defeat may arise from a desire, little known to oneself, to slough off the influence of a parent or other authority-figure, where this influence is felt to be oppressive. The desire then is to defeat an aspiration whose fulfillment would constitute victory for the authority-figure whose influence or power over oneself one wants to reject. In the case of such self-defeating behavior, self-knowledge attained through therapy or otherwise can bring to awareness the background causal factors and hence help one to overcome the behavior. Self-defeat, then, is one of the main factors that can inhibit aspiration-fulfillment.[16]

[16] For graphic portrayals of this phenomenon, based partly on Freudian sources, see Samuel J. Warner, *Self-Realization and Self-Defeat* (New York: Grove Press, 1966).

Whatever its causes, self-defeat may operate in other ways to defeat aspiration-fulfillment. As I noted above (2.1), persons may act in ways contrary to their professed aspirations: the man who aspires to professional success may defeat his aspiration by alcoholism or womanizing, and so forth. Many tragedies of personal life result from such conflicts.

Persons may act contrary to their aspirations in other ways. Especially in our efficiency-oriented society, they may become so obsessed with various means that they lose sight of the ends to which they aspire. A married couple, for example, may devote so much of their energies to money matters that the mutual love they aspire to preserve is diminished or destroyed. It may be difficult to focus on one's aspirations when the cost of maintaining or fulfilling them becomes prohibitive. The aspiring self must keep in mind the fundamental values that are the contents of its aspirations, and must fit the means into an appropriately subordinate role. In conditions of scarcity this may be an especially difficult assignment. Moreover, the means must be carefully scrutinized to see that they are not in other ways antithetical to the aspired-to end. This condition can be satisfied while taking due account of the continuum of means and ends.

These considerations also bear in other ways on the envisaged product or outcome of aspiration-fulfillment. A central question is this: how sure are you that a given envisaged outcome is what you really want? Psychological literature is full of cases where persons renounce the ends or desires they had previously embraced. "They realize that they do not value such purposes or goals even though they may have lived by them all their lives up to this point."[17] Here it is especially important to try to be clear about the relation between the self one aspires to be and the values one aspires to attain—not only about their attainability by oneself but also about one's estimation of their worth. To deal with this problem, one may use certain prudential choice procedures involving an elementary kind of experimental inductive reasoning. If you do become a famous novelist, will you be truly satisfied? You may feel that this is not enough, that you also need a family or a circle of friends. In that case you will have to revise your conception of what it is you aspire to, what you need for self-fulfillment; and this may well influence

---

[17] Carl R. Rogers, *On Becoming A Person* (Boston: Houghton Mifflin, 1961), p. 170. See also the poignant remarks of John Stuart Mill, *Autobiography*, chap. 5 (ed. Jack Stillinger [Boston: Houghton Mifflin, 1969], p. 81): "it occurred to me to put the question directly to myself, 'Suppose all your objects in life were realized; that all the changes in institutions and opinions which you are looking forward to, could be completely effected at this very instant: would this be a great joy and happiness to you?' And an irrepressible self-consciousness distantly answered, 'No!' At this my heart sank within me: the whole foundation on which my life was constructed fell down. . . . I seemed to have nothing left to live for."

the steps you take in the course of writing your novels: you will be careful not to alienate your friends or family, and to acquire a family or at least a mate.

Besides a method of agreement, methods of concomitant variations and of difference may also be needed. You may try to examine whether, by varying the envisaged aspirandum in certain respects—such as the kind of novel you aspire to write, or the kinds of friends you want to have—this will make the envisaged outcome more desirable for you. Also, you must try to imagine whether, if you remove some part of the envisaged means, this will remove some part of the aspirandum set.

These tidy rational recommendations, based largely on the general patterns of cause-effect and means-end reasoning, may mask the complexities that actually confront persons who cope with the process and the product of their aspirations. There are the familiar difficulties of strong emotions that resist prudential calculations, including the weakness of will whereby one fails to follow the course one regards as best for oneself. This may be viewed as a conflict between two "selves," wherein one's "emotional self" resists one's "rational self." Here a training of the will in the direction of behavior-autonomy may be undertaken. Moreover, persons often become enmeshed in a web of prior commitments both to themselves and to others that may greatly inhibit their ability to have and maintain a rational approach to their aspirations. They may find it difficult to extricate themselves from their pasts and to begin anew both their processes of aspiration-formation and their conceptions of the desired outcomes, including salient aspects of their self-conceptions. But even in such cases it may be possible to bring rational methods to bear on their aspirations in midstream.

These points also bring out two other interrelated aspects of aspiration-fulfillment: aspects that serve to modify but not to cancel my emphasis above (2.1) on the centrality and perspective of having aspirations. First, flexibility rather than rigidity is needed in determining the object of one's aspiration. As one's strivings and deliberation proceed, one should be prepared to revise one's conception of what one aspires to. Revision, however, does not mean cancellation. A "simple" goal like becoming a famous novelist can become specified in many different ways; the cost of achieving some of them may be deemed too great by the aspirant, so that he may shift to others or give up the goal altogether. Sagacity is needed here; the aspirant must try to be wise both about himself and about the aspects of the world that bear on his attainment of his goal. He should try both to avoid giving up too early and to make the revisions that enable him to achieve some reasonable approximation of his goal.

Second, in the process of aspiration-fulfillment, a pluralism of ends may be developed. You deeply desire to become a famous novelist; but this presupposes various means, ranging from staying alive to having supportive friends. Some of these means may be deemed so important that they become part of the end itself, so that your deepest desire comes to take on a large variety of aims or contents. Such pluralism need not be antithetical to the superlativeness of aspirations; it may be to the combination one arrives at that the superlativeness pertains.

This variety, however, raises problems of consistency: what one aspires to may be found, before or after being fulfilled, to conflict with other deep desires. As was noted above, poignant contemporary examples of such conflicts are found in the choices confronting many women between family and career. Many women have aspirations toward each of these, but find it very difficult or impossible to satisfy both. Social institutions, to be discussed more fully below, may help to mitigate such conflicts.

Both because certain of one's aspirations may be frustrated and because a person may have different kinds of interests, it is often prudent not to put all one's eggs in one basket but to provide for some diversity of aspirations. This diversity is compatible with the deep general and culminative features of aspirations; there need not be a conflict of aspirations if they are carefully organized while taking due account of one's abilities and circumstances. Thus, for example, one can be both a good scientist and a good family man despite the difficulties that sometimes attend the combination of these roles. There are, of course, limits to the possibility of such combinations;[18] but some pluralism is both prudent and feasible.

These considerations about the self-knowledge that enters into autonomous aspiration-fulfillment must themselves be qualified in several ways. To the ancient dictum "Know thyself" Freudians and others have responded not only that it is often extremely difficult to know oneself in sufficient depth but also that such knowledge may be dangerous and hence unwelcome. A person, whether or not as a result of psychotherapy, may come to recognize that "at bottom" he is cowardly, lascivious, arrogant, or unfeeling, and he may be unable to change these traits even if he tries. Moreover, in an age of genetic testing one may fear and reject the disclosure that one carries some disease-causing gene.[19] In addition, the very kinds of cautious, calculative inductive reasoning that were recommended as a way of bringing aspirations under autonomous control may have negative effects: not only may they remove the spontaneity that enters into one's acting on one's deepest desires, but they may also diminish their perceived value.

[18] See William James, *Principles of Psychology* (New York: Dover Publications, 1950), vol. 1, p. 309.

[19] See, e.g., U. S. Office of Technology Assessment (Washington, D.C., 1988), *Mapping Our Genes: The Genome Projects: How Big, How Fast?*

So attempts at aspiration-fulfillment are risky. But this does not mean that they should be given up. As I noted above, they add zest, direction, and meaning to one's life. The likelihood of success is strongly affected by relevant traits of oneself. But these traits need not be conceived as fixed and unalterable; on the contrary, just as the traits may affect the achievement of the desired outcomes, so, conversely, the desire for these outcomes can serve to modify the traits themselves. The lazy person who aspires to be a professional ball-player or a scientist may be sparked by his aspirations to change in the direction of zealous industriousness. So self-knowledge, guided by one's aspirations, retains its vital role for autonomous self-fulfillment.

These considerations raise two further sets of problems, one quantitative, the other qualitative. The quantitative problem is this: is there any limit to aspiration-fulfillment? The idea of fulfillment seems to suggest that there is a culmination of the process such that once one's aspiration is fulfilled, no further strivings or desires need or will arise. But if, as thinkers like Hobbes and Freud have emphasized, the sequence of desires is unlimited, the fulfillment of one being but the means to fulfilling another, then this static picture must be rejected or at least revised.[20]

There is indeed no reason why aspiration-fulfillment may not be successive and consecutive. But this should not be interpreted in Hobbesian fashion as simply a succession of atomistic desires. On the contrary, because aspirations are one's deepest desires, they can operate as organizing principles for subordinate desires. Moreover, their culmination should not be regarded as a kind of static nirvana; rather, as was suggested above, their objects or contents are a continuing process of fulfillment, whether as having someone's love or as pursuing some artistic, scientific, or other profession, or as living in accordance with some other highly valued ideal. In this way one's conception of the self one aspires to become can be modified concomitantly with the values one aspires to achieve.

This brings us to a second set of problems, qualitative ones: whose aspirations should one try to fulfill? Leaving aside for now the problems of egoism and elitism, the direct answer is, of course, one's own. But which aspect of oneself should figure here? I noted above that the multiplicity of desires should not be construed as entailing a multiplicity of selves in any literal sense: it is the same self that has both higher-order and lower-order desires and that can gain knowledge bearing on each of these. But let us for now adopt the language of multiple selves as a metaphorical way of dealing with the multiple aspects of the single, en-

---

[20] See Thomas Hobbes, *Leviathan*, chap. 11: "the Felicity of this life consisteth not in the repose of a mind satisfied. . . . Felicity is a continuall progresse of the desire, from one object to another; the attaining of the former, being still but the way to the later."

during self. Now if each person is in some sense multiple, and if not all the aspirations of this multiple self can be fulfilled, then our question is: how should one choose among them?

An obvious example of this multiplicity of selves is temporal: the distinction between earlier and later selves.[21] Let us suppose that A when young aspires to be a movie actor, and that he succeeds in fulfilling this aspiration. But when he is older he may repudiate this aspiration, because his life turns out to be tawdry and superficial or because he no longer has the looks that helped to contribute to his earlier success, or for other reasons. At this later stage he bitterly regrets not having become a public-interest lawyer who would devote his life to defending the interests of the poor.

Here the question of whose aspirations A should have tried to fulfill— those of his earlier self or his later self—merges into a further distinction, between degrees of self-knowledge. The dictum "Know thyself" may be construed as suggesting a division between two parts or phases of the self. One part is that which is to be known, but does not yet know itself, or does not know itself as fully as is needed in the conditions that confront the self. The other part is that which knows this first part: it attains an understanding of itself which it previously lacked. Now when it is said that one should try to fulfill one's aspirations, the prudent course would seem to be that what should be fulfilled is one's self-knowing self's aspirations. But at the time when one projects one's aspirations having a certain envisioned object, one may not yet be such a self-knowing self; one may be ignorant of important and relevant parts of oneself. This is again a reason for holding that aspiration-fulfillment may carry serious risks.

This problem is to be dealt with in a way similar to the problem of infinity of desires. The self is not to be atomized into a series of discrete entities. Rather, self-knowledge involves a continuous process wherein the later stage learns from what has been experienced at an earlier stage and modifies its aspirations and expectations accordingly. In an important sense, then, it is the same person that both knows and is known: the enduring self gradually comes to know itself better. The general point here is essentially the same as that whereby, in the history of modern epistemology, Leibniz overcame Locke's skepticism about our knowledge of physical substance. As against the sharp distinction or barrier set up by the theory of representative perception or in other ways, Leibniz

[21] See Derek Parfit, *Reasons and Persons* (Oxford: Clarendon Press, 1984), pp. 304–6. The problem I consider here is not the same as Joel Feinberg's "paradox of self-fulfillment" (*Freedom and Fulfillment* [Princeton: Princeton University Press, 1992], pp. 94–97), which bears on parents' assisting in their children's self-fulfillment, as against a person's own successive aspirations.

maintained that the gradual growth of knowledge operates to overcome these barriers: we are brought ever closer to knowing the essential nature of substance as that which "underlies" our perceptions.[22] In a parallel way, without any pretension to complete knowledge, the self that makes itself its own cognitive object can, on the basis of its experiences and its reflection thereon, come to know itself better, and can develop its aspirations accordingly.[23]

2.4. TO WHAT DOES ONE AND SHOULD ONE ASPIRE?

I have thus far discussed the nature, formation, and fulfillment of aspirations with only slight reference to their objects. Examples of these objects have indeed been mentioned, such as becoming a famous novelist, a movie actor, or a lover; but I have taken such aspirations as given, as definitive of certain modes of life and value. To go more deeply into this matter, let us first ask: Is there any general object of all aspirations? Happiness might seem to be a plausible answer. But here we confront a well-trodden path of difficulties. If happiness is defined as fulfillment of aspirations, this gets us nowhere. And if happiness is given a substantive definition as having a certain content, such as love and meaningful work, there are the difficulties not only of making these sufficiently specific but also that aspirations may also have many other objects, such as the contemplation of beauty, mystical experience, social betterment, and many other ways of being, having, and doing. Similar difficulties arise if one tries to derive the general objects of aspirations from "natural desires" construed as reflecting the nature of the self (1.3). As we saw earlier, there are also difficulties in the attempt by utilitarians and others to give, as a general answer about the objects of aspirations, that these objects consist in having certain feelings or other mental states. But we also noted certain contexts in which the general answer is partly correct in cases of overpowering desires.

Aristotle's report on the conceptions of "happiness" current in his day—physical pleasure, honor or reputation, and money-making[24]—is still descriptive of widely accepted current objects of aspiration in many other societies, including ours. But there is a difference between regard-

[22] See John Locke, *Essay concerning Human Understanding* II. 23. 2 ff; G. W. Leibniz, *New Essays on Human Understanding* II. 23 (trans. P. Remnant and J. Bennett [Cambridge: Cambridge University Press, 1981], pp. 217–26).

[23] For other modes of multiple selves, see Jon Elster, ed., *The Multiple Self* (Cambridge: Cambridge University Press, 1986); and, for more extreme (including schizoid) divisions, R. D. Laing, *The Divided Self* (Baltimore: Penguin Books, 1965).

[24] Aristotle, *Nicomachean Ethics*, 1.4.

ing any one of these as the sole or chief good or object of aspiration and regarding each of them as a vital component of aspiration-fulfillment but not as the sole or chief component. As we shall see, each can enter in various ways as a part of self-fulfillment. But the development of this point will require that we move from aspiration-fulfillment to capacity-fulfillment.

The question of the object of aspirations is important for several reasons. It calls attention to the important fact, emphasized near the beginning of this chapter, that things other than the self are involved in self-fulfillment, that it aims to achieve values that may go beyond the self. This has a significant bearing on the alleged egoism of self-fulfillment. More generally, the question of the object of aspirations is important because it bears on the more basic question of what aspirations are good for, why we should try to have and fulfill them. I have previously given a very general answer: the having of aspirations adds zest and meaning to life. But this leaves open the question of whether aspirations are necessary for this purpose, whether life can have zest and meaning in other ways. Moreover, the question of what aspirations are good for, if not directly normative, leads quickly to the normative question of what aspirations should we have; what should one aspire to? This question has perhaps been implicit in some of the inductive strategies I sketched above regarding the autonomous agent's use of self-knowledge to modify the processes and objects of his aspirations. But this discussion was entirely relative to the agent's own desires and outlook; it did not refer to what value the objects of aspiration might or should have independently of those desires. But it is the normative independent question that is now being considered.

A certain liberal position holds that moral philosophy should not concern itself with this independent normative question; that the requirements of both moral and political freedom and autonomy entail that persons should be free to form and pursue whatever aspirations they may have without interference, either moral or legal, from other persons so long as they do not harm anyone besides themselves. Persons should be permitted to form their own conceptions both of the kinds of selves they aspire to be and of the values they aspire to attain. An epistemological argument has also been given for this position: each person knows what is best for herself, what gives her pleasure or the absence of pain, and this self-knowledge renders nugatory the attempts of other persons to advise her about what she should aspire to. To intervene in the aspirations of adults is an unjustified form of paternalism.

Despite these arguments, there have been at least two important criticisms of the quest for self-fulfillment bearing on their envisaged objects. One is that self-fulfillment is simply a form of egoism or narcissism: in seeking to fulfill oneself one is concerned only with satisfying one's own desires or self-conceptions, regardless of their impact on other persons. The other, "elitist" criticism is that by focusing simply on desires with their almost unlimited range of possible objects, and with no independent consideration of their value, the quest for self-fulfillment can lead to and indeed encourage a concern for objects and ways of life that are superficial, tawdry, narrow, and benighted. These two criticisms merge into one another because the self-centeredness of aspiration-fulfillment is held to be so engrossed with whatever pleases oneself or nurtures one's own ego that it allows little or no independent concern for evaluating the quality of what one desires.

These criticisms rest on the far-reaching thesis that, contrary to the general conception of self-fulfillment that I sketched at the beginning of this book, aspiration-fulfillment is not the sole or primary criterion of value, that it is not self-sufficient in the general realm of value; that, on the contrary, it may and should be confronted by other values with which it may conflict. If this thesis has any plausibility, which I believe it does, it raises the question of the criteria for upholding values other than self-fulfillment, and how, or by what criteria, we are to resolve conflicts of values like the ones just cited between self-fulfillment and the values adduced in criticism of it. This large question will have to be addressed in several steps; ultimately it requires that we move from aspiration-fulfillment to capacity-fulfillment. But in the present context certain preliminary answers can be given from within the context of aspiration-fulfillment itself.

The charge that aspiration-fulfillment entails egoism can be answered by noting that, as I have just pointed out, aspiration-fulfillment as such does not have any specific object. As so far considered, what one aspires to may run a vast gamut of objects. These may indeed include aspects of oneself: a superbly healthy body, a very keen intellect, a strong sense of personal identity, great wealth, domination over others, and so forth. I shall refer to such objects of aspirations as "internal" ones. These objects are not the same as the feelings or other mental states that figured above in the utilitarian account of the objects of aspirations. The internal objects can be quite "objective" features of oneself. There is a difference between having, for example, a healthy body and having a feeling of health, and similarly with other aspects of oneself.

An especially influential kind of internal aspiration, deriving from the Romantic movement, has taken "authenticity" to be the prime object of aspiration. This is partly intimated in the famous injunction, "To thine own self be true." The central ideas are that there is a core self which defines or demarcates what one is as a unique person, as having a certain identity; one is conscious of this core self and the demands it makes on one to live up to it; and these demands are the proper objects of one's aspirations, so that self-fulfillment consists in this way in being "authentic" or true to oneself. With certain modifications, this view may also be attributed to Nietzsche.[25]

This conception of aspiration-fulfillment can be interpreted in several different ways. In one way it embodies an emphasis on a kind of individualist spontaneity wherein what is supremely important is to "do one's own thing;" it may reflect an extreme egoism in its disregard of the needs of other persons, and it may also be imprudent in its neglect of the calculation of consequences. Some aspects of the "sexual revolution" may exemplify this emphasis. The drive for such ideal authenticity also incurs the danger of vacuity. Unless one can tie the self to a content or a conception of value that gives it significance, the ideal may result either in contemplating one's own navel or in striking out toward whatever object arouses one's fancy. If, to solve this problem, one insists on the self's ineradicable ties to other persons—a view I endorse—there remains the sobering fact that one may pursue these ties in ways that are deeply immoral.[26]

Now it is a further sobering fact that aspiration-fulfillment as I have discussed it so far may be attributed to Hitler and Stalin at the points where the respective tyrants had achieved their greatest triumphs. But, by the same token, aspiration-fulfillment may also be attributed to Mother Teresa and Mahatma Gandhi. More generally, there may be persons whose deepest desires are for states of the world other than themselves, such as for a more just or healthy or beautiful society. I shall refer to such objects of aspirations as "external" ones. Persons like those just cited whose aspirations are for such external objects strive to fulfill themselves by contributing to the development of such societies. The urge toward this development comes from within themselves, so that by engaging in it they are bringing to fruition important parts of themselves, their deepest desires for what they regard as supremely valuable, so that they are still seeking, finding, and expressing their personal identity. Nevertheless, it is at their external objects, not at states of themselves, that their aspirations are directly aimed. As we have seen, in aspirations one desires not only some object but also that one be a certain kind of person who has and fulfills the aforementioned desire. But here

---

[25] See Charles Taylor, *The Ethics of Authenticity* (Cambridge, Mass.: Harvard University Press, 1992). On the relevance to Nietzsche, see Alexander Nehamas, *Nietzsche: Life as Literature* (Cambridge, Mass.: Harvard University Press, 1985), chap. 6: "How One Becomes What One Is" (pp. 170–99).

[26] For Charles Taylor's attempt to solve this problem, see *The Ethics of Authenticity*, chaps. 4–5. I think his attempt, though suggestive, is unsuccessful in its final leap to moral egalitarianism.

the desire about oneself is dependent and sequential upon the external desire; it need not be one's sole or exclusive desire.

We must, then, distinguish between the desiring self or subject and the desired object. Not all desires that one has, or that emanate from oneself, are reflexive or internal in that they have only oneself, or states of oneself, as their objects. It is a fallacy to infer that because one invests oneself in producing some result, that result must be some aspect of oneself. While, as we have seen, many cases of self-fulfillment do have some aspect of the aspiring self as their object, not all do—let alone by the very concept of self-fulfillment. On the contrary, for many persons their self-fulfillment and their awareness of it emerge as "by-products" of their achieving the direct external objects of their aspirations, whether these consist in composing beautiful music or pursuing political objectives or whatever. Indeed, the connection between aspiration-fulfillment and impersonal idealism may be pressed further. It may be held that if one would fulfill oneself one should forget oneself and lose oneself in some cause—aesthetic, scientific, political—that is greater than oneself and that gives meaning to one's life. On this view, to focus one's aspirations and efforts on oneself is not so much immoral as imprudent: paradoxically, in seeking to benefit oneself one harms oneself. A version of this paradox is Jesus' dictum that if you want to save yourself you should lose yourself (Luke 9:24). One may identify oneself with one's desires or the desired objects without thereby desiring exclusively some aspect of oneself. In this regard there can be selfless desires or aspirations, for even though they emanate from oneself and are recognized as such, their direct objects are things other than oneself. One's self-conception still figures in one's aspirations, but as intrinsically bound up with one's sought-for values. This is also familiarly true of the quest for happiness: the way to attain it is not by directly seeking it but by engaging in activities that engross one and that one regards as worthwhile.[27]

This externalist point has limits. One may successfully seek for oneself, as bases of one's self-fulfillment, such internal states as tranquillity or excitement. To be sure, these states may be externalized in various ways: tranquillity may be achieved by listening to soothing music, excitement by attending raucous parties. Still, the results explicitly aimed

---

[27] "I never, indeed, wavered in the conviction that happiness is the best of all rules of conduct, and the end of life. But I now thought that this end was only to be attained by not making it the direct end. Those only are happy (I thought) who have their minds fixed on some object other than their own happiness. . . . Ask yourself whether you are happy, and you cease to be so. The only chance is to treat, not happiness, but some end external to it, as the purpose of life" (J. S. Mill, *Autobiography*, chap. 5, pp. 85–86). On self-realization as "by-product," see also A. Macbeath, *Experiments in Living* (London: Macmillan, 1952), p. 417; Jon Elster, "Self- Realization in Work and Politics," p. 100.

at may focus on one's inner feelings. So why shouldn't this also be true of happiness and of self-fulfillment as aspiration-fulfillment?

One answer is that self-fulfillment and happiness, as such, are too general to provide determinate objects at which to aim. As can be seen in the first book of Aristotle's *Nicomachean Ethics*, specific criteria are needed for evaluating such proposed objects. But these criteria, for some persons, may include internal states like peace of mind or tension and turbulence. It then becomes a factual question whether such states, for the persons in question, yield the desired results of aspiration-fulfillment. In any case, it would be a mistake to construe all aspiration-fulfillment on this internal model.

So aspiration-fulfillment is not to be identified with the kind of "unrestricted desire-fulfillment theory" which holds that "what is best for someone is what would best fulfill all of his desires, throughout his life," where "best for someone" is construed in internal terms as what "is good for me and makes my life go better."[28] There may be kinds of aspiration-fulfillment which, because their objects are external, do not meet or require this condition. It would be a mistake to hold that all aspirations have only internal objects and that aspiration-fulfillment can occur only when such objects are attained.

Let us now consider the other criticism of aspiration-fulfillment mentioned above: that it takes no independent account of the value of the objects one aspires to attain, so that they may be in various ways tawdry, benighted, or valueless. This criticism assumes that there are criteria of value other than the desires of the aspiring subject. Let us now consider an opposed thesis which I shall call the autonomy of aspiration-fulfillment. According to this thesis, aspirations are their own justifications; they neither need nor permit judgment from any external source. On this view aspirations, as consisting in each person's deepest desire for himself, cannot and should not be corrected or judged by some other desire on the part of the aspiring person; and to intrude on a person's aspirations by judgments from without is to violate the aspirer's own autonomy and "authenticity."

It may be objected that one person's aspirations may conflict with another's, as when A's aspiration to exert domination over the persons he associates with conflicts with the aspiration of B (one of A's associates) to avoid being dominated. Such conflict, however, need not constitute an insuperable obstacle to accepting the autonomy of aspiration-fulfillment; one may simply resign oneself to the inevitability of conflict, recognizing it as part of the regular order of things. Such recognition would reflect a realistic awareness of how things are. Alternatively, one

[28] Parfit, *Reasons and Persons*, p. 499.

may seek agreements of various sorts whereby opposed aspirations are brought into some harmony with one another. In this way the autonomy of aspiration-fulfillment may be preserved.

2.5. THREE TYPES OF MORALITY

Confronted by monsters like Hitler and Stalin, who pursued their aspirations with no such agreements among their victims, we may well rebel against acceptance of such autonomy; we may insist on the appropriateness and indeed the necessity of subjecting aspirations to moral evaluation and criticism. But such a plausible, well-recognized tendency may incur several types of objections, each based on a different meaning assigned to "morality." On the one hand, morality may be defined as *universalist*, in terms of universal impartiality. On this definition a morality is a set of precepts which require that all persons be treated with impartial affirmative consideration for their respective goods or interests. Such a morality is interpersonally egalitarian: it requires that a person give equal consideration to other persons' needs or interests as well as one's own, so that it is morally wrong to treat other persons as mere means to one's own ends. On such a definition the aspiration-fulfillments of a Hitler or a Stalin would be categorically rejected as morally wrong, and other aspiration-fulfillments would be morally acceptable only if they did not involve violating other persons' rights.

Interpersonal morality may, however, be defined more broadly so that it may lack the egalitarian universalist restrictions just mentioned. In this broader definition, a morality is a set of rules or directives that purport to be categorically obligatory and that set requirements for actions and institutions, where the requirements are held to support what are taken to be the most important interests of persons or recipients other than or in addition to the agent. This definition would permit us to talk of "Nazi morality," "Stalinist morality," and so forth because such "moralities," while interpersonal in their scope, are not universalist or egalitarian since they support the interests only of some persons as against others, and not of all persons equally. They are, then, interpersonal *particularist* moralities. So on this definition Hitler and Stalin could be depicted as embracing the particularist moralities of Nazism and Stalinism, respectively.

There are other particularist moralities of a quite different sort. They include the requirements of family, love, friendship, patriotism, and other human relations whose concern is to promote not the interests of all persons equally but only of some persons as against others. I shall subsequently argue (3.4) that egalitarian universalist morality has a privileged status in relation to these other moralities because it has a necessary rational cogency the others lack, so it can be used to evaluate the rational justifiability of these other moralities. So for the present I shall restrict interpersonal morality to the universalist rules or directives which require that all persons be treated with equal and impartial positive consideration for their most important interests.

When such universalist morality is invoked to criticize certain aspirations on the ground that they are morally wrong and hence ought to be rejected, it incurs familiar difficulties. Why should morality in this sense be regarded as "overriding," such that its values are to be taken as sitting in definitive judgment over the needs or interests of the person who seeks to fulfill his aspirations? Why should the requirements of "the moral system" be allowed to interfere with a person's own projects of self-fulfillment? Morality on this view appears as an "alien," external intrusion into the actions or aspirations of persons, and questions arise both about the justification of such intrusion and about a person's motivation for accepting it.[29] Even if one admits that certain kinds of aspiration-fulfillment are morally wrong, this still leaves open the question of why moral wrongness should be regarded as dominating the justification that a given individual finds in fulfilling his own aspirations.

We might try to deal with this problem by deriving interpersonal universalist morality from aspiration-fulfillment. We might, for example, appeal to the reply given above to the charge that the concern with self-fulfillment is egoistic. This, however, would not close the gap between interpersonal morality and aspiration-fulfillment. For even if it is not the desiring self but the desired objects that are the goal of self-fulfillment, these objects may still be morally wrong. Idealistic, selfless villains are still villains, and the aspirations of Hitler and Stalin for "purifying" the human race and for building a regimented "classless society" were no less morally vicious for transcending their purely personal interests. A similar point emerges if we try to overcome the potential immorality of self-fulfillment as concerned with individualist self-aggrandizement by appealing to the social character of the self. It may be held that the self in its true nature is not an atomic individual; on the contrary, it is intrinsically constituted by being part of a larger social whole or community. Consequently, the self cannot fulfill itself without at the same time fulfilling this social whole, so that its fulfillment is moral because other-regarding rather than being purely self-centered.

---

[29] See Bernard Williams, *Ethics and the Limits of Philosophy* (Cambridge, Mass.: Harvard University Press, 1985), chap. 10; Philippa Foot, *Virtues and Vices* (Berkeley: University of California Press, 1978), chaps. 11–13; Thomas Nagel, *Mortal Questions* (Cambridge: Cambridge University Press, 1979), p. 37; James Griffin, *Well-Being* (Oxford: Clarendon Press, 1986), pp. 127, 128, 133.

This argument raises the question of the degree to which the self is indeed constituted by its environing social context.[30] But even if it is so constituted, there remains the further question of how inclusive is this social context. After all, Hitler had his henchmen, his party, indeed the whole Nazi state; and even if he was in some way constituted by these larger units and fulfilled them in fulfilling himself and his own aspirations, this did not prevent the fulfillments from being deeply immoral.

Let us now consider another alternative definition of morality which also has a distinguished lineage. On this definition, morality is *personalist*; it consists in counsels or precepts for living a good life, a life that best fulfills one's intellectual, aesthetic, and other capacities in ways that contribute to one's development and dignity. According to this definition, morality has no direct or necessary reference to the goods or desires of persons other than the individual agent, and there is no necessary appeal from the agent's own desires to the desires or needs of other persons. On this view, accordingly, the quest for aspiration-fulfillment could itself be a moral enterprise. Moral criticism of any one person's aspirations would consist in appealing not to the aspirations of other persons but only to the more fully enlightened awareness of the individual person himself. Such awareness might include a concern for the freedom or well-being of other persons, especially of one's family and friends. Since friendship is normally an important component of the good life, a person may recognize that what friends he has and how he relates to them have an important bearing on the fulfillment of his own aspirations. Nevertheless, these interpersonal considerations would be only instrumental to his own individual aspiration-fulfillment. They would be only means, albeit very important ones, to the fuller satisfaction of his own strongest desires.

The personalist conception of morality may face less of a problem of motivation than does the universalist conception because the former sanctions the individual's pursuit of the good life. But it may still incur difficulties of both motivation and justification insofar as it sets up standards for such a life that go beyond persons' own desires or aspirations. Familiar problems of the interpersonal comparison of values or conceptions of the good arise here. Why is poetry or "high culture" better or more desirable than pushpin or "low culture"? Even if one's society refrains from imposing one set of conceptions of the good as against others, what warrant is there for saying that a person's self-fulfillment consists in his voluntarily following one set of standards as against others, so long as he does not harm other persons thereby?[31]

[30] See Alan Gewirth, *The Community of Rights* (Chicago: University of Chicago Press, 1996), pp. 91–96.

[31] For good recent discussions of particularist and personalist conceptions of morality,

Despite these difficulties and diversities among the three types of morality, it should not be thought that "morality" is an equivocal term in this context. The three types have it in common that they set requirements for action which further what are taken to be vitally important interests of persons. They differ not only in their conceptions of what these interests are (see also 4.1)—such differences are also found in each type—but also on the distributive issue of who are the persons whose interests are to be promoted. In universalist morality it is the interests of all persons equally; in particularist morality it is the interests of some favored groups as against others; and in personalist morality it is the interests of the individual agent herself. These distributive differences should not, however, be interpreted so rigidly as to overlook their possible interpenetrations. Personalist morality may also affect the interests of persons besides the agent; particularist morality may affect the interests of the individual agent who pursues its requirements; universalist morality may in various ways also redound to the benefit of the individual agent by virtue of his other-directed concerns. These interpenetrations help to moderate possible conflicts among the precepts of the respective moralities, including their varying relations to self-fulfillment. One of my main concerns in what follows will be to ascertain how these conflicts are to be dealt with.

We can begin to deal with this question by noting that the three types of morality are both teleological and deontological. They are teleological in that they require the promotion of persons' interests, which, as we shall see, are in various ways objects of moral rights. But the three types are also deontological in that they impose duties that limit the pursuit of interests. Thus, for example, particularist interests require limiting the pursuit even of certain eminent personalist interests (3.7); universalist interests may require limiting certain particularist interests (4.7); personalist interests may require limiting certain universalist interests when these may seem to require self-sacrifice (3.5); and so forth. These varying relations among the three types of morality will have an important bearing on the kinds of self-fulfillment that persons can attain.

It seems, then, that each of the above conceptions of morality faces difficulties both of its own and of its relations to the others. Hence it may be concluded that the idea of a moral critique of the objects of self-fulfillment as aspiration-fulfillment either must be given up or must be regarded as a purely tentative, hypothetical enterprise severely limited in rational cogency. I now want to suggest, however, that there is a way

---

see Lawrence A. Blum, *Friendship, Altruism, and Morality* (London: Routledge and Kegan Paul, 1980), and Robert B. Louden, *Morality and Moral Theory* (New York: Oxford University Press, 1992).

out of this impasse, one that shows that an invocation of the criteria of universalist interpersonal morality is neither limited nor question-begging in the ways so far indicated. As we have seen, one of the root difficulties with applying the standards of interpersonal universalist morality to the objects of aspiration-fulfillment stems from the fact that such morality is conceived as being "alien" or external to the individual agent, as deriving from considerations that are imposed on him from without. On such a conception, it is plausible to ask why requirements that are foreign to one's own deepest desires should be credited as having a justified bearing on those desires, especially when they purport to limit or restrict their fulfillments.

The situation is different, however, if it can be shown that the requirements of interpersonal universalist morality come not from outside the individual agent but rather from within herself. For in such a case these requirements are self-imposed and are therefore products of the agent's own autonomy. Thus, while the requirements are in part external to the agent so far as concerns the persons whose desires or needs must receive affirmative consideration, they are internal to the agent so far as concerns their rational source and acceptance. The agent must recognize that universalist morality sets requirements that she is logically committed to accept by virtue of rational standards that not only are within her powers to accept but also impose themselves on her insofar as she is even minimally rational. The standards in question are intrinsic parts of herself and of her self-conception as a rational person. Or, to put it otherwise, the self that is the direct object of self-fulfillment must be construed as including standards that logically commit the self to an acceptance of the requirements of universalist morality.

The reference to the "rational" and the "logical" may well leave one skeptical. They may seem to be question-begging if they are somehow identified with the impartial requirements of universalist morality. The case is different, however, if the "rational" and "logical" are restricted to criteria that are themselves entirely nonmoral in that they do not directly include any specifically moral considerations, and if they are confined to requirements that must be accepted by any even minimally rational person or agent. This is not to construe the self as an exclusively rational person; it is not to lose sight of the irrational and nonrational parts of the self. Nevertheless, insofar as the self can hearken to certain minimal rational criteria, to be spelled out below, the derivation of universalist morality from this rational self can serve to ground its acceptance of such morality as deriving from within its own norms and capacities.

It may be helpful at this point to note briefly some of the traditional ways in which philosophers have tried to show that it is rational to be moral in the universalist sense. These ways may be construed as seeking to connect aspiration-fulfillment with universalist morality by arguing that one will not succeed in fulfilling one's aspirations, whatever they may be, unless one is universalistically moral. On this view reason compels you to accept the norms of universalist morality, so that there is no need to leave the sphere of aspirations and their fulfillments in order to motivate and justify the self's acceptance of the requirements of universalist morality.

Omitting for now the familiar Kantian doctrine of universalizability, we may briefly consider four such bridging attempts. Plato held that to be just or universalistically moral is in a person's own self-interest because only so can he be mentally healthy.[32] Hobbes maintained that it cannot be rational to be unjust or immoral because one cannot count on being able to deceive all the persons who would be adversely affected by one's injustice.[33] Hume declared that a person's own happiness requires that he be moral or honest because otherwise he will not have "inward peace of mind," including "peaceful reflection on [his] own conduct."[34] And, most recently, John Rawls has defended the rationality of justice by arguing that if rational, self-interested persons were to choose the constitution of their society from behind a veil of ignorance of all their personal qualities, they would opt for principles that provide for certain equal rights for all persons.[35] So by such arguments persons who seek to fulfill their aspirations would be motivated to accept the norms of universalist morality.

I think these attempts at reconciling aspiration-fulfillment and universalist morality are suggestive, but they all incur serious difficulties. Within present space limits I must deal with them briefly. If the mental health of which Plato speaks is not to be question-beggingly identified with being moral, there is much evidence to show that persons can be immoral without suffering the perturbations of the soul that Plato said invariably ensue on injustice in action and even in character. A similar point applies to Hume's position. Hobbes's thesis that one cannot get away with being unjust is similarly contradicted by the examples of unjust rogues throughout history; moreover, history attests even more to the ubiquitousness of the successful unjust treatment of some groups by other groups, as in genocide and slavery. As for Rawls's doctrine of rational choice from behind a veil of ignorance, this raises at least two familiar questions. First, how rational can the choice be when all knowledge of one's own particular desires and other characteristics is

[32] *Republic*, iv. 444.

[33] *Leviathan*, chap. 15, paras. 4 ff.

[34] *Enquiry concerning the Principles of Morals*, ed. Selby-Bigge, sec. 9, part 2 (Oxford: Clarendon Press, 1962), pp. 283, 284.

[35] *A Theory of Justice*, chaps. 2, 3.

withheld? Second, why should actual rational persons, who are concerned with achieving their particular ends or aspirations, accept principles based on ignorance of those ends?

Despite these difficulties, I shall undertake to use certain fundamental rational standards to find an appropriate criterion for the value of the objects of aspirations, including their moral value. To deal with this issue and other basic aspects of self-fulfillment, we must turn from aspiration-fulfillment to capacity-fulfillment.

CHAPTER 3

Capacity-Fulfillment and Universalist Morality

3.1. CAPACITIES AND THEIR FULFILLMENT

It will be recalled that the basic question for self-fulfillment as capacity-fulfillment is: How can I make the best of myself? Put affirmatively, the general formula of such fulfillment may be stated as follows: For you to fulfill yourself is for you to achieve the best that it is in you to become.

These references to "best" already suggest that self-fulfillment can be not only elitist but also very demanding. It presumably requires distinguishing "best" from "worst" and also from "better." But how can one tell which of one's capacities is (or are) one's "best"? Even if one can, does the same capacity always remain the best for each person, or may it vary from one time to another? Anyway, why should I be concerned with this "best," even if it is in some way my own? Why not just leave well enough alone, rather than embarking on an arduous quest for some sort of optimal condition? Why not seek, at most, some incremental improvements that may be within my ready reach, as against seeking for some sort of will-o'-the-wisp perfectionism?

These questions should be taken seriously, and I shall try to provide answers to them. But they indicate, among other things, that if self-fulfillment is to be other than an ineffectual ideal reserved at most for an elitist few—if it is to be the object of a genuine desire—then it must make contact not only with the aspirations but also with the actual capacities of persons as they are. Within these limitations, however, self-fulfillment as the development of one's best capacities can be both an attractive and an attainable ideal for persons who, even while being aware of their deficiencies, seek to achieve their most cherished purposes in ways that are enlightened and valuable for themselves. This, in part, returns us to aspirations, but with the addition of relevant knowledge in its bearing on excellences that are within one's reach.

As against lives that are frustrated or disappointing, to seek after one's best can be not only challenging but also rewarding and exhilarating. It can help one to find out who one truly is, where this involves fulfilling those of one's capacities that can make one's life as worthwhile to oneself as possible. As we have seen, in its most effective form, such a quest for capacity-fulfillment is also an object of one's aspirations, so that the two modes of self-fulfillment go together, but with aspirations now receiving normative guidance by one's search for what is best in oneself. Just as an unexamined life may not be worth living, so an unfulfilled life, where one falls far short of one's best capacities, may make one's life disappointing and bitter, in ways that go far beyond the strivings demanded by self-fulfillment. So to fulfill yourself is to find yourself, since it is in yourself that the capacities reside that you bring to fulfillment. Let us now consider somewhat more fully the ramifications of this quest for capacity-fulfillment.

When it is said that to fulfill yourself is to achieve the best that it is in you to become, the phrase "in you" signifies that the self-fulfillment involves not the imposition of certain conditions or results from outside yourself but rather that it is your own inherent potentialities or capacities that you develop. The person is not only the achieving subject and the achieved object, but also what she achieves or develops derives from within herself, as implicit or latent potentialities or capacities that she actualizes or brings to fruition. This point also bears on the idea of development. The best that "is in" you is not in you as something that is preexisting or ready-made; it is not like a pearl that already exists in an oyster and needs only to be extricated. Rather, it gets developed out of preexisting materials that can be turned in different directions through autonomous choice and habituation (see also 1.3). These preexisting materials are a person's capacities.

These considerations indicate further why, in the quest for self-fulfillment, we must move from aspiration-fulfillment to capacity-fulfillment. Both modes of self-fulfillment involve superlatives—one's deepest desires, one's best abilities. The self and its fulfillment or development are not, however, exhausted by its aspirations, not only because these may be erroneous or inimical but also because they may in other ways not suffice to fulfill the self in the sense of developing it at its best. A more direct route is needed to get at the self and the values it is capable of achieving from within its own resources. Capacities are parts of the self that enable it to act to attain goods, so that they are inherent abilities. These enablings directly evoke activity on the part of the self. They may also yield for this self goods or satisfactions that go considerably beyond one's original aspirations.

These distinctions do not mean that in the analysis of capacity-fulfillment aspirations and aspiration-fulfillment are left completely behind. Rather, as we have seen, they are still present, but as having to be modified by the further criteria that we shall find involved in capacity-fulfillment.

In working out the contents of self-fulfillment as capacity-fulfillment in this and the next two chapters, we shall be following a long and somewhat involved route. To enable the reader to see somewhat more clearly the guiding threads of the argument, it may be helpful if I summarily present here three of the main conclusions I shall be reaching. They represent an elaboration of the three conceptions of morality that I distinguished in section 2.5: the universalist, the personalist, and the particularist. Within universalist morality, the conclusion will be that if a person is to fulfill himself and thereby be true to what is best in himself, he must be a reasonable self, one who is considerate of the generic rights of other persons as well as of his own. The society as a whole must reflect this reasonableness by upholding certain equal rights. Within personalist morality, the conclusion will be that if a person is to fulfill herself she must be able to make maximally effective use of her practical capacities of freedom and well-being. This involves that she is an agent who controls her behavior by her unforced choice while having knowledge of relevant circumstances, including self-knowledge, with a view to achieving purposes that reflect the fullest development of the virtues that are available to her. Within particularist morality, the conclusion will be that self-fulfillment requires deep interpersonal preferential relations of love, friendship, and familial devotion, as well as various communal loyalties. All of these modes of capacity-fulfillment will make extensive use of reason as the best of human veridical capacities. This use will help to resolve potential conflicts between the three areas of capacity-fulfillment. In the remainder of this book I shall present analyses and arguments aimed at supporting these conclusions about capacity-fulfillment in sufficient detail.

Let us now return to the general formula of capacity-fulfillment presented at the beginning of this chapter. Two concepts in this formula require further analysis. First, as regards "best," it will have been noted that this word figures in two different ways in the description of capacity-fulfillment: (1) as making the "best of" oneself; (2) as achieving the "best that it is in you to become." We may contrast each of these expressions with another, which is perhaps more familiar: (3) what is "best for" you. In certain respects these three applications of "best" coincide: what is best for you is to develop what is best in you, and to achieve this development is to make the best of yourself. Nevertheless, there are distinctions between them that are important both in themselves and in interpreting the relation between capacity-fulfillment and aspiration-fulfillment. In (3) "what is best for you," there is suggested a relation of passivity or recipience whereby your desires are fulfilled, or your life is made to go as well as possible. Even where you are your own agent, in that it is you who does what is best for yourself, the focus is still on what happens to you as a result of your action. In the other two "best" expressions, on the other hand, "best" suggests rather a kind of personal agency. In (2) "what is best in you," this is a perfectionist-agent "best" in that it signifies that part or aspect of you which excels in some phase of agency or in capacities for agency. And in (1) "making the best of yourself," there is again the idea of agency, but also that of recipience. Unlike in "best for you," the "best" that is envisaged in making the best of yourself is that you act in such a way as to lead to (2) the prior, perfectionist condition of what is best in you.

The relevance of these distinctions in the present context is that for you to fulfill what is best in yourself may in certain ways not be what is best for you. You may be made very unhappy if you develop your highest talents; for example, a person who by intense concentration and practice becomes a superb violinist may come to feel very discontented with his life.[1] Although we saw something similar in connection with aspirations (2.4), the salient present point is not that aspiration-fulfillment may conflict with happiness but that capacity-fulfillment may conflict both with aspiration-fulfillment and with happiness construed as general satisfaction with one's life.

This conflict may be moderated by an appeal to what Rawls has called the "Aristotelian Principle": "other things equal, human beings enjoy the exercise of their realized capacities (their innate or trained abilities), and this enjoyment increases the more the capacity is realized, or the greater its complexity."[2] This principle, if sound, would go far toward removing a conflict between what is best in you and what is best for you. But the conflict would not be completely removed if the contingencies of your "enjoyment" of your "realized capacities" were superseded by a new set of desires or aspirations. So there remains a severe problem for the analysis and evaluation of capacity-fulfillment.[3]

Let us now turn to "capacity." I have said that to make the best of oneself is to fulfill certain of one's capacities. The idea that there is an important connection between the self and its capacities can be traced back to the dictum in Plato's *Sophist* that the very "definition" of real things is "that they are nothing but power."[4] The power in question is

---

[1] For a good recent discussion of this point, see L. W. Sumner, "Two Theories of the Good," *Social Philosophy and Policy* 9, no. 2 (summer 1992): 1–14.

[2] John Rawls, *A Theory of Justice* (Cambridge, Mass.: Harvard University Press, 1971), p. 426.

[3] Thomas Hurka, in *Perfectionism* (New York: Oxford University Press, 1993), recognizes a possible conflict between desire and perfection (p. 27), but nevertheless undertakes to reconcile perfection with personal liberty by making autonomy a perfection and advocating a government that, while not coercing, "steers enough people into better activities" (p. 156). This may still leave it open that persons may seek their happiness or satisfaction of desires in many values short of perfection, so that the conflict adduced above between aspiration-fulfillment and capacity- fulfillment would not be removed. Hurka makes some sound remarks in this connection on the appropriate limits and scope of governmental intervention (chap. 11).

[4] Plato, *Sophist*, 247.

the capacity or ability to affect other things or to be affected by them, but it may also extend to a thing's bringing about changes in itself. Since self-fulfillment is a reflexive relation, the capacities involved in it are both passive and active: they both undergo development and they bring about this development. So capacities are two-faced: on the one hand they are abilities or powers that are latent before they are exercised or actualized; on the other hand they are abilities to bring about this exercise. On this model, the human self consists in its capacities for bringing about changes in things, including itself; it is a kind of energizing force whose functioning stems from within itself. "Capacity" differs from "power" mainly by referring more specifically to the extent or scope of the internal or external objects that would be affected or developed by its exercise.

So I here use "capacity" in a very broad sense. Where Aristotle, for example, distinguishes among emotions, powers or capacities, and states of character in terms of their different relations to virtues or vices,[5] I classify each of these under capacities insofar as they can affect or issue in actions. In this regard, also, capacities need not be normative; unlike "capabilities," they need not enable persons to "function" or to function well; the actions in which they eventuate may be dysfunctional as well as functional. So this raises the challenge of which capacities enter into self-fulfillment viewed as achieving the best that it is in one to become. Criteria of "best" will thus be a major concern.

Viewed so far, then, capacity-fulfillment consists simply in the activation or playing out of certain internal forces of the self; it is the actualization of inherent potentialities (cf. 1.3). To make capacity-fulfillment relevant to self-fulfillment, at least two further distinctions are needed.

---

[5] Aristotle, *Nicomachean Ethics*, 2.5. In view of the plethora of "ability-" words that figure in the present discussion, it may be helpful to note a few distinctions. First, as between "capacity" and "potentiality," the latter is more general and can serve as the ground of the former. See, for example, Alan Donagan (*Philosophical Papers* [Chicago: University of Chicago Press, 1994], vol. 2, p. 98), who refers to "the complex specific potentiality . . . to develop certain capacities." Capacities can be developed as stemming from certain diffuse potentialities, but not conversely. Second, as between "capacity" and "capability," the latter has been used as a quasi-technical term by Amartya Sen: "The *capability* of a person reflects the alternative combination of functionings the person can achieve, and from which he or she can choose one collection" (in Martha C. Nussbaum and Sen, eds., *The Quality of Life* [Oxford: Clarendon Press, 1993], p. 31). While "capacity" is close to "capability" in meaning, I think, on the basis of Sen's discussion of the latter, that there may be three interrelated differences. (a) "Capability" is primarily active; it enables persons to "function" in certain ways, where "functionings" represent what a person "manages to do in leading a life" (p. 31). "Capacity," on the other hand, may be passive as well as active; it is an ability not only to develop but also to be developed in certain ways. (b) "Capacities" may be less directly tied to actual functionings; they may be more latent and may require to be developed in order to function in one way or another. (c) Capabilities are always valuable, while capacities are more general.

First, we must distinguish between necessary and contingent activations of capacities. Some capacities, such as the circulation of the blood or the blinking of eyelids, are activated in an automatic way independently of the self's control. But other activations are subject to the self's choice and control and are brought about by the self as active cause. It is capacities of the latter kind that pertain to self-fulfillment. This involves the important point that the capacities in question are primarily capacities for *action*. Actions are, of course, of many different kinds; but action in the most general relevant sense consists in voluntary and purposive behavior, i.e., behavior that is controlled by the agent who has knowledge of the relevant circumstances of his behaviors and who intends to attain some end or goal (see 3.4). In action, then, one not only exercises capacities but also controls this exercise with a view to certain purposes. As we shall see, this idea of action is basic both to morality and to other segments of capacity-fulfillment.

A second distinction about capacity-fulfillment bears on the self's control of its activations of capacities, including its objects or outcomes. Some controls are relatively simple and easy and their outcomes are relatively trivial, such as twiddling one's thumbs or turning from left to right. Other controls are more arduous, and their outcomes have more value for the person who controls them. It is to this latter context that self-fulfillment as capacity-fulfillment pertains. For fulfillment involves the idea of a sequence of choices and strivings that culminate in an achievement or product that is a full development of the end or aim of the strivings. And self-fulfillment adds the idea that these strivings emanate in important part from within the person as chooser and controller, and that the achievement in which they culminate represents a full development of the person. For these reasons, the outcome of the development has great importance for the person, whatever her desires in the matter.

The reflexive character of self-fulfillment involves various paradoxes, some of which I have touched on above. How can it be the self that fulfills itself? If it is capable of fulfilling itself, then mustn't it in some sense be already fulfilled? Let us put this in terms of capacity-fulfillment. If self-fulfillment is fulfillment of certain of one's capacities, then if one fulfills oneself mustn't one already have at least the capacities that are necessary and sufficient for such fulfilling? If, on the other hand, one is unfulfilled, then doesn't one lack the capacity to bring it about that one is fulfilled? How can that which is incomplete or uneffectuated bring about that it is complete? In the case of plants and animals, this bringing about is an automatic process of growth with no interventions of choice or planning by the entities involved. But in the case of humans who fulfill themselves by actualizing their inherent powers or potentialities, it would seem that these powers must already be exercised or actualized if they are to have the ability to bring the actualization about.

One answer to this question is similar to the answer given above to the question of the temporally multiple selves that figure in the formation and fulfillment of aspirations (2.3): we must distinguish between prior and posterior capacities. One uses the capacities one has antecedently to the process in order to attain subsequent capacities, just as one can use a hammer to make another hammer. This analogy is not quite right, however, because capacity-fulfillment is a matter not of using an already complete capacity in order to make an entirely new capacity, but rather of exercising capacities one already has, although only in an indeterminate form. This exercise is an actualization of pre-existing, though diffuse, potentialities. It is a creative process: in fulfilling the self one creates oneself, but along lines that are implicit in such of one's prior capacities as one chooses to fulfill because they are what is best in oneself. So to fulfill oneself requires not that one already be fulfilled but rather that one moves from relatively indeterminate powers to exercise them as one chooses so as to make them more determinate. To become a good violinist, for example, you use your relatively crude initial capacities of fingering, bowing, and tone discrimination, and by practicing you gradually improve these capacities in the light of the criteria you acquire for better violin-playing. The awareness of these criteria is a second-order capacity to reflect on your first-order capacity so as to move toward improvement. But by the same token one may, at a second level, reject what one now is at the first level; and this rejection may call upon aspirations or capacities to move beyond what one now is. This movement is included among persons' capacities. So in this way you may fulfill yourself in attaining various aspirations or capacities without having already attained those very aspirations or capacities, because at the earlier stage you have the capacity to aspire to and to attain them.

What one attains thereby is a self-fulfillment in several respects. In fulfilling one's aspirations one becomes what one most deeply wants to be, and thereby one reaches what, from one's own perspective, is a higher or better stage of oneself. In fulfilling one's capacities, similarly, one develops powers that are latent in oneself but that are eminently worthy of being brought to fruition. These powers, in a certain important sense, constitute who one is. This "is," however, is normative; it involves an overcoming of one's limitations, a bringing out of what is best in oneself. This "best" is, in a certain respect, inherent in oneself, but to bring it out involves a selection from among the many other characteristics that one has or may have. In the self-fulfillment which consists in capacity-fulfillment, it is one's best capacities that must be actualized. This, then, marks an important difference from aspiration-fulfillment.

The latter, especially as regards first-order desires, is relative to the aspirations persons happen to have, whereas one's best capacities are not thus relative.

3.2. WEIGHING VALUES TO DETERMINE THE BEST CAPACITIES: THE PURPOSIVE RANKING THESIS

If a person's capacity-fulfillment consists in her achieving the best that it is in her to become, this raises the question of how we determine what is this "best." But a prior question, already broached above, should be considered here: why must capacity-fulfillment be construed as requiring the development of what is *best* in one? Why shouldn't all one's capacities that are subject to one's control and desire figure equally in capacity-fulfillment? There is, indeed, a certain value-egalitarian position which holds that all capacities and the goods they enable one to attain are on a par so far as concerns their value. On this view there is no hierarchy of goods or of capacities for achieving them. Some capacities, of course, are more efficient than others in that they are more effective in achieving their goals. But the goals themselves, the goods aimed at, and thus the capacities directed at these goods, are all equal so far as concerns their value. One can find such a position in William James: "Take any demand, however slight, which any creature, however slight, may make. Ought it not, for its own sake, to be satisfied? If not, prove why not. . . . The only possible reason there can be why any phenomenon ought to exist is that such a phenomenon is actually desired."[6] Or, as John Dewey puts it, "Anything that in a given situation is an end and good at all is of equal worth, rank, and dignity with every other good of any other situation."[7] On this view, then, the question of which capacities are the best to fulfill is given a completely nondiscriminating answer. There may, of course, be conflicts between ends or "demands"; but these are to be dealt with either by bringing about "the very largest total universe of good which we can see"[8] or by a concern for "growth" as "the only moral 'end.'"[9] By such considerations the potential conflict noted above between what is "best in" you and what is "best for" you would be partly removed.

This position has important merits as serving to avoid invidious elitist distinctions between "higher" and "lower" kinds of interests and capac-

---

[6] William James, "The Moral Philosopher and the Moral Life," in James, *The Will to Believe and Other Essays in Popular Philosophy* (New York: Dover 1956), p. 195.

[7] John Dewey, *Reconstruction in Philosophy* (Boston: Beacon Press, 1948), p. 176.

[8] James, *Will to Believe*, p. 209.

[9] Dewey, *Reconstruction*, pp. 177, 184.

ities. But, taken in its unqualified form, the position is to be rejected on at least two grounds. First, even within the sphere of aspirations or other desires there is found a distinction between means and ends: some things are desired for the sake of other things, and the latter rank higher than the former as objects of desire. This does not mean that ends are fixed once and for all; they may be modified in the light of the means that are used to attain them. Still, there remains a relative difference between ends and means that justifies a higher ranking for ends. Second, among ends themselves and the capacities for achieving them, as we shall see later in this section, nonarbitrary rankings can be ascertained whereby some capacities are better than others, and they can be pursued, among their competitors, to the point where some of them emerge as best. These can, moreover, be linked to desires in ways that help to overcome the possible conflicts between capacities and aspirations. As we shall soon see, however, there are distinctions among kinds of "best" that enable us to accommodate at least part of the value-egalitarian position.

Returning to the question of the best capacities, let us consider two further preliminary questions, one of scope, the other of content. The question of scope is: whose best is at issue here? The question of content is: which best is at issue here? Put together with our initial question, we are asking: How do we determine what is the best in which persons?

We may approach the question of scope by taking a leaf from Aristotle's discussion of the varieties of political constitutions. He distinguished three different questions concerning "the best constitution": first, which constitution is best absolutely; second, which constitution is best in which particular circumstances; third, which constitution is best for states in general.[10] Aristotle held that these different questions must be given different answers: what is best absolutely is to be determined by reference to the maximal development of the moral and intellectual virtues; what is best in particular circumstances is to be determined by reference to the contingent material conditions, geographic, economic, sociological, in which different groups of people live; and what is best for states in general is to be determined by reference to the moderate circumstances that characterize the "middle class" of the average state.

If we were to apply Aristotle's distinctions to the question of what is the best of human capacities, we would distinguish three parallel questions: first, which human capacities are the absolutely best to be developed; second, which capacities are such that their development is best for different persons amid their different qualities and circumstances; and third, which capacities and their development are best for persons in

[10] Aristotle, *Politics*, 4.1.

general, or for most persons. If we were to follow Aristotle further, we would hold that theoretical reason is the absolutely best of human capacities, and that human self-fulfillment at its absolute best consists in the development and pursuit of reason in the theoretical sciences.[11] But it is at least equally important to hearken to Aristotle's salubrious discussions of the diverse constitutions of democracy and oligarchy that are best suited to populations of various economic and geographic circumstances, and of the "polity" that is best suited to states having a large middle class.[12]

A similar pluralism will be at least implicit in my discussions of the best human capacities. While at some points I shall focus on a kind of perfectionism that reflects ideally best human capacities, my main concern will be with capacities that are best in more moderate kinds of personal development that are within the reach of most persons. This will involve a greater appreciation of individual differences while also taking account of what persons can do to develop the best of their capacities. And this point also enables us to accommodate at least part of the value-egalitarian position that was described at the beginning of this section, as well as the distinction between what is best in you and what is best for you.

Let us now turn to the question of content: what are the best capacities to be developed in persons? Since a person's capacity-fulfillment consists in her achieving the best that it is in her to become, we may look at this question from two standpoints: that of the process and that of the product. The formula of capacity-fulfillment refers to the best as product: it is what is achieved. But because of the reflexive nature of self-fulfillment, to achieve the best that is in one requires that the process leading to this achievement be also controlled or directed by the best that is in one. As we saw above, the fulfillment of aspirations must be controlled by the aspiring self if it is to have the stability and security required for success. The same considerations hold for capacity-fulfillment.

I have already discussed the apparent paradox whereby self-fulfillment seems to involve that the self that controls the process of fulfillment must itself be already fulfilled (3.1). But the salient present question of content is whether the self has a capacity which is best for it as enabling it to achieve the fulfillment of other capacities. The hypothesis would then be that these other capacities, when fulfilled, would share the optimality or bestness of the capacity that brought them about. In such a case, the bestness of the process would lead to the bestness of the

---

[11] Aristotle, *Nicomachean Ethics*, 10. 5–9.
[12] *Politics*, books 4 and 6.

product, or at least the process would make the product as good as possible.[13]

Is there, among human capacities, one that is best? This raises the whole question of the possibility of comparing and measuring human values, to which various answers have been given.[14] In view of the many different human capacities that are sources of value and subject to control and choice, such as desire, emotion, reason, love, and the many more general capacities that figure in intellectual, practical, technical, athletic, and myriad other activities, it may seem that they are too incommensurable with one another to allow any one or more of them to be singled out as the best. Etymologically, "commensurable" means measurable together, and this presumably requires a common scale or unit of measurement, as when one uses a yardstick to ascertain the relative lengths of two physical objects. But is there any common scale among the various human capacities that would enable us to measure them with a view to ascertaining not their relative lengths but their relative values?

We can imagine many different scales, bearing on such questions as: Which are the capacities whose exercise would give you the most pleasure? Which would give you the most long-term satisfaction? Which would pose the greatest challenge? Which would use your highest intellectual powers, or your greatest physical powers? Which would contribute the most to your well-being? While each of these possible bases of value-comparisons has some plausibility, they either do not dig deeply enough or they involve serious difficulties of application.

I shall now propose a different answer, based on the idea of inherent rankings. These are rankings that derive from within the purposes of activities. These purposes serve to determine what is better, worse, or equal in capacities and activities that are defined by those purposes. We may therefore distinguish three components in what I shall call the *Purposive Ranking Thesis*: (a) a kind or context of activity, (b) the purpose of that activity, and (c) the comparison or value-ranking of capacities according to their contribution to that purpose. This contribution may

[13] This point is not the same as the one criticized by John Broome, "A Cause of Preference Is Not an Object of Preference," *Social Choice and Welfare* 10 (1993): 57–68. Among the differences are: (a) Broome proceeds entirely in terms of "preferences," whereas my "best" is more objective; (b) I view reason not as causing preferences but as providing grounds for ranking capacities with regard to value.

[14] For good recent discussions, see James Griffin, *Well-Being* (Oxford: Clarendon Press, 1986), chaps. 5–7; Joseph Raz, *The Morality of Freedom* (Oxford: Clarendon Press, 1986), chap. 13; John Broome, *Weighing Goods* (Oxford: Basil Blackwell, 1991); Thomas Hurka, *Perfectionism* (New York: Oxford University Press, 1993), chaps. 7–10; S. L. Hurley, *Natural Reasons* (New York: Oxford University Press, 1989), chap. 13.

be of the means-end sort, but it may also be of other kinds, such as the constitutive conditions of some activity or other whole.

Let us take an example from the activity of baseball. Here the capacity reflected in a higher batting average is better, other things being equal, than the capacity of a lower average, and this superiority derives from the point or purpose of the activity of baseball construed as the winning of games. But a certain variability must be noted in the concept of "purpose." To take major-league baseball again, its purpose may be construed in other ways, such as providing entertainment for spectators. In this case a player's capacity to perform frolicking antics on the field may rank higher in value than a sober, self-effacing player's capacities. And of course other activities, including chess, plumbing, medical practice, banking, teaching, and so forth have their own respective purposes and their consequent inherent criteria for ranking values and capacities. But despite their differences, all these spheres of activity have a common structure according to the Purposive Ranking Thesis: in each the basis of comparison of capacities is inherent in the respective activity, in that what capacity is better or best can be ascertained in each case from the activity's point or purpose.

Two limitations must be noted in this account. First, it is one thing to say that the ranking in each kind of activity derives from *within* the activity's point or purpose. It is another thing to say that we can rank or compare *across* activities, unless some more general purpose can be found to include them. We may know how to rank hitters in baseball and entrepreneurs in business, but this does not, as such, enable us to rank baseball as against business. We could rank them if the purpose of each were to make money or to thrill onlookers; but then this would confront us with the problem of conflicting purposes and thus of conflicting evaluations and rankings. And if we try to rank them according to utilitarianism in terms of some super-purposes, such as promoting utility or the good or pleasurable feelings, this would be too vague and general to be helpful.

A second, closely related limitation of the Purposive Ranking Thesis is that it can apply just as well to capacities for trivial or immoral activities as to activities or capacities that are morally permissible. Consider, for example, the activity whose purpose is to count blades of grass on some broad lawn. Given this purpose, that capacity would rank higher which proceeded more accurately and also, perhaps, more rapidly. Or again, consider the Nazi activity of murdering Jews. The Nazi who committed more murders more efficiently would, according to the Purposive Ranking Thesis, rank higher in the relevant scale of values. As we shall see, however (3.4), universalist morality sets important limits to the kinds of activities and purposes that can justify rankings of capacities.

The Purposive Ranking Thesis is very close to the traditional principle of distributive justice, the contribution principle; indeed, the Thesis can serve as the principle's genus. According to the contribution principle, distribution should be determined by contribution; i.e., the distribution of rewards in some project should be determined by the relative contribution that persons make to attaining the purpose of that project, so that the ranking of rewards is to be proportioned to the relative contributions.[15] The Purposive Ranking Thesis is simply a more general version of this principle: the relative ranking of goods or capacities is to be determined by, and so be proportional to, the purposes of the goods. In the contribution principle's application the relevant purposes may be more determinate than in applications of the Purposive Ranking Thesis, but the main idea in each case is the same. Thus the baseball example can be used to illustrate both items.

3.3. IS REASON THE BEST OF HUMAN CAPACITIES?

Where, then, does this leave us with regard to ascertaining which capacity is the best in us to fulfill? I shall be offering several answers to this question. But let us begin from a very traditional answer that can be fitted into the Purposive Ranking Thesis. The honored status of being the best of human capacities has often been assigned to reason. It has indeed been said that reason is "what each person is," or one's "best part."[16] But this traditional answer has also been perennially challenged. A whole host of competitors against reason have been upheld throughout the ages, including desire, emotion, compassion, intuition, imagination, religious faith, aesthetic sensitivity, sexual or other love, animal instinct, personal authenticity, and many others. The plausibility of many of these competitors is reinforced if you think of the capacities or qualities that you would find maximally desirable in your friends or associates. You may well feel that a kindly, compassionate character is far preferable to the cold austerity that is sometimes associated with the "man of reason" or intellect.

It is sometimes held that such an objection against reason is not sound because reason is involved in one way or another in these other capacities. Compassion, for example, requires reason in order to ascertain its proper object; so too in different ways does religious faith and perhaps some of the others as well. This point, however, brings out the

---

[15] See Aristotle, *Politics*, 3. 9. 1281a3; Karl Marx, "Critique of the Gotha Program," in Robert C. Tucker, ed., *The Marx-Engels Reader*, 2nd ed. (New York: W. W. Norton, 1978), p. 530.

[16] See Aristotle, *Nicomachean Ethics*, 9. 8. 1169a1–3; 10. 7. 1177a1–3.

importance of having an appropriate conception not only of what reason consists in but also of the relevant context of activity and purpose in which it is compared with or measured against other human qualities or capacities. According to the Purposive Ranking Thesis, to say that reason is the best of human capacities tells us little until we know what is the context or criterion of "best" in terms of purpose. This criterion may well be irrelevant to, or at least different from, the criteria that are invoked, such as personal comfort or affection, when the various competitors of reason are acclaimed as in various ways superior to reason. Moreover, whether reason is the best of human capacities in the relevant respect is independent of the traditionally debated question of whether reason is the unique or distinctive capacity of humans: whether it belongs only to humans or whether it alone belongs to all humans. Reason could be unique or distinctive and still be inferior to other capacities on some criteria; on the other hand, it could be superior or best even if it is not unique or distinctive.

To deal with these issues, we must return to the Purposive Ranking Thesis. Reason has traditionally been defined as the power or capacity of ascertaining and preserving truth. It is to be noted that this is an epistemic definition which focuses on the point or purpose of the activities in which reason is exercised. This purpose does not bear on the psychological or moral characters or dispositions of the persons who use this power or on the feelings or other effects brought about by its use. The definition bears rather on reason as a truth-ascertaining activity, including the logical norms that directly enter into it. I shall refer to this as reason's "veridical capacity." It is this purpose of the use of reason that sets the criteria inherent in the activity of reason and that provides the basis for evaluating and ranking it. The norms by which this activity proceeds are primarily the canons of deductive and inductive logic, including in the former the operations of conceptual analysis and in the latter the deliverances of sense perception.

The point we have reached so far is that, on the question of the content of the best of human capacities, reason is that best according to the Purposive Ranking Thesis insofar as the purpose of the activity is to ascertain and preserve truth. But various doubts may arise here. We may hesitate to move from a definition of reason to a substantive conclusion about reason's being the best means of ascertaining truth. This is, of course, a large issue. I shall here briefly consider two specific objections. First, some of the above-noted competitors of reason, such as faith or intuition, have been upheld as providing sources or grounds of truth that are superior to reason. But none of these other capacities have the sureness and nonarbitrariness that are found in the canons and operations of reason. Moreover, concerning any of these other capacities questions may be raised about the justificatory reasons for accepting them as bases of truth, and any such attempted justification must make use of reason in the sense of induction or deduction or both.

A second objection is that the canons of deductive and inductive reason have themselves been criticized on various epistemic grounds.[17] But these grounds have been based on reason; more specifically, while there have been historical demands that reason pass various justificatory tests set by religious faith, aesthetic sensitivity, and so forth, the very scrutiny to determine whether these tests are passed must itself make use of reason. For example, salient powers of reason must be used in order to check whether propositions upheld on the basis of faith are consistent with the products of logical and empirical rationality, or whether the use of reason is compatible with the experiencing of aesthetic feelings, and the like. Thus any attack on reason or any claim to supersede it with regard to truth by some other human capacity or criterion must rely on reason to justify its claims. On the other hand, despite Hume's dictum that "reason is nothing but a wonderful and unintelligible instinct in our souls,"[18] the logical validity and necessity achieved by deduction and the empirical ineluctableness reflected in induction are directly constitutive of reason, and they give it a cogency and nonarbitrariness that provide a sufficient justification for relying on it with regard to truth.

At this point, however, we must take account of an important aspect of the Humean critique of reason. It is one thing to hold that the canons or rules of reason serve to ascertain truth; it is another to say that persons' actual use of these canons always fulfills this purpose. In other

---

[17] See, e.g., Karl Popper's claim that the "rationalist attitude," with its emphasis on "argument and experience," rests on an "irrational faith in reason" (*The Open Society and Its Enemies*, 2nd ed. [London: Routledge and Kegan Paul, 1952], vol. 2, pp. 23–31). See also such critiques of deductive inference as Lewis Carroll, "What the Tortoise Said to Achilles," *Mind* 4 (1895): 278–80; and A. N. Prior, "The Runabout Inference Ticket," *Analysis* 21 (1960): 38–39; and M.A.E. Dummett, "The Justification of Deduction," *Proceedings of the British Academy* 59 (1973). Cf. Wittgenstein's remark that "the laws of inference can be said to compel us; in the same sense, that is to say, as other laws in human society" (*Remarks on the Foundation of Mathematics* [Oxford: Basil Blackwell, 1956], I.116, p. 34). For a criticism of "liberal" conceptions of reason as excluding or inhibiting practical social activity, see Roy Edgley, "Reason and Violence: A Fragment of the Ideology of Liberal Intellectuals," in Stephan Körner, ed., *Practical Reason* (New Haven: Yale University Press, 1974), pp. 113–35. See also the essays collected in Bryan R. Wilson, ed., *Rationality* (Oxford: Basil Blackwell, 1970); Martin Hollis and Steven Lukes, eds., *Rationality and Relativism* (Oxford: Basil Blackwell, 1982). See also Ernest Gellner, *Reason and Culture* (Oxford: Basil Blackwell, 1992).
[18] David Hume, *Treatise of Human Nature*, 1. 3. 6 (ed. Selby-Bigge, p. 179). See ibid., 1. 4. 1 (pp. 180–87: "Of scepticism with regard to reason."

words, we must distinguish between the canonic and the operational aspects of reason. In the canonic aspect the canons of reason are directly followed. This is clearest in simple deductions, such as in the first figure of the Aristotelian syllogism or in the addition of two and three to equal five. On the other hand, in the operational aspect of reason, in persons' actual applications of the canons of reason, persons may make mistakes; in particular, the more one uses the empirical canons of inductive logic, the more fallible one's operations may be. It will therefore be important, in the various invocations of reason that I shall be making here, to be clear about which aspect of reason is being referred to.

In connection with the use of reason to justify the supreme principle of universalist morality, I shall be claiming an apodictic status for reason. I shall here be using conceptual analysis, which I construe on the model of deductive logic, in that when a complex concept A is analyzed as containing concepts B, C, and D, these concepts belong to A with logical necessity so that it is contradictory to hold that A applies while denying that B, C, or D applies. In my argument for the supreme principle of universalist morality, the concept of action, while representing the actual phenomena of human conduct, will be obtained and used by such conceptual analysis. On the other hand, in connection with personalist and particularist moralities, elements of probabilism will have to be recognized. In any case, this distinction does not militate against the general point that reason is the best of human capacities with regard to ascertaining truth.

As our next step, let us try to connect the point just made with the ideal of capacity-fulfillment. If this ideal requires fulfilling the best of our capacities, and if reason is the best capacity with regard to ascertaining truth, then capacity-fulfillment requires that we develop and use this capacity when the activity we engage in has as its purpose the ascertainment of truth. But here we must distinguish two different meanings of "the use of reason" bearing on two different kinds of activities or contexts in which reason is used. One kind is purely intellectual; it consists in the theoretical use of reason in the sciences and in much of philosophy. The other kind is much more inclusive; it comprises the application of rational criteria to the many other, practical contexts of human life, including the moral, the aesthetic, the technical, and so forth.[19] If the use of reason is confined to the former purely intellectual context, then what emerges as the best that it is in one to become—the best kind of life—is solely that of the scientist or theoretical philosopher. For it is in

[19] This distinction corresponds to the distinction drawn by W.F.R. Hardie between happiness as consisting in a single "dominant end" or in an "inclusive end." See Hardie, "The Final Good in Aristotle's Ethics," *Philosophy* 40 (1965): 279.

such a life that the ascertainment of truth is pursued for its own sake. This would exclude from "the best kind of life" the myriad activities of the masses of ordinary persons who are not scientists or philosophers, and as capacity-fulfillment it would confine self-fulfillment to a narrow range of intellectuals.

Here, however, we must recur to the point about individual differences with regard to "best" that we noted above in discussing the question of scope. It is not only scientists and philosophers who can and should make use of theoretical reason. The learning of mathematical and scientific knowledge, and especially of the skills that come from using the methods involved in practicing these kinds of knowledge, is indeed an important basis for developing the rational capacity and thus for achieving capacity-fulfillment. But the use of reason need not be confined to the theoretical sphere, and in the practical context of human self-fulfillment it is inapposite to do so. For reason as the veridical capacity can be used to help humans to deal with the many problems they face other than those of science and philosophy. It is indeed true that science and philosophy themselves can and should be used to deal with practical human problems. But in these other uses science and philosophy are ancillary or instrumental; they are pursued not for their own sakes but rather to help resolve problems that arise in many other contexts of human life. And, as we shall see, it is this inclusive, instrumental use of reason that figures both in the justification of universalist morality as required for self-fulfillment and in the ascertainment of many other components of self-fulfillment as capacity-fulfillment. In these contexts, reason becomes practical.

This point requires a partial reinterpretation of the idea that reason is the best of human capacities. What is meant is still that reason is the only sure way of attaining and preserving truth. But truth may be and is pursued not only for its own sake but also for the sake of attaining many other values. It will be by the use of reason that the connection of these other values with self-fulfillment will be ascertained. Such self-fulfillment will achieve the best that it is in one to become because it will be the veridically best part of oneself that guides such achievement.

As a long philosophical tradition from Plato through Spinoza to Freud has emphasized, the application of reason to practical life involves that one try to know oneself, that one candidly confront and recognize aspects of oneself that are relevant to the fulfillment of one's other capacities. It requires a kind of self-acceptance as opposed to hypocrisy, while at the same time one takes note of one's possibilities for self-improvement. In this way one can move toward greater maturity in relation both to oneself and to others, and thereby one can achieve an important part of one's capacity-fulfillment. The operations of reason may here be fallible, but they are still the best means of ascertaining the relevant practical truths.

In these and other practical applications of reason, capacity-fulfillment is enabled to avoid two extremes. It avoids the relativism whereby the immense varieties of human capacities are all equally accepted as bases of human good. It also avoids the dogmatism whereby a single capacity is set up as the sole end which is to be fulfilled, without having an adequate basis for this exclusiveness and without recognition of the value of other capacities. Reason can thus serve to ground a more realistic pluralism of capacity-fulfillments while at the same time being sensitive to warranted rankings. So to ask what is the best of human capacities does not commit us to the view that there is only one such capacity. Moreover, the components of capacity-fulfillment will include not only qualities or values that are directly constitutive of this "best" but also capacities that are ancillary to it. Getting food is an obvious example.

When we ask about what is the best of human capacities, and when we specify that the relevant context is self-fulfillment, our question concerns the process that is intended to lead to achieving the best that is in the person. This achievement may require various capacities other than reason, such as deep desire and perseverance. But these other capacities must here be ancillary to reason insofar as the achievement requires that one ascertain the truth about what is best, as giving the mark at which to aim. And, according to the definition given above, reason is the primary capacity, the best means, concerned with the ascertainment of truth. So, to this important extent, reason is the practically primary faculty, as setting the ends that are to be desired. But, as we shall see, the desires involved in the purposiveness of action also play an essential role.

If, then, reason is the best human capacity for ascertaining and preserving truth, it follows that we must use reason to ascertain what is best in human beings other than their epistemic or veridical capacities. This point can be associated with the orders of desire discussed above in connection with aspiration-fulfillment. We saw that in aspirations one desires not only to have a certain object but also to be a kind of person who has and fulfills that desire (2.1). Now reason, by virtue of being the best veridical capacity, can be fitted into this structure in that it can help to ascertain what kind of person one should try to be, what kinds of aspirations one should have. In this way reason, and with it the universalist morality it justifies, can both evaluate and reinforce the several orders that enter into aspiration-fulfillment. This raises the question of whether there is any "truth" to be ascertained in these other areas, such as with regard to moral, aesthetic, and other capacities of human beings. I shall now begin to deal with this question.

3.4. THE RATIONAL JUSTIFICATION OF
UNIVERSALIST MORALITY

I now want to examine whether and how reason can be used to ground universalist morality as an important part of capacity-fulfillment. It will be recalled that this morality was invoked as a basis for criticizing various objects of aspiration-fulfillment (2.5). The present concern with universalist morality is thus important both for carrying on the critical evaluation of aspiration-fulfillment and for establishing a central component of capacity-fulfillment.

We saw earlier that a serious objection to making such morality one of the required objects of self-fulfillment as aspiration-fulfillment is that this would obtrude an "alien" consideration on the self (2.5). The above discussion of reason as veridical provides an answer to this objection. For reason is an essential part or capacity of the human self; hence, if it can be shown to justify precepts requiring that persons act in accordance with universalist morality, then to impose such precepts on self-fulfillment is not to introduce a point of view that is alien to the self on which those requirements are imposed. It is rather to hearken to an essential part of that self.

In undertaking this project, it is important not to include in the meaning of "reason" the very conception of morality whose grounding in reason is to be demonstrated. I have tried above to accommodate this requirement by confining the criteria of reason as veridical to the canons of deductive and inductive logic. The salient present point is that if the contents attributed to self-fulfillment as capacity-fulfillment are to be regarded as a justified ideal for human action, they must satisfy the requirements of rational justification. So my project in this section is to give a rational justification of universalist morality.

Some philosophers have expressed doubts about the need for such a project. They have held that certain moral judgments are self-evident or necessarily true, such as that it is at least prima facie wrong to inflict pain on other persons or to break one's promises. From this it is held to follow that such judgments need no argument or justification. It has also been maintained, more specifically, that "human rights foundationalism . . . is outmoded and irrelevant" and that "the most philosophy can do is to summarize our culturally influenced intuitions about the right thing to do in various situations."[20]

---

[20] See William H. Gass, "The Case of the Obliging Stranger," *Philosophical Review* 66 (1957): 193ff.; J. R. Lucas, "Ethical Intuitionism II," *Philosophy* 46 (1971): 9–10; Renford Bambrough, "A Proof of the Objctivity of Morals," *American Journal of Jurisprudence* 14 (1969): 37ff.; R. F. Holland, "Moral Skepticism," *Aristotelian Supplementary Vol. 41*

While this intuitionist position has some plausibility, it incurs at least two difficulties. First, intuitions vary from group to group, so to rely on the intuitions of one group does not, as such, show why they should be preferred to the intuitions of other groups, including groups that reject human rights or any kind of rights talk. While it may be objected that the intuitions of some groups should not be taken seriously, the alternatives to what is declared to be self-evident or necessarily true have been upheld by various philosophers and ordinary persons going back at least to Glaucon in the second book of Plato's *Republic*. These alternatives restrict in various ways both the persons whose interests are to be favorably considered and what these interests are. The classic conflicts of moral philosophy represented in these alternatives cannot be rationally resolved simply by refusing to contend with one of the competing positions. The accusation that upholders of such restrictive alternatives are 'blind' or 'mad' stops argument when argument on the distributive and substantive issues they raise is both needed and possible. The assertion of madness is also confronted by the fact that persons upholding and practicing the castigated alternatives emerge as quite 'normal' in the psychiatric sense.[21]

A second difficulty with the intuitionist position concerns how far it can carry us. If we hold, as against the older intuitionists, that there are many complex moral issues that require argument rather than peremptory assertion, such issues as euthanasia and economic justice, then the problem arises of whether generalization from the purportedly self-evident judgments can deal adequately with those issues. Conflicts may arise between generalizations, and to resolve them recourse must be had not only to a still more general moral principle but also to the ranges of argument that enter into its justification. As we shall see, the argument for the universalist moral principle to be developed here will provide important bases for ascertaining the justified contents of capacity-fulfillment.

Let us now examine how the use of reason can show that universalist

---

(1967): 185ff.; G. J. Warnock, *The Object of Morality* (London: Methuen, 1971), pp. 122–25; Judith Jarvis Thomson, *The Realm of Rights* (Cambridge, Mass.: Harvard University Press, 1990), pp. 15–16. I have previously discussed this intuitionist position in *Reason and Morality* (Chicago: University of Chicago Press, 1978), pp. 7–12. For the attack on "human rights foundationalism," see Richard Rorty, "Human Rights, Rationality, and Sentimentality," in Stephen Shute and Susan Hurley, eds., *On Human Rights: The Oxford Amnesty Lectures 1993* (New York: Basic Books, 1993), pp. 116, 117.

[21] See Douglas M. Kelley, *22 Cells in Nuremberg: A Psychiatrist Examines the Nazi Criminals* (New York: Greenberg Publisher, 1947). See also Maria Jahoda, *Current Concepts of Positive Mental Health* (New York: Basic Books, 1958), especially pp. 77–80. Cf. Hannah Arendt, *Eichmann in Jerusalem: A Report on the Banality of Evil* (New York: Viking Press, 1963).

morality is intrinsically connected with self-fulfillment, i.e. that self-fulfillment as capacity-fulfillment necessarily involves that the self effectively accept egalitarian moral requirements, first in its actions, but then also in its attitudes, motivations, and character. The self in question is now viewed as a rational agent. As an agent she acts for various purposes she wants to attain. As rational she uses reason as truth-ascertaining to regulate her pursuit of these purposes. The conclusion to be drawn from this use of reason is that every rational agent logically must accept that she and all other rational agents have certain equal moral rights, i.e. rights to freedom and well-being as the necessary conditions of her action and generally successful action. Because of these rationally grounded rights, correlative moral duties or practical requirements logically must also be accepted by all persons as rational agents. In this way it will have been shown that reason requires all persons as rational agents to act in accordance with universalist morality as a necessary part of their self-fulfillment as capacity-fulfillment. The reason that is here in question is the deductive use of conceptual analysis. For persons to fulfill themselves through guidance by reason as the best of veridical capacities, they must be reasonable persons who respect the moral rights of other persons as well as of themselves. The logical necessity here attributed to the acceptance of the moral judgments in question, through the canonic aspect of reason, provides the basis for holding that they are necessarily true.[22]

To see how this argument for universalist morality works, we must note that, in the contexts both of capacity-fulfillment and of morality, there is a direct connection between being a self and being an agent. On the one hand, it is by agency or action that the relevant capacities are exercised and fulfilled; and the capacities themselves are powers or potentialities of human action. On the other hand, the main context of morality is human action; for all moralities, amid their diverse contexts, are concerned with telling persons how they ought to act, especially toward one another. Many moralities focus directly not on actions but on virtues, on what kinds of character persons ought to have. But since virtues include, as vital components, dispositions to act in certain ways, there is at least an implicit concern with actions even in moralities that focus on virtues. Moreover, actions are also the objects of all other practical precepts, including technical, artistic, prudential, religious, and so forth.

Now the action that is thus relevant both to morality and to capacity-fulfillment has two generic features. *Voluntariness* or *freedom* is the procedural generic feature of action; it consists in controlling one's

---

[22] I have discussed the truth of moral judgments much more fully in *Reason and Morality*, pp. 171–90. For a fuller development of the whole argument, see ibid., chaps. 1–3.

behavior by one's unforced choice while having knowledge of relevant circumstances. *Purposiveness* or *intentionality* is the substantive generic feature of action; it consists in aiming to attain some end or goal which constitutes one's reason for acting; this goal may be either the action itself or something to be achieved by the action. Since, moreover, the aim of acting is to succeed in one's purposes, when purposiveness is extended to the general conditions required for such success, it becomes the more general feature which I shall call *well-being*. Viewed from the standpoint of action, then, well-being consists in having the various substantive conditions and abilities that are proximately required either for acting at all or for having general chances of success in achieving one's purposes through one's action. Such well-being falls into a hierarchy of three different levels. *Basic well-being* consists in having the essential preconditions of action, such as life, physical integrity, mental equilibrium. *Nonsubtractive well-being* consists in having the general abilities and conditions needed for maintaining undiminished one's general level of purpose-fulfillment and one's capabilities for particular actions; examples are not being lied to or stolen from. *Additive well-being* consists in having the general abilities and conditions needed for increasing one's level of purpose-fulfillment and one's capabilities for particular actions; examples are education, self-esteem, and opportunities for acquiring wealth and income. As we shall see, such additive well-being is a vital basis both of what is best in human selves and of achieving this best. But more generally the connection between being a self and being at least a prospective or potential agent suggests that there is an important connection between self-fulfillment and purpose-fulfillment. This connection was already present in the area of aspiration-fulfillment. But capacity-fulfillment extends and deepens the connection because of the ways in which, as we shall see, it involves the use of reason to criticize and develop the purposes that may be sought in action.

In order to understand how the application of reason to action logically involves that every rational agent must accept a certain universalist moral principle, it is important to note the connection between action with its generic features and goodness or value. This connection stems from the fact that action as purposive is conative in that the agent tries by his action to bring about certain results or consummations that he wants, at least intentionally if not inclinationally, to attain. From this conativeness it follows that the purposes for which he acts seem to him to be good. The goodness in question need not be moral or definitive, but it involves that his purpose seems to him to have at least sufficient value that he regards it as worth trying to attain. In this way all the purposes that figure in the Purposive Ranking Thesis are grounded in the very structure of human action. Since, moreover, freedom and well-being, as the generic features of action and generally successful action, are the necessary conditions of the agent's attaining by his action what he regards as goods, he also must regard his freedom and well-being as necessary goods.

The next step in the argument is to see that action has not only a valuational structure but also a deontic one, i.e. it involves the notions of rights and correlative 'oughts'. The central point of the argument is that rights and rights-claims arise logically and fundamentally out of the concern of all human beings, as prospective purposive agents, that the proximate necessary conditions of their action and generally successful action be protected.

I shall now give a brief outline of the dialectically necessary rational argument from the generic features of action to the ascription of human rights and thereby to the supreme principle of universalist morality. The argument undertakes to establish two main theses. The first is that every agent logically must accept that he or she has rights to freedom and well-being. The second is that the agent logically must also accept that all other agents also have these rights equally with his or her own, so that in this way the existence of universal moral rights, and thus of human rights, must be accepted within the whole context of action or practice.

Reduced to its barest essentials, the argument for the first main thesis is as follows. Since the agent has at least a minimum of self-awareness, when he acts for some purpose there can be attributed to him a statement of the form (1) "I do X for end or purpose E." This is a statement form that logically must be accepted by every agent for himself, so that it serves to ground the categoricalness of the rights-principle generated by the argument. From (1), as we have seen, the agent logically must accept (2) "E is good." For while the goodness in question need not be moral, and the ascription of goodness need not be definitive, it involves the agent's acceptance that the purpose for which he acts has for him at least some value sufficient to merit his trying to attain it. Now since freedom and well-being are the proximate necessary conditions of the agent's acting to attain any of his purposes and thus any goods, the agent, on the basis of his accepting (2), must also accept (3) "My freedom and well-being are necessary goods." Hence he must also accept (4) "I must have freedom and well-being," where this 'must' is practical-prescriptive in that it signifies the agent's advocacy or endorsement of his having the conditions he needs to have in order to act and to act successfully in general.

The next step is especially crucial. On the basis of his accepting (4), the agent logically must also accept (5) "I have rights to freedom and well-being." At this step the normative (though not necessarily moral) concept of rights (in the strong sense of claim-rights) is introduced, as an essential element in the thinking of every rational agent. That the agent logically must accept (5) on the basis of accepting (4) can be shown as follows. Suppose he rejects (5). Then, because of the correlativity of claim-rights and strict 'oughts,' he also has to reject (6) "All other persons ought at least to refrain from removing or interfering with my freedom and well-being." By rejecting (6), he has to accept (7) "Other persons may (i.e., It is permissible that other persons) remove or interfere with my freedom and well-being." And by accepting (7), he also has to accept (8) "I may not (i.e., It is permissible that I not) have freedom and well-being." But (8) contradicts (4). Since every agent must accept (4), he must reject (8). And since (8) follows from the denial of (5), every agent must reject that denial, so that he must accept (5) "I have rights to freedom and well-being." I call them generic rights because they are rights to have the generic features of action and successful action characterize one's behavior.

The argument for the first main thesis has thus established that all action is necessarily connected with the concept of rights. For every agent logically must hold or accept that he has rights to the necessary conditions of action and successful action in general.[23]

---

[23] Alasdair MacIntyre has presented the following objection to this argument: "It is first of all clear that the claim that I have a right to something is a quite different type of claim from the claim that I need or want or will be benefited by something. From the first—if it is the only relevant consideration—it follows that others ought not to interfere with my attempts to do or have whatever it is, whether it is for my own good or not. From the second it does not. And it makes no difference what kind of good or benefit is at issue" (*After Virtue* [Notre Dame, Indiana: University of Notre Dame Press, 1981], pp. 64–65). MacIntyre here overlooks two relevant points: first, that the whole argument proceeds from within the conative purview of the purposive agent; second, that the argument is confined to the generic necessities recognized by the agent from within that purview. Thus, while I have rendered the direct antecedent in step (4) as "I must have freedom and well-being," MacIntyre presents it as "the claim that I need or want or will be benefited by something." Now from such a general "claim" to "something," it indeed does not follow either that one has a right to that something or that one must claim a right to it. But the antecedent in my argument is presented as a truly necessary statement, in that the agent correctly holds that, in order to act, he must have the necessary conditions of his action. From this it does indeed follow that the agent holds that "others ought not to interfere with" his having these conditions, for the reasons given in the text of my argument. If the agent were to deny this 'ought'-judgment, then he would have to accept that it is permissible for other persons to remove or interfere with his having freedom and well-being. And from this it would follow that he accepts that he may not—it is permissible that he not—have freedom and well-being. But this would contradict his prior statement (4) "I must have freedom and well-being." Hence, on the basis of his having to accept this 'must'-statement, each agent, on pain of contradiction, must accept the 'ought'-judgment, and thus the right-claim, with which MacIntyre has said the agent may dispense. So MacIntyre's objection does not stand up. I have dealt with his theses more fully in "Rights and Virtues," *Review of Metaphysics* 38 (June 1985): 739–62. On the 'ought'-judgment invoked here, see also my "'Ought' and Reasons for Action," *Southern Journal of Philosophy* 35 (summer 1997): 171–77.

It will have been noted that this dialectical argument applies to even completely self-interested agents. Their self-interested purposes generate the prudential right-claim of step (5), because their rejection of this claim would entail their acquiescing in removal from them of the necessary conditions of their action.

Let us now turn to the argument for the second main thesis. This is also of special importance because it involves the transition from prudential to moral rights. On the basis of his having to accept that he has the generic rights, every agent logically must accept that all other actual or prospective agents have these rights equally with his own. This generalization is an application of the logical principle of universalizability: if some predicate P belongs to some subject S because S has a certain quality Q (where the 'because' is that of sufficient condition), then P logically must belong to all other subjects S1 to Sn that also have Q. Thus, if any agent holds that he has the generic rights because he is a prospective purposive agent, then he also logically must hold that every prospective purposive agent has the generic rights.

Now every agent logically must accept (9) "I have rights to freedom and well-being because I am a prospective purposive agent." For suppose some agent A were to object that the necessary and sufficient justifying condition of his having the generic rights is his having some property R that is more restrictive than simply being a prospective purposive agent. Examples of R might include his being a wage-earner or an entrepreneur or a banker or a landlord or an American or white or black or male or being named "Wordsworth Donisthorpe," and so forth. From this it would follow that A would logically have to hold that it is only his having R that justifies his having the generic rights, so that if he were to lack R, then he would not have the generic rights.

But such an agent would contradict himself. For we saw above that, as an agent, he logically must hold that he has the generic rights, since otherwise he would be in the position of accepting that he normatively need not have what he has accepted that he normatively must have, namely, the freedom and well-being that are the necessary conditions of action and successful action in general. Hence, since no agent, including A, can consistently hold that he does not have the generic rights, he must give up the idea that any such restrictive property R can be the necessary as well as sufficient justifying condition of his having these rights. From this it follows that every agent logically must acknowledge that, simply by virtue of being a prospective purposive agent, he has the generic rights, so that he also logically must accept (10) "All prospective purposive agents have rights to freedom and well-being." At this point the rights in question become universalist moral rights, because the agent is now committed to taking favorable account of the interests of all other persons, as prospective purposive agents, as well as of himself.

The argument has thus shown that it is not rational for any agent to be exclusively self-interested, where 'rational' signifies conformity to the principle of noncontradiction as the fundamental principle of reason.

Since the universalized judgment (10) sets a prescriptive requirement for the action of every agent toward all other prospective purposive agents, who are or may be the recipients of his action, every agent logically must also accept for himself a universalist moral principle which may be formulated as follows: (11) Act in accord with the generic rights of your recipients as well as of yourself. I call this the Principle of Generic Consistency (PGC), because it combines the formal consideration of logical consistency with the material consideration of the generic features and rights of action. This concludes the argument for the second main thesis. Since the generic rights are rights had equally by all agents, and since all humans are actual, prospective, or potential agents, the generic rights are now seen to be human rights. So the PGC is the universalist moral principle of human rights.[24]

---

[24] In *Reason and Morality* (pp. 89–95) I raised against myself the objection that the agent might be an "amoralist" who rejects all deontic concepts, including rights. I gave a lengthy reply to this objection. Gilbert Harman, in *Moral Relativism and Moral Objectivity* (Cambridge, Mass.: Blackwell, 1995), pp. 51–52, raised this same objection on behalf of the "nihilist" without noting that I had already raised and answered it. In personal correspondence Harman has acknowledged his oversight on this matter. In *Ethics and the Limits of Philosophy* (Cambridge, Mass.: Harvard University Press, 1985), Bernard Williams has presented four criticisms of my argument for the PGC; but the criticisms are based on misconceptions and misinterpretations. First, he says that an agent may act for some purpose without regarding it as good (p. 58). But Williams fails to distinguish here between definitive judgments of goodness and judgments that ascribe only some minimal, even tentative, good or value to one's purposes. In my argument I held that the agent need not accept more than the latter when he thinks that his purpose merits his acting to attain it. Such a minimal attribution of goodness is all I require for this stage of my argument. Second, Williams says that when the agent A prescribes that B and other agents not interfere with his freedom of action, A must recognize that B can similarly prescribe to A; but, Williams objects, this does not commit A to accepting B's prescription (p. 61). This, however, is a misinterpretation of my argument. I do not argue from the similarity of A and B as making claims or prescriptions; rather, I argue that A, in claiming rights to freedom by virtue of his being a purposive agent, must recognize that B, as a purposive agent, also has the same rights. The whole argument remains within each agent's own perspective, as to what he must rationally acknowledge. Thus, when A acknowledges B's rights, this is not (as Williams says) because B "can have thoughts like his (A's) own" but rather because A must recognize that B fulfills the same sufficient condition for having rights that A has had to accept for himself. And, of course, since A is here operating as a rational agent, the same line of analysis and argument characterizes every rational agent: each must claim rights to the necessary conditions of agency for himself and hence must acknowledge the same rights for all others. But the basis of A's having to respect B's rights is A's recognition of B's similarity to A not as making claims but rather as having the same justifying attributes as A adduces to justify his own right-claims. Williams's third objection is that the agent need not prescribe any rules about rights either to himself or to anyone else (p. 62). Williams here overlooks my extensive consideration and refutation of this possibility, which

If the above argument is sound, it has shown that the principle of egalitarian universalist morality has been established by reason through the use of conceptual analysis to ascertain the requirements both of logical consistency and of action. And since the reason that has been so used is an essential capacity of the self, indeed its best capacity in the ascertainment of truth, it follows that the requirements of universalist morality, far from being imposed by considerations alien to the self, derive from resources that are intrinsic to the self. Since, moreover, self-fulfillment as capacity-fulfillment consists in achieving the best that it is in one to become, it follows from this use of reason that to accept and act in accordance with the requirements of universalist morality is an essential part of such self-fulfillment. This provides further evidence that self-fulfillment, far from being egoistic, is not only compatible with but is required by universalist morality. And, as noted above, the principle of such morality is a necessary truth.

The above argument for the PGC shows that self-fulfillment includes both the having of rights—the generic rights—and their effectuation in personal situations and in social institutions. This involves not only that one's freedom and well-being are protected but also that there is social recognition that these necessary goods of action are due or owed to the person as her personal property, as what she is personally entitled to have and control for her own sake. Correlatively, other persons have a mandatory duty at least not to infringe this property, and, under certain circumstances, to assist the person in attaining this property. By this requirement all persons, in seeking their own self-fulfillment through their

---

I attribute to the "amoralist" (*Reason and Morality*, pp. 89–95). His final objection is that there is no warrant for restricting the agent's right-claims or prescriptions to his freedom, as against "whatever particular purposes I may happen to have" (p. 62). Apart from the fact that I hold that the agent claims rights to well-being as well as to freedom, Williams here overlooks my emphasis on modality: since right-claims embody claims to necessary conduct on the part of other persons, as to how they must act, the claims can be logically derived only from premises that themselves also embody such necessity. Hence, within the purview of rationally necessary argument that is alone at issue here, the objects of the claims can only be the necessary goods of agency, not all goods or purposes indiscriminately (see *Reason and Morality*, pp. 77–78, 81–82). Near the end of his book (p. 189) Williams recognizes this very distinction, but without referring back to its bearing on his criticism of my argument.

In view of these shortcomings in Williams's critique of my attempt to provide an "Archimedean point" for moral philosophy, I conclude that he has not shown that my project of establishing an "objective foundation" for morality has failed. And with this, his general assertion of the incompetence of philosophy in the field of "ethical theory" is likewise quite defective. On these and related issues, see also the cogent discussions in Deryck Beyleveld, *The Dialectical Necessity of Morality: An Analysis and Defense of Alan Gewirth's Argument to the Principle of Generic Consistency* (Chicago: University of Chicago Press, 1991), pp. 166–73, 308–10, 405–7, and 423.

rights to freedom and well-being, must also take positive account of the equal rights of other persons. This taking account proceeds both through the conduct of individuals and also, in large part, through institutional protections of human rights. These protections involve that all persons have effective rights to equal opportunity for their capacity-fulfillment, so that the PGC provides, to this extent, the basis of an egalitarian society. In this way, also, effectuation of the principle of human rights helps to remove some of the main social obstacles to persons' effective formation and fulfillment of their aspirations (see above, 2.2, 3). Because of their derivation from reason as justifying their mandatoriness, the requirements of universalist morality are important parts of that "best" whose achievement is constitutive of self-fulfillment as capacity-fulfillment. And to recognize and accept these requirements in one's thought and action may involve a kind of self-transformation whereby one becomes more fully a moral and social being.

The appeal to consistency in ethics—the thesis that the immoral person contradicts himself and thus is inherently irrational—goes back to Kant and indeed to Plato. It may be and has been objected, however, that such an appeal goes beyond what ethical argument needs and is capable of, and that it reflects a kind of rationalistic or intellectual fallacy, in that it reduces moral evil to logical error. There are two replies. First, the modality of logical necessity is the only way of accounting for, and doing justice to, the categorical obligatoriness of moral judgments, especially those concerning human rights, whereby compliance with them is rationally mandatory for all actual or prospective agents regardless of their personal inclinations or institutional affiliations. Here, the canonic aspect of reason is especially important. Second, since the general sphere of morality is in important part one of great dissensus, its competing claims and counter-claims can be rationally adjudicated in a nonquestion-begging way if we can show that one principle is such that logical inconsistency results from rejecting it, while this is not so with the other principles. For this provides a conclusive argument in favor of the first principle, since a proposition whose denial is self-contradictory is itself necessarily true. This, then, is the point of emphasizing the criterion of logical consistency: not that of superseding moral criteria that use specifically moral concepts of persons and their interests, but rather that of providing a culminating structural argument where other arguments fail of conclusiveness (see also below, 5.8).

Reason, as the veridical capacity, can be used for evil purposes as well as for good ones. But this familiar point does not remove the ground for basing on reason the justification of universalist morality. For the evil purposes cannot themselves be justified by reason, in contrast to freedom and well-being as the necessary goods of action and the rights and universalization that derive therefrom. Whether the purposes are based on hate or prejudice or other malevolent emotions, or on factual errors, impeccable reasoning to the means for carrying out the purposes does not militate against the crucial consideration that the premises themselves are not based on reason. So this leaves standing the justificatory use of reason in the present moral context.

3.5. UNIVERSALIST MORALITY AND FULFILLMENT OF THE REASONABLE SELF

The grounding of universalist morality in reason is not antithetical to its having an important emotional component. The argument brings to awareness the principle that other persons have moral rights equal to one's own; and this awareness can both be furthered by and serve to foster feelings of compassion, solidarity, and respect for other persons. The rational grounding of the principle can itself help to motivate its conscientious acceptance as an important part of self-fulfillment. Moral education guided by the reasonableness inherent in the rational argument for the principle's equality of rights can bring to vivid appreciation its requirements about the goods and rights of other persons. This appreciation, at its best, also takes the form of a firm state of character, or moral virtue, on the part of the persons who follow the argument or at least accept its conclusion. Most directly this is the virtue of justice, of acting in accord with the rights of other persons as well as of oneself, and of having a firm disposition so to act because of its rightness. Such persons are morally good because of their deep-seated motivations and corresponding practical acceptance and understanding. Through the argument given above, it can be seen that possession of this moral virtue is an important part of capacity-fulfillment.

Even if the requirements of universalist morality are established by reason and hence derive from within the epistemically best self, it may be objected that those requirements cannot pertain to or be parts of self-fulfillment because their objects—what they require to be protected or provided—are the goods or interests of other persons, not those of the self or agent. It has indeed been contended that a fully moral person would be a "moral saint" who would be so obsessed with promoting the good of other persons or of society that she would completely overlook or reject her own needs and desires.[25] So moral goodness would entail not self-fulfillment but self-abnegation or self-sacrifice.

The unsoundness of this thesis can be seen from the fact that rationally justified universalist morality requires the rejection not only of one-sided egoism but also of one-sided altruism. This double require-

---

[25] See Susan Wolf, "Moral Saints," *Journal of Philosophy* 79 (August 1982): 419–39.

ment is found in the famous second version of Kant's categorical imperative: "Act so that you always treat humanity, whether in your own person *or in that of another*, always as an end and never as a means only."[26] Essentially the same requirement is also found in the PGC: "Act in accord with the generic rights of your recipients as well as of yourself." It must be kept in mind that the whole argument for the PGC as the principle of human rights begins from the purposes of the self-interested agent. By the argument, the agent is brought to see that he cannot consistently maintain an exclusively self-interested position, that his rational self-fulfillment requires concern for the rights of others. This does not mean, however, that he must surrender all concern for his self-interest; for in requiring that he act in accord with the generic rights of his recipients the principle sets up what may be called a moderate altruism.

There may, of course, be conflicts between the agent's rights and those of other persons. But there are rational criteria for resolving these conflicts, based upon the PGC's derivation from the necessary conditions of action. An especially important criterion is what I shall call the degrees of needfulness for action, which may be stated as follows: when two rights are in conflict with one another, that right takes precedence whose object is more needed for action. This is why, for example, the rights not to be stolen from or lied to are overridden by the rights not to starve or be murdered if the latter rights can be fulfilled only by infringing the former.[27]

In place of the extreme of "moral saints," the PGC as the principle of human rights upholds a conception that may be called the reasonable self.[28] Such a self, in attaining its capacity-fulfillment, is aware of its own

---

[26] *Foundations of the Metaphysics of Morals*, chap. 2 (Akad. ed., p. 429; trans. L. W. Beck [Indianapolis: Bobbs- Merrill, 1959], p. 47; emphasis added).

[27] I have discussed this criterion in some detail in *The Community of Rights* (Chicago: University of Chicago Press, 1996), pp. 45–54.

[28] On the reasonable self, see also Alan Gewirth, *Political Philosophy* (New York: Macmillan, 1965), pp. 14–16, and "The Rationality of Reasonableness," *Synthese* 17 (1983): 225–47. Seyla Benhabib has criticized my argument for the PGC by comparison with "communicative ethics," on two grounds (*Critique, Norm, and Utopia* [New York: Columbia University Press, 1986], pp. 356–57): "First, Gewirth proceeds from a strictly monological or self-centered (although not egotistical) point of view in constructing his dialectically necessary method, while communicative ethics proceeds from the standpoint of dialogue and constructs the standpoint of agents as members of a linguistic community. Second, Gewirth dissolves all 'interaction' into 'transactions' among selves. . . . From the standpoint of communicative ethics, this dissolution of interaction into transactions is completely unacceptable, for it puts the cart before the horse. It ignores that individuals become beings capable of transactions by first learning to interact according to rules of mutuality and reciprocity." These criticisms are deficient for at least two reasons. First, Benhabib ignores the fact that in what she calls my "strictly monological" approach I have the agent addressing other agents with the requirement that they recognize his rights, and

agency needs and rights, but it also takes due account of the agency needs of other persons, respecting their rights as well as one's own and maintaining a certain equitableness or mutuality of consideration between oneself and others, as required by the universality of human rights. Thus the reasonable self recognizes that it has rights against others as well as obligations toward others, and that these must be embodied not only in individual actions but in social and political institutions, which thereby constitute a community of rights. Individuals, as part of their self-fulfillment, have duties to support such communities precisely because of this embodiment; this includes responsibilities of political participation. Thus in requiring respect for the human rights of each person, the conception of the reasonable self requires also support of the whole system of mutually sustaining rights and duties. In this way, the emphasis on individual rights is not only compatible with, but requires a conscientious concern for, the common good, where 'common,' from its initial distributive meaning, takes on also the collective meaning of the community that is constituted by and is the protector of human rights. Military service in a just war is one form that this support may take, but there are many others. More generally, the reasonable self is also a good citizen in a polity that respects human rights, accepting the burdens as well as the rewards of citizenship. At the same time, awareness of the complexities of applying the principle of human rights to concrete cases requires that one take account of the probabilism involved in the actual applications of reason, its operational aspect (3.3).

So to fulfill oneself in that part of capacity-fulfillment which concerns the universalist morality of how one treats other persons, one must be a reasonable self. One thereby makes the best of oneself and is true to what is best in oneself. The status of the reasonable self's being an important part of one's best self can also be derived from the Purposive Ranking Thesis, where the relevant activity and purpose involve treating other persons in ways that are rationally justified. Since it is the reasonable self that best fulfills this purpose, it follows that the reasonable self

---

then acknowledging that these other agents also have the same rights, so that he is a "reasonable" person. If this approach is "strictly monological," it is so only in a very attenuated sense. Second, my approach, unlike that of "communicative ethics," does not beg the question of moral justification by incorporating into my starting-point the requirement of individuals' "first learning to interact according to rules of mutuality and reciprocity." This requirement, which Benhabib accurately takes over from Jürgen Habermas, incorporates into its starting-point the very qualities of "mutuality and reciprocity" which it is the project of a noncircular moral philosophy to justify. In my starting-point, by contrast, it is assumed only that the persons addressed are rational as being able to understand the canons of deductive and inductive logic, but not as accepting any moral principle, including those that the argument is intended to justify.

is at least part of one's best self: it is this self that fulfills the rationally justified requirements of universalist morality. From this it also follows that self-fulfillment cannot rightly be extended to such other selves as the one epitomized in Freud's id, because of their violations of universalist morality.

As I noted above, there may be conflicts between the rights of the self and the rights of other persons. Among the most extreme examples are cases where other persons' rights to life conflict with one's own right to life. This could occur in several ways. One is where tyrannical regimes set out to murder parts of their populations, as in the Nazis' Holocaust and the "ethnic cleansing" perpetrated in the former Yugoslavia in 1993. Here it may be difficult or impossible for individual persons to intervene without risking their own lives; but it is their duty to press their governments to take appropriate measures. Where, within the limits set by geographic and other factors, including comparable costs to agents, individual actions of rescue are possible, the principle of human rights prescribes the moral duty to perform them. Fulfillment of this duty is an important part of self-fulfillment. In any case, indifference in the face of such evils is entirely unacceptable morally.

We must look more closely at the question of how far rights extend in such extreme situations, including the rights both of the threatened persons and of their possible individual rescuers. According to the criterion of degrees of needfulness for action, acts of rescue are morally required of persons if they are in a position to effect the rescues without comparable costs to themselves. The threatened persons have rights to be rescued in such circumstances. But their rights to life do not extend to the lives of any other innocent persons. In general, if a person has a right to X, then she has a right to anything else Y that may be necessary for her having X, unless someone else already has a right to that Y and Y is as needed for action as is X. For example, if Jones is starving and cannot obtain food by her own efforts, while Smith has abundant food, then Jones has a right to as much of Smith's food as she needs to prevent starvation even though Smith has a property right in the food. But if Smith has only enough food to prevent his own starvation, then Jones has no right to it because Smith's not starving is as needed for his action as Jones's not starving is for hers. In such a case, the correct description of the situation may be put in either of two ways: (a) Jones's right not to starve or her right to Smith's food is overridden; (b) Jones does not have a right not to starve when her nonstarvation requires the infringement of Smith's equal right.

It is for this reason that the rights to life of the persons who are threatened by murder do not include the right to have their possible rescuers murdered. The lives of the possible rescuers are as needed for their action as the lives of the threatened persons are for theirs. But by the same token, when acts of rescue are possible, with the realistic expectation that the rescuers are not risking their own lives, those acts are morally mandatory positive duties. Obviously in such tragic situations the results of miscalculation can be terrible. But the risks can be and have been shouldered by persons who have sufficiently strong convictions about the community of rights (see also below, 5.2).

There remain further questions about how far this requirement of individual responsibility extends, beyond the governmental provision emphasized above. The questions concern especially the rightness of persons' living their own lives while confronted by other persons whose extreme hardships and sufferings prevent them from having the freedom and well-being needed for living their own lives. I want to suggest that a sound answer to these questions is provided by recourse to the full context of capacity-fulfillment with its locus of human purposive agency. We have duties to help persons to fulfill their generic rights of agency when they cannot do so by their own efforts. Through such fulfillment, persons are enabled to act, with general chances of success, in pursuit of their own purposes, whatever they may be, so long as they do not violate the generic rights of other persons. But by the same token, the helpers, the respondents of the duties, should also be able to act in pursuit of their own purposes, in accordance with their own rights to freedom and well-being. An accommodation must, then, be reached between persons' duties to help others and their rights to be free purposive agents on their own behalf. This accommodation is indicated in the PGC's injunction to act in accord with the generic rights of one's recipients as well as of oneself. It would be morally wrong to emphasize either of these poles to the exclusion of the other. But since, and insofar as, the duties to help may more readily be under-supported, there is required vigorous advocacy on the part of individuals and groups, together with action by the state as indicated above. Persons who have the moral character based on the principle of human rights will feel deep regret when they are unable to help persons who are in such dire need.

Thus far in this section I have argued that the ground for including practical respect for universalist morality within capacity-fulfillment is that such respect is required by veridical reason as the epistemically best of human capacities. I shall now try to show that this inclusion can also be justified by consideration of the Purposive Ranking Thesis that I discussed above. It will be recalled that the pattern of argument invoking this thesis moves from (a) a kind of activity or context which has (b) certain characteristic purposes to (c) the ascertainment of what is best according to the criteria inherent in those purposes. Now in the case of universalist morality the context (a) concerns how one should treat other persons, and the purpose (b) of this context is to ascertain what is justified by reason. I have tried to show that what is best, according to the criteria inherent in this purpose, is (c) adherence to the universalist morality of human rights. So in this way it emerges again that capacity-fulfillment, as achieving the best that it is in one to become, requires practical respect for universalist morality. The criterion of "best" is provided by the rational purpose of the relevant interpersonal activity.

My argument in this section has rested on the premise that since reason is the epistemically best of human capacities, whatever is justified by reason must also be among the best of human capacities and thus must be a part of capacity-fulfillment. It was on the basis of this premise that I held that practical acceptance of the universalist morality of human rights is itself a part of capacity-fulfillment. In this way the bestness of the process—the justificatory use of reason—gets transferred to the bestness of the product—the universalist morality of human rights.

But consider this objection: the theorems of higher mathematics are justified by reason; hence, on the above premise, knowledge of those theorems would be a part of capacity-fulfillment. This would then mean that knowledge of an immense plethora of rationally justified propositions in all the sciences would also become a part of capacity-fulfillment. But since nobody can know all the sciences, it would follow that capacity-fulfillment is not only dauntingly difficult but indeed impossible.

A main answer to this objection is that it does not take account of the distinctions of the different scopes of "best" presented above (3.3). Since capacity-fulfillment as we are considering it here must be achievable by most persons, the best that it is in one to become must take account of persons' limited capacities. As I suggested above, there is indeed a place in capacity-fulfillment for the development of one's intellectual capacities in the learning of mathematical and scientific skills. But this does not mean that the whole vast range of propositions that can be justified by reason must be parts of capacity-fulfillment. On the other hand, acceptance of the universalist moral principle of human rights is a vital part of capacity-fulfillment both because of its bearing on the practical question, which actually confronts persons, of how they ought to treat one another, and because the grasp of the principle and of its justificatory argument is within the reach of all minimally rational persons. Every such person can understand that just as he holds that he has certain rights on the basis of his being a prospective purposive agent, so he must accept that all other prospective purposive agents also have these rights.

The argument I have given for the PGC can provide support for a traditional, controversial Kantian thesis about universalist morality: that its requirements are overriding in that they take precedence over all other practical requirements, including those set by various aspirations and by personalist or individual moralities of the good life insofar as they may conflict with universalist morality.[29] The activities and purposes that can justify rankings according to the Purposive Ranking Thesis are also limited as to their contents by this morality. The argument for the PGC helps to ground this thesis because it shows how universalist morality involves two elements of necessity. On the material side, because the objects that enter into the argument for the PGC are the generic features of human action, it follows that no agent can reject these features for himself while remaining an agent; and, as we have seen, action or agency is the direct or indirect object of all moral and other practical precepts. On the formal side, the argument has been that any agent who violates the PGC's requirements contradicts himself. Since noncontradiction is the most basic criterion of reason and truth, conformity to the PGC is a necessary requirement of all justified action. Here the canonic aspect of reason serves to ground the PGC's apodictic status. The overridingness of universalist morality follows from these two elements of necessity. In view of this, hereafter when I use "moral" without qualification, it will be to egalitarian universalist morality that I shall be referring. Because of these elements, every practical precept, to be rationally justified, must conform to, or at least not violate, the requirements set by the PGC.

3.6. SELF-RESPECT AND DIVERSE WAYS OF LIFE

Effective possession of the rights to freedom and well-being is an essential part of capacity-fulfillment. This was seen to follow from the double consideration about the use of reason: that it is a part of capacity-fulfillment and that it justifies the universal possession of these rights. We have also seen that such fulfillment disjustifies aspirations and policies whose objects are violations of the rights. Important cases of such violations occur when persons' autonomous control and fulfillment of their aspirations are subjected to socially imposed limitations that are themselves unjustified (see 2.2). The limitations violate the PGC's requirement that all persons have equal rights to freedom and well-being. This equality of rights does not involve that all persons have equal inherent ability to form and fulfill their aspirations, let alone that they should or

---

[29] This overridingness thesis has been contested, among others, by Philippa Foot, "Are Moral Considerations Overriding?," in her collection *Virtues and Vices* (Berkeley: University of California Press, 1978), and Bernard Williams, *Ethics and the Limits of Philosophy*, chap. 10.

must be equally enabled to fulfill them. Rather, it involves two other kinds of rights, one negative, the other positive.

The negative rights require that limitations not be imposed by social conventions or political power on persons' ability to aspire realistically to whatever goals their inherent capacities may render feasible, so long as these aspirations do not have the moral wrongness discussed above. These negative rights bear especially on the social determination of roles and accompanying aspirations. Feminists in particular have held that patriarchal societies constrict women's choices so that any aspirations beyond being mothers and housewives are discouraged. Disadvantages imposed by race and class also operate to diminish persons' aspirations: lack of opportunities leads to lack of confidence that certain of one's possible aspirations can realistically be regarded as fulfillable. The effectuation of the negative rights requires political, economic, and social changes in institutions that impose such aspiration-diminishing handicaps. I have discussed the contents and methods of these changes elsewhere.[30]

The positive rights require social arrangements whereby persons are helped to develop their abilities of aspiration-fulfillment so long as they cannot do so by their own efforts. Such help should be general rather than specific or particular: it must enable persons to obtain the general tools of aspiration-fulfillment, such as education, rather than the specific means of fulfilling some particular aspiration or set of aspirations. In these ways the PGC as the principle of human rights entails a general right to aspiration-fulfillment, a right that is itself based on the use of reason as an essential part of capacity-fulfillment.

The human rights also have other important connections with capacity-fulfillment. Not only does the use of reason in capacity-fulfillment serve to ground the human rights; those rights serve in turn to ground other parts of capacity-fulfillment. A main one is self-respect. Without self-respect, there can be no self-fulfillment as capacity-fulfillment. To see why this is so, let us compare self-respect with self-esteem.

Both self-respect and self-esteem are virtues that are parts of what I have called additive well-being; but they are virtues of different kinds because they differ in their objects, i.e., in what aspect of the self is valued. Self-respect is a moral virtue, where the "moral" is based on universalist morality. In self-respect what one values is one's moral qualities, including one's dignity as a moral person who is worthy of the respect of other persons. One respects oneself insofar as one treats other persons fairly or justly. For a person to respect herself, she must be realistically aware that she has fulfilled the essential requirement of univer-

---

[30] See *The Community of Rights*, chaps. 4–8.

salist morality of acting in accord with the generic rights of others as well as of oneself. Such self-respect is thus an essential condition for action upholding the principle of human rights and hence for capacity-fulfill-ment as requiring such action. On this basis, to have self-respect is to have a proper appreciation of one's dignity or worth as a human being and reasonable self. As we shall see, duties to oneself also enter here (4.6).

Self-esteem, on the other hand, is a prudential virtue. It may also be called a "moral" virtue, but here the relevant morality is what I have called personalist morality (2.5). In self-esteem, what one values are var-ious of one's prudential qualities, including one's effectiveness in attain-ing one's desired goals or aspirations. To have self-esteem is to have a secure sense of one's own merits, and thus includes having the convic-tion that one's plans and purposes are worthwhile and that one has the ability to carry them out. Such self-esteem is a significant component of additive well-being for it enables one to increase one's capabilities of purpose-fulfillment and hence to fulfill more of one's goals or aspira-tions (see 4.4).

Self-esteem is an essential part of capacity-fulfillment, but only under two conditions. First, its objects may not include any violations of human rights. The objects of self-esteem, what one values oneself for, may, like the objects of aspirations, vary enormously. Hitler and Stalin could have had self-esteem as well as Mahatma Gandhi and Mother Teresa, but the former two did not have capacity-fulfillment. Second, the objects of self-esteem must be sufficiently important to qualify as corresponding to what is best in oneself. This allows much relativism, but within limits to be spelled out below.

Self-respect, on the other hand, is directly a part of capacity-fulfill-ment because, as a universalist moral quality, it is based upon the human rights that are grounded in the use of the capacity of reason. This basis in human rights can be brought out more fully in two interrelated ways. The first bears on the self's own having of rights. To have a right is to have an interest that ought to be protected and promoted; and this 'ought' involves, on the one side, that the interest in question is some-thing that is due or owed to the subject or right-holder as her personal property, as what she is personally entitled to have and control for her own sake; and, on the other side, that other persons, as respondents, have a mandatory duty at least not to infringe this property. The having of rights, then, entails that one is in a justified position to demand of other persons that they at least not interfere with one's having the ob-jects of one's rights and, in certain circumstances, that they help one to attain or maintain these objects. So the right-holder's self-respect fol-lows from the idea that other persons must not only give affirmative consideration to her needs and interests but also that she is in a justified position to require or demand such consideration. In this way the right-holder is a full-fledged member of the moral community. She has that status by virtue of the rational moral principle whose proof is given by reason as the best of her epistemic capacities. But in the United States and many other countries persons who are poor are often looked down upon, are not given the help to which they have rights, are not respected, and hence may suffer a deep loss of self-respect.

A second way in which self-respect derives from the moral principle of human rights bears directly not on the self's own having of rights but on her effective recognition of the rights of other persons. The PGC requires that one be a reasonable person who acts in accord with the generic rights of one's recipients as well as of oneself. So a person who acts in this way recognizes that he satisfies an essential moral requirement. He thereby acts in accord with reason and thus achieves an important part of capacity-fulfillment.

It may be objected, on grounds of cultural relativism, that this grounding of self-respect in recognition of universal moral rights is parochial, for it ignores the fact that in many societies the moral code is not universalist but particularist, requiring invidious discriminations against some classes of persons. To take an extreme example, the Nazis' moral code required not recognition of the rights of Jews but rather their oppression and murder. For Nazis, then, self-respect as based on their moral code would require participation or at least acquiescence in genocide.

The answer to this objection is that since the Nazis' moral code violated the universalist moral principle based on reason, it did not derive from what is best in human beings. Hence, no genuine self-fulfillment or self-respect was achieved by the Nazis' immoral practices or by adherence to other immoral codes. It must be kept in mind that the criterion of "best" in the definition of self-fulfillment as capacity-fulfillment is objective as based on the veridical use of reason; while taking account of persons' different capacities and circumstances (3.2), it is not relative to the variable beliefs or preferences of different persons or groups.

But how far does this objectivity and invariability go? It may be contended that while it is all very well to appeal to certain invariant standards in connection with the universalist morality of human rights, there are many other areas of self-fulfillment in which such invariance is far less plausible. Once the requirements of universalist morality are satisfied, what of the many alternative ways of life that may figure in different personalist moralities and aspirations? Such alternatives cover an enormously wide range, from idlers, surfers, full-time television viewers, drinkers, eaters, billiard players, and so forth to many other kinds of activity. Can or should any one or combination of those ways of life figure rightly in self-fulfillment as capacity-fulfillment?

As we have seen (2.4), a certain liberal outlook would give an affirmative answer to this question. Any way of life is as good as any other so long as other persons' moral rights are not violated. Pushpin is as good as poetry. For one thing, according to this view there is no nonarbitrary way of measuring or comparing these values so as to rank some as better and others as worse. Moreover, regardless of possibilities of evaluative comparison, persons should be free to choose their own ways of life so long as they do not violate other persons' rights. A liberal democratic society should not legally distinguish among different conceptions of the good; it should simply provide a neutral framework within which different persons may freely pursue their own conceptions.

In addition to the criteria of personalist morality to be discussed below (4.1), there are at least two more social grounds for modifying such liberal neutrality. One derives from the political requirements of liberal society itself, the other from its economic structure. Both of these grounds are provided by the use of reason as the epistemic capacity for ascertaining the means to certain ends and the constituents of certain values, including especially the requirements of universalist morality. First, the liberal democracy that is here in question includes the institutional protection of human rights briefly discussed above (3.4), and it also involves effective use of the civil liberties to be dealt with below in connection with particularist morality (4.8). Such liberal democracy requires an intelligent electorate, whose citizens can go some way toward rationally evaluating alternative proposed lines of policy. To have such citizens requires a publicly supported system of education whereby children can acquire relevant tools of learning. Such a system should inculcate habits of self-discipline whereby students learn to apply themselves with appropriate seriousness to develop their mental and other capacities. Educational endeavors of this kind are antithetical to the anarchy of "conceptions of the good" which an extreme version of liberal neutrality might be held to accept. Since it is by reason that the need for and the contents of education are ascertained, the pursuit of education and the development of its intellectual and emotional capacities is an intrinsic part of self-fulfillment as capacity-fulfillment. Persons' self-respect is fostered when they can participate intelligently in a morally justified political system.

It will have been noted that my argument has moved from the educational requirements of liberal democracy to the capacity-fulfillment of its citizens. The connection between these considerations is not accidental. The Purposive Ranking Thesis can be invoked here. Given the context of liberal democracy with its purpose of self-government, this purpose is best achieved by having an intelligent citizenry. So the intelligence relevant to political participation is, in this context, the best that it is in persons to become and hence an important part of capacity-fulfillment.

There have indeed been arguments in defense of citizen apathy, on the ground that this prevents rocking of the political boat and is, for many citizens, a "rational" response to the perceived impact of government on their utilities.[31] But such arguments are defective in many ways. The vast unmet needs of the masses of deprived persons in modern democratic societies can be met only if they actively support certain measures as against others, and this requires the use of reason in fitting means to ends. Persons' self-respect, moreover, requires that they not be free riders on the political efforts of other persons. Political participation can be an important part of capacity-fulfillment whereby persons bring their intellectual and conative capacities to bear toward what they regard as requirements of justice.

A second ground for rejecting the kind of liberal neutrality sketched above concerns economic activities within the moral framework of human rights. Those rights entail a relation of mutuality whereby all persons have not only rights against one another but also duties to each other. This mutuality bears, among other things, on the acquisition of economic goods ranging from the needs of basic well-being (food, shelter, health care, and so forth) to other levels of goods. According to the PGC, all persons have rights to these goods; but to fulfill these rights as matters of personal moral responsibility they must also contribute to fulfilling the comparable rights of other persons. In other words, a system of economic exchange whereby persons supply one another's wants is justified by the mutuality of human rights.

Now to participate in such a system, persons must have capacities of productive agency.[32] We may distinguish between broader and narrower kinds of such agency. In the broader sense, productive agency is the effective ability to achieve one's purposes; it is hence equivalent to that additive well-being which was distinguished above (3.4) as one of the three components of well-being, for it involves increasing one's level of purpose-fulfillment and one's capabilities for successful action. In its narrower sense, productive agency is economic; it consists in having the effective ability to acquire wealth and income by one's work. By such productive agency one provides objects or services that have use-value for other persons and are also exchange values that are effectively de-

---

[31] See Charles A. McCoy and John Playford, *Apolitical Politics: A Critique of Behavioralism* (New York: Crowell, 1967); Anthony Downs, *An Economic Theory of Democracy* (New York: Harper and Row, 1957).

[32] See *The Community of Rights*, chap. 4.

manded by persons who are able and willing to pay for them. Such economic productive agency involves participation in relations of mutual exchange with other persons. The effective right to have the wealth and income that are needed for one's successful purposive agency (including productive agency in the broader sense) is thus contingent on one's fulfilling the duty to produce equivalent goods for other persons.

By virtue of participating in such a morally justified economic system, persons have self-respect: they have a sense of their worth or dignity. This derives from one's awareness that one effectively acknowledges in other persons the same right to purpose-fulfillment as one claims for oneself. The productive agency whereby one participates in such a morally justified economic system is thus an important part of self-fulfillment as based on rational moral justification. Such agency includes the development of virtues of self-discipline, self-reliance, resourcefulness, and skills of analysis and problem-solving. At the same time it must be emphasized that the morally justified use of productive agency requires various protections bearing on wage-income and conditions of work. But in any case the goods and virtues that enter into economic productive agency set important limits to the liberal neutrality concerning conceptions of the good.

Marx wrote that in the fully developed communist society "labor has become not only a means of life but life's prime want." This would occur, he said, "after the enslaving subordination of the individual to the division of labor, and therewith also the antithesis between mental and physical labor, has vanished."[33] But whatever the prospects of this ideal, labor for millions of persons in the modern world is very different. It must be recognized that, amid the vast variety of kinds of work, there are two broad modes of work that are at extreme opposites to one another, and that have very different relations to self-fulfillment. One mode may be called "depressive," the other "creative." I shall here characterize them in words largely taken from Marx; for the passage of over a century has not altered their defining features.

Depressive work is toil, drudgery, stressful and deadening. Marx called this mode of work a "curse, a negation of tranquillity," whereby one sacrifices one's freedom and leisure in order to obtain commodities. Such work is "done out of necessity." "Its alien character emerges clearly in the fact that as soon as no physical or other compulsion exists it is avoided like the plague." And as to the process of work, the worker has "little choice about how and when the work is done." His work

[33] "Critique of the Gotha Program," in Tucker, ed., *The Marx-Engels Reader*, 2nd ed., p. 530.

procedures are dictated to him by others: managers, supervisors, efficiency experts, so that his work situation is characterized by powerlessness and loss of initiative and autonomy. It is the opposite of fulfilling for the worker.

At the opposite extreme from this depressive mode of work is what may be called a creative mode. One reason for this terminology is that in this mode of work the emphasis often falls on its valuable product, as in "work of art" or "master work," rather than on the arduous process. But the process of work itself is also very different from the depressive mode. In the creative mode work is not only instrumental to the fulfillment of needs but is itself a need, for in its overcoming of obstacles it is "a liberating activity," a "positive, creative activity," so that it is intrinsically satisfying to the worker. Such work makes use of persons' higher mental faculties; it is taken on freely and gladly and the worker has a justified sense of personal responsibility and achievement, for it is a form of "self-realization."[34]

While work as actually undergone by most persons exhibits a wide diversity between these two extremes, there is abundant evidence that for most workers in America it is far closer to the depressive extreme than to the creative one.[35] The principle of human rights requires that persons be given realistic hope that they can develop their capacities of productive agency so that they are not forced to work at the lowest levels of their competence, but are instead enabled to come as close as their latent abilities permit to the creative mode of work. In this way work can become a valuable part of capacity-fulfillment whereby persons make the best of themselves.[36]

Women face special problems in connection with work. First, it must be recognized that raising children and nurturing family life are themselves important kinds of productive agency. When women do not work outside the home, recognition of this importance justifies their fully sharing in their husbands' income. Second, when women do work outside the home, husbands must share with their wives the making of adequate provisions for child care. In these ways, self-fulfillment as capacity-

---

[34] Karl Marx, *Grundrisse*, trans. M. Nicolaus (Harmondsworth, England: Penguin, 1973), pp. 610–16; "Economic and Philosophic Manuscripts of 1844," in Tucker, ed., *The Marx-Engels Reader*, p. 74. See also Gregory Pence, "Towards a Theory of Work," *Philosophical Forum* 1, nos. 2–4 (1978–79): 307; Robert Blauner, *Alienation and Freedom: The Factory Worker and His Industry* (Chicago: University of Chicago Press, 1964); Harry Braverman, *Labor and Monopoly Capital* (New York: Monthly Review Press, 1974).

[35] See, e.g., *Work in America: Report of a Special Task Force to the Secretary of Health, Education, and Welfare* (Cambridge, Mass.: MIT Press, 1973), pp. 30ff., chaps. 2–3. See also Studs Terkel, *Working* (New York: Pantheon Books, 1972).

[36] Cf. Jon Elster, "Self-Realization in Work and Politics: The Marxist Conception of the Good Life," *Social Philosophy and Policy* 3, no. 2 (spring 1986): 110–15.

fulfillment involves making the best of oneself in conditions of work, where the criterion of this "best" is derived from the application of universalist morality to the requirements of economic life.

3.7. THE MORAL CRITICISM OF ASPIRATIONS

According to the above argument, reason as the best of human epistemic capacities has shown that practical respect for human rights is an essential part of self-fulfillment as capacity-fulfillment. On the other hand, to violate human rights is to act counter to such capacity-fulfillment. To put it otherwise, when one acts in accordance with human rights one makes the best of oneself in so acting; because reason is the best of epistemic capacities, to act in accordance with reason is, to this extent, to achieve the best it is in one to become.

We can now use this result to double back to aspiration-fulfillment. For the grounding of universalist morality in reason provides a rational basis for evaluating the objects of various aspirations. In this way, capacity-fulfillment can sit in reasoned judgment over aspiration-fulfillment. The direct basis of this judgment derives from the fact that the human rights to freedom and well-being entail more specific rights bearing on the formation and fulfillment of aspirations; and these rights set rational requirements that aspirations must satisfy if they are to be rationally and hence morally acceptable. Important parts of these rights are negative; they involve that the objects of aspirations cannot justifiably include actions or institutions that violate the equal human rights to freedom and well-being. At the same time, these specifications of the general human rights come gradually to involve the probabilities of the operational aspect of reason (3.3).

We may distinguish three kinds of aspirations whose objects raise serious problems of such moral wrongness. One kind, epitomized by Hitler and Stalin, is inherently wrong because it violates, and aims to violate, the most basic human rights of other persons. These and other tyrants, as defined by their aspirations and corresponding actions, ought not to have fulfilled themselves and ought to have been prevented from fulfilling themselves. As we have seen, such tyrants may be depicted as upholding various particularist interpersonal moralities, in that they set requirements for actions and institutions that purported to be categorically obligatory and that aimed to promote the interests of other persons restricted in various ways. But the moral wrongness of these requirements is readily apparent from the PGC.

A second kind of aspiration we may characterize as indirectly wrong. It does not aim at violating human rights as such, but the violation is

102 CAPACITY-FULFILLMENT, MORALITY

nonetheless a constitutive part of the aspiration. Viewed morally, the aspiration has a dual aspect. In one of its parts, its object is morally permissible, but in another part it is not. An example is adultery. When a married person has sex with someone other than his or her spouse, the dual aspect seems clear: the aspiration to give and receive love is morally permissible, but the adulterer violates his spouse's right based on the marriage contract by breaking the solemn promise to "forsake all others."

Can this dual aspect also be found in the first kind of morally wrong aspiration? Stalin and Hitler, it may be said, had morally permissible aspirations: the former to promote the collective good, the latter to purify the human race. These aspirations, however, were so intrinsically bound up with extreme violations of the rights to freedom and well-being, the infliction of terrible suffering on so many innocent people, that they cannot even minimally be characterized as morally permissible.

In the case of adultery, on the other hand, the aspiration for love is sometimes a salient element that is distinct from violation of the marriage bond. This was brought out starkly in the three sets of quotations I presented earlier (2.1) from *Madame Bovary, Anna Karenina,* and *Sister Carrie.* As a counterpoint to these aspirations, adulterers may find abysmal unhappiness in their present marriages. For Emma, her husband was "boring"; for Anna, he was "loathsome"; George Hurstwood's "wife had developed a cold, commonplace nature which to him was anything but pleasing."[37]

But even if adultery may be explained as fulfilling aspirations for love, this does not excuse, let alone justify it. For it is attained by violating the rights of the victimized spouse. Marriage involves a mutuality of rights, whereby each partner has an exclusive right to the closest intimacy and support of the other (see also below, 4.7). There may indeed be polygamous and other cultures that reject this exclusivity of marriage. But, entirely apart from the familiar arguments against polygamy, such as that it degrades women and contributes to tyranny on the part of the husband, there is a difference between a consensual, institutionalized relationship wherein a wife (or husband) agrees that her spouse may take several other sexual partners and a relationship where this prior institutionalized consent is not found and is indeed rejected. It is the latter kind of situation that figures in adultery, which therefore amounts to a betrayal of trust and of mutuality that violates the rights of the victimized spouse.[38]

[37] Dreiser, *Sister Carrie,* p. 113.

[38] For possible mitigations of this judgment, see Richard Wasserstrom, "Is Adultery Immoral?," in Wasserstrom, ed., *Today's Moral Problems,* 2nd ed. (New York: Macmillan, 1979), pp. 288–30. For a valuable critique, see Jacob Joshua Ross, *The Virtues of the Family* (New York: Free Press, 1994), pp. 172–75.

These considerations are only partially mitigated by the disappointments and resentments that arise in many monogamous marriages. Such negative features, especially as they affect the wife, are sometimes adduced as not merely explaining adultery but as making it inevitable. Thus Simone de Beauvoir has written, "In frustrating women, by depriving them of all erotic satisfaction, in denying them liberty and individuality of feeling, marriage leads them toward adultery by an inevitable and ironical dialectic."[39] The wife "is thus fated for infidelity; it is the sole concrete form her liberty can assume."[40] These dogmatic statements, presented as assured matters of fact, are contradicted by the existence of many stable, happy marriages in which wives as well as husbands find fulfillment both of their aspirations and of their capacities. In any case, divorce rather than adultery is the honorable solution to an irredeemably conflicted marriage. It is also relevant to note that adultery, through its flouting of ties of honor and intimacy, may lead to deep unhappiness on the part of the adulterer, and indeed (as is illustrated by the above examples of Bovary, Karenina, and Hurstwood) to suicide. Such tragic outcomes show again the overwhelming importance of striving mightily for the enormously difficult goal of self-knowledge on the part of persons who seek to fulfill their aspirations. The problems of the relation between the earlier self and the later self (2.3) again arise here, including the question of which self does the fulfilling and which self is fulfilled.

There is often an important social background to such tragedies. Married persons may rebel against the further unjustified bonds or obligations that society may impose on the married persons. Especially when the adulterer is a woman, there may be deep resentment against the double standard whereby the wife is regarded as her husband's property and subjected to rigid social conventions of propriety. Such a double standard is a violation of the equal rights to freedom and well-being.

Let us turn to a third kind of aspiration that raises serious moral problems. Like the second kind, this has both a morally permissible and a morally wrong component. The morally permissible component, however, is more extensive in two interrelated ways. First, its actions are not merely permissible but also admirable and indeed supererogatory and eminent. Second, it has this feature because its aspired-to purpose or envisaged outcome is not simply to personally benefit or gratify oneself but to produce a more general good and thereby to fulfill a valuable capacity. For example: as in the second kind of aspiration, a married man may desert his family, but he does so, as in the case of Gauguin, in order

[39] Simone de Beauvoir, *The Second Sex*, trans. H. M. Parshley (New York: Vintage Books, 1989), p. 548.
[40] Ibid., p. 188.

to produce beautiful works of art,[41] or, as in the case of a cancer re-searcher, in order to relieve human suffering.[42] Such eminent persons aim to fulfill themselves by developing important capacities for additive well-being and thereby making the best of themselves. The artistic and scientific aspirations and capacities, taken by themselves, are admirable because of the high, interpersonally appreciable quality of their envis-aged objects. But they take on a serious component of moral wrongness when they are pursued at the expense of deserted spouses or children or violate the moral rights of persons in other ways. In general, these two phases are only contingently connected: one can pursue high artistic or scientific endeavors without deserting one's family or otherwise violat-ing moral rights for reasons that have nothing to do with benefiting other persons. But in view of my thesis of the practical overridingness of the requirements set by universalist morality (3.5), how can this thesis be reconciled with the eminence and admirableness of the values of per-sons who choose to infringe those requirements in order to pursue such values? The case is not appreciably altered if the requirements that are infringed are regarded as stemming from particularist morality rather than universalist morality, for, as we shall see, the former receives its justification from the latter (4.7). On this complex issue there emerges especially strongly the need to take account of the probabilism involved in the operational aspect of reason, the actual use of the canons of reason in their applications to a concrete subject-matter.

The single-minded, eminent pursuit of what one regards as supremely valuable raises issues that I partly discussed above in connection with aspiration-fulfillment, including the need for concentrated effort and the ideal of "authenticity" (2.1, 4). In the present context this ideal may be characterized in at least two different ways. One way, which reflects the influence of Romanticism, is self-oriented; it comprises a single-minded self-affirmation on the part of the protagonist. "This is what I must do, regardless of consequences." "This is my project, and that is all that counts." The agent here appeals to no values except his own vehe-ment desires or aspirations. This position rests on a certain conception of autonomy whereby one sets one's own rules without consideration of any external criteria for their adequacy.

Such a conception should be faulted for its arbitrariness in upholding the self's aspirations as the sole basis of action and value. If reason enters

---

[41] See Bernard Williams, *Moral Luck* (Cambridge: Cambridge University Press, 1981), pp. 22–26. See also Michael Slote, *Goods and Virtues* (Oxford: Clarendon Press, 1983), chap. 4; Owen Flanagan, "Admirable Immorality and Admirable Imperfection," *Journal of Philosophy* 83 (1986): 41–60.

[42] See Rush Rhees, "Some Developments in Wittgenstein's View of Ethics," *Philosophical Review* 74 (January 1965): 22.

here at all, it is only as calculating means to the end; but the end, self-aggrandizement, is not itself subjected to any rational scrutiny. From this stems the Romantic exaltation of the "irrational" as the mark of value. Besides being egoistic, the conception is marked by a dangerous irresponsibility.

A second interpretation of the "authentic" pursuit of eminence is object-oriented. Here the agent regards himself as acting not simply as a matter of self-affirmation but rather as affirming also the supreme value of the objects of his pursuit. What drives him is the eminent value he aims to further or achieve as well as to exemplify; it is so eminent that it overrides all other values, including the needs of his spouse or family. Such an object-oriented conception may be expressed in terms that come close to the self-oriented approach, as in the following depiction of "master morality" by Nietzsche:

> The noble type of man experiences *itself* as determining values; it does not need approval; it judges, "what is harmful to me is harmful in itself"; it knows itself to be that which accords honor to things; it is *value-creating*. Everything it knows as part of itself it honors; such a morality is self-glorification.[43]

Despite its reference to the noble man as "value-creating," there is in the near background of Nietzsche's ideal a set of object-values which the master morality recognizes as having independent validity, including honoring oneself "as one who has power over himself, who knows how to speak and be silent, who . . . respects all serenity and hardness" and who has a "profound reverence for age and tradition . . . the faith and prejudice in favor of ancestors."[44] The basis in objective values is more explicit in Aristotle's "great-souled" man, who has "greatness in every virtue" and hence is "good in the highest degree."[45] Such an object-oriented pursuit of eminence is close to the capacity-fulfillment which consists in achieving the best that it is in one to become. But since it violates the rights of one's spouse and children, to this extent the conception fails the moral test of reason in its canonic, apodictic aspect. When it acknowledges that certain objective values underlie its claims to eminence, it is confronted by the question of whether those values are indeed so supreme that they completely override the moral values represented in the needs of one's family. So at this point it is not enough to declare the exclusive weight of one's own eminent goal; rational fairness and indeed consistency require that these other needs also be given

[43] Friedrich Nietzsche, *Beyond Good and Evil*, sec. 260 (trans. Walter Kaufmann [New York: Vintage Books, 1966], p. 205; emphases in original).

[44] Ibid.

[45] Aristotle, *Nicomachean Ethics*, 4. 3. 1123b30–35.

positive consideration. The exclusivist claimant of eminence thus fails an important test of truth.

At least one form of utilitarianism would sanction the eminent claimant's desertion of his family because of the greater "utility" that would be generated thereby. But on the basis of the PGC, which requires that one act in accord with one's recipients' rights as well as one's own, such a simple solution is not available. What is required, rather, is the moderate altruism whereby one tries to accommodate both sets of rights, in this case one's own freedom and well-being together with the well-being of the persons who are affected by one's actions. Unless one artificially stacks the cards in advance by making the artist's or scientist's eminent aspirations so adamant that they can in no way be compromised, a solution that recognizes the rights on each side is both morally justified and feasible.

CHAPTER 4

Capacity-Fulfillment and the Good Life

4.1. FREEDOM AND WELL-BEING AS THE BEST OF PRACTICAL CAPACITIES

In the preceding chapter I tried to show how adherence to the rights of universalist interpersonal morality, as required by reason, is an important part of self-fulfillment as capacity-fulfillment. But the argument's invocation of freedom and well-being as the necessary goods of action can also be used to provide central components of personalist morality as further parts of capacity-fulfillment. It will be recalled that personalist morality is concerned with the goodness of a person's life, where the criterion of goodness is individual or prudential rather than based on universalist morality. "Goodness" here signifies a life that is, variously, eminently worthwhile or happy or flourishing for the person who lives it. In the present context of self-fulfillment as capacity-fulfillment, the criterion of goodness is not, as in aspiration-fulfillment, persons' deepest desires. Instead, personalist morality here gives counsels and precepts for the self's having a good life through personal development of one's capacities whereby one makes the best of oneself.

Personalist morality cannot be derived from universalist morality by direct deduction. Universalist morality is primarily interpersonal; it is concerned with persons' generic rights against one another and hence with how persons ought to treat one another, and it is an essential part of self-fulfillment as capacity-fulfillment both because its norms are ascertained by canonic reason as the best of human veridical capacities and because the conduct it prescribes enables persons to be reasonable selves who make the best of themselves as moral beings. Personalist morality, on the other hand, deals primarily with the individual's conduct in relation to herself; it concerns how she can fulfill herself by making her life go as well as possible. The norms for such a life will indeed have to observe the requirements for being a reasonable self as these are set by universalist morality. Moreover, the rights of universalist morality will also apply here as requiring both noninterference and assistance. But this still leaves a large expanse to be filled in by personalist morality.

There are, however, at least three ways in which personalist morality can be related more directly to universalist morality. One way is by focusing on the personal virtues or excellences that enable persons to be reasonable selves. This involves the duties persons have to inculcate in themselves personal qualities that can be operationally-rationally ascertained to be necessary or highly conducive to their obeying the PGC. A second way is more analogical. The total self is viewed as having parts or aspects that act on one another in ways that can be good or bad for the parts acted on, by affecting their freedom and well-being. Here the requirements of personalist morality are modeled on those of universalist morality, in that each part of the total self must take favorable account of the rights of the other parts. I shall deal more fully below with each of these ways of deriving personalist morality from universalist morality, through the idea of duties to oneself (4.6).

In much of this chapter I shall pursue a third, more directly substantive way of deriving the contents of personalist morality. As we have seen, freedom and well-being are the necessary goods of action and generally successful action, and universalist morality requires that every person's rights to these goods be respected as an essential part of self-fulfillment. But because freedom and well-being are thus necessary goods, their development for each person is also an essential part of personalist morality concerned with the good life. If persons are to fulfill themselves by making the best of themselves, they must have good lives that are based on these necessary goods.

Discussions of "the good life" have long been a staple of both Western and non-Western moral philosophy. But the discussions have been beset by serious disputes.[1] The adjective "good" suggests that not all life is good or equally good; but this apparently plausible thesis has been contested by thinkers who uphold "reverence for life" as a general ethical ideal.[2] Even if we waive this point, other implications of the phrase "the good life" also raise difficulties. The definite article suggests that there is only one (kind of) good life. But this is controverted by the fact that there have been many different conceptions of the good life, varying not only with different persons' aspirations but also, more generally, with different criteria of value. The conceptions have run a vast gamut; there are, for example, the contrasts between religious conceptions of the good life and secular ones; between pacific conceptions and militaristic or bellicose ones; between theoretic or intellectual conceptions and political or activist ones; between both of these and romantic or aesthetic conceptions; between biological or economic conceptions and more spiritual ones; between conceptions that focus on pleasure or hap-

[1] See Lawrence C. Becker, "Good Lives: Prolegomena," *Social Philosophy and Policy* 9, no. 2 (summer 1992): 15–37.
[2] See John Kleinig, *Valuing Life* (Princeton: Princeton University Press, 1991), esp. chap. 3.

piness and those that focus on duty or dignity; between conceptions that emphasize freedom and those that emphasize security or order; and so forth. This plurality of conceptions represents not only different objects of aspirations but also different ways in which persons have been thought to make the best of themselves. But the plurality is so extensive that it is held to yield conflicts of values that are irreconcilable. And if, to avoid such conflicts, one offers a conception of the good life that somehow subsumes these other conceptions under a broader idea, as utilitarianism for example tries to do by invoking "preferences," then either the superordinate idea is so vague as to be unhelpful or it sets forth a standard that is beyond the reach of most persons. As we have seen, similar difficulties beset the idea that the good life consists in the "realization of potentialities" or in the fulfillment of a "natural end" based on human nature (1.3).

While taking due account of these difficulties, I want to suggest a way of surmounting them. This way appeals to the freedom and well-being that I have earlier said are ascertained by reason to be the proximate necessary conditions of all successful action (3.4). The idea may be put as follows: Since freedom and well-being, as proximate enabling capacities, enter into all successful action, and since in all action the agent aims to achieve something he regards as good, it follows that freedom and well-being are the general components of any and every life that an agent regards as good. So concerning all the contrasting conceptions that I listed above as criteria that have been upheld for the good life, since all of them involve various modes of action both as attaining freedom and well-being and as embodying them, they can all be rationally subsumed under freedom and well-being as the proximate values that underlie them. And because, as we have seen, all persons have rights to freedom and well-being, they have to this extent rights to develop the personalist morality of the good life. These rights are partly negative in that they require noninterference with this development. But they are also positive insofar as the development can be assisted by supportive institutions and other measures when persons cannot achieve this development by their own efforts.

Let us tie this point to the general idea of capacity-fulfillment as achieving the best that it is in one to become. Because freedom and well-being, as the proximate necessary goods of action, are collectively the capacities that enter into such capacity-fulfillment, they are the best means that agents have for achieving the purposes for which they engage in action. To put it somewhat more formally, following the model of the Purposive Ranking Thesis, we have (a) the general context of action and (b) the general purpose of action as achieving the specific purposes for which one acts. Now because (c) freedom and well-being are the proximate generic features of action and generally successful action, it follows that they are the best available means of achieving the specific purposes of action. Any more specific means to these ends would have to include freedom and well-being as its controlling components. So, as against all the varying purposes that may be used in the Purposive Ranking Thesis to supply the criteria for ranking values and performances (3.2), the general context of action provides the most general, all-encompassing rational criterion for such ranking. And from this there follows the rational ranking of freedom and well-being as the best of practical capacities. Hence, to fulfill oneself by way of capacity-fulfillment, one must make the most effective use one can of one's freedom and well-being, within the limits set by the overriding authority of universalist morality (3.5).

This argument is, of course, very general and abstract, so it incurs the danger cited above of excessive vagueness. Do freedom and well-being, as the generic features of successful action, have contents that are sufficiently specific to account for "the," or even "a," good life as ordinarily conceived, including the contrasting conceptions listed above? I shall now try to work out an affirmative answer. My main points will be that capacity-fulfillment, as achieving the best that it is in one to become, comprises a good life for the persons who attain it, and that such fulfillment includes the use of freedom and well-being in ways that are maximally effective for the agent. This effectiveness involves the development of prudential virtues that are directly incorporated into the various phases of these generic features of action. Such virtues are excellences of action as well as of character, in that persons can act to develop for themselves their possession of the necessary goods of successful action.

Three cautions from earlier sections (3.2, 3.5) must be stressed here. First, there is the caution about scope: the fact of individual differences brings out that what is maximally effective, and hence what constitutes a good life, will vary with individual abilities and preferences. Second, there is the caution about content: the uses of freedom and well-being must respect the rational limits set by the universalist moral principle of human rights. Third, there is the caution about modality: the specifications of freedom and well-being, as involving the operational aspect of reason, will be largely probabilistic rather than apodictic.

Although freedom and well-being are the generic features of all successful action, they can be used and developed with different degrees of effectiveness. Parental upbringing, education, and social conditions are among the factors that can affect this development. A society based on the human rights of the PGC, and the maintenance of reasonableness in personal relations as also required by the PGC, can be important helps toward enabling each person to make the best use of her freedom and well-being. So when we here ask about capacity-fulfillment as achieving the best that it is in one to become, it is these capacities for action that figure most generally in such fulfillment. For the process of the fulfillment is a process of action, and the outcome of the fulfillment consists in various modes of action.

It may be objected that "action" is here stretched too broadly to encompass all the varying conceptions of the good life. The contention would be that the PGC, with its focus on freedom and well-being as the necessary goods of action, ignores the many kinds of values, whether morally relevant or not, that stem from human concerns other than those of practical agency. As was suggested above in the varying conceptions of the good life, there is a whole array of human situations and ideals whose orientation is quite different from practical well-being, such as those of the aesthete and the artist, the religionist, the intellectual, the libertine, and so forth. For such persons, the focus of what they regard as a good life is not on action but on contemplation, worship, thought, or pleasure. Thus, although the specific comparative ordering wherein basic well-being is rated as the most important good is inescapable when the requirements of action supply the criterion of measurement, it is objected that a different ordering emerges when aesthetic contemplation, for example, is made the decisive purpose or criterion. This is why some persons prefer to starve in garrets for the sake of painting or to give money to museums rather than to organizations that help the victims of famine. The upshot is that universalist morality, with its focus on freedom and well-being, is not conclusive as to what all persons ought to do in order to have a good life, so that these necessary goods of action do not have the centrality for capacity-fulfillment that I have claimed for them. For insofar as duties are based on nonpractical values like those just mentioned, the duties derive not from the generic features of action but from concerns other than action, and the ordering of capacities must hence be based on criteria other than their degrees of needfulness for action.

In answer to this objection, it must first be noted that in this book 'action' is used in a sense that includes the activities of the artist, the intellectual, the religionist, and so forth (3.4). For all of these are voluntary and purposive behaviors. Hence they all fall under the generic features of action and necessarily incur the right-claims and 'ought'-judgments that follow from these. Amid the myriad answers to the question of what constitutes a good life, there is one kind of answer whose rational justification is invariant because it is based on the objective necessary conditions for the pursuit of any and all goods or interests. All such pursuits are purposive actions, and it is from the freedom and well-being that are the necessary conditions of all successful purposive actions

that the duties both of universalist and of personalist morality are derived. Hence, the requirements of the PGC can rationally be evaded by
no agents regardless of their diverse values, so that freedom and well-
being necessarily enter into every aspect of human activity, including
personalist morality as a part of self-fulfillment.

It may be helpful at this point to indicate some of the ways in which
freedom and well-being (with their bases in voluntariness and purposiveness, respectively), can be distinguished from one another as en-
tering into the general context of action. This should at least suggest
why they are exhaustive and exclusive among the generic features of action. Freedom involves a procedural aspect of actions in that it concerns
the way actions are controlled as ongoing events. Well-being, on the
other hand, while also having a procedural aspect, involves the substantive aspect of actions, the specific contents of these events. Freedom refers to the means, well-being to the end; freedom comprises the agent's
causation of his action, whereas well-being comprises the object or goal
of the action in the sense of the good he wants to have or achieve
through this causation. Thus freedom is a matter of initiation or control
while well-being is at least in part a matter of consummation. Other can-
didates for generic features of action, such as adherence to rules or principles or calculations of consequences and so forth, either do not characterize all actions or else are derivative from and subsumable under one
or the other of the two features discussed above.

The point we have reached is that, with regard to capacity-fulfillment
as achieving the best that it is in one to become, what is best here is
whatever is found by reason to lead to or consist in the fullest development of freedom and well-being, within the limits set by the universalist
morality of human rights. By virtue of this achievement's contribution
to the good life, it also forms the rational basis for certain precepts or
counsels of personalist morality regarding various virtues that persons
should try to develop for themselves. These virtues are traits of character
and of action whereby persons attain and maintain for themselves the
necessary goods of successful action. This development is also a part of
self-fulfillment as capacity-fulfillment. I shall now try to spell out some
of the components of such fulfillment as a way of coming to more specific grips with the contents of the good life.

4.2. PERSONALIST MORALITY AS BASED UPON FREEDOM

Let us first consider the capacity for freedom. As we shall see, the exercise of this capacity is affected by subtle internal aspects of the self. But
in its external manifestations the fullest development of freedom bears

partly on the rights of its negative phase, wherein your control of your behavior is not obstructed or interfered with by other persons. When such freedom is developed to its fullest, there are no interferences with your behavior except where these are required by the PGC, including the degrees of needfulness for action and laws in a constitutional democracy that rests on and secures the human rights. There is also a positive phase of freedom, consisting in the power or ability to act as you choose. This element of choice is important not only occurrently but also dispositionally; it contributes not only to your performance of particular actions but also to your long-range ability to act. Both these aspects enter significantly into your development of character; as Aristotle famously noted, it is by your particular chosen actions that you build up your character, your habitual way of doing and feeling.[3] This intervention of choice is one of the ways in which capacity-fulfillment differs from the bare actualization of potentialities discussed above (1.3).

The idea of control is central to freedom; it is what gives freedom its value as a generic feature of action. It involves being master of oneself, including not only one's external behaviors but also one's inner experience; and it extends to relevant parts of one's environment as they impinge on oneself. To have a justified sense of such control contributes importantly to one's making the best of oneself.[4]

Both the negative and the positive phases of freedom as control include having knowledge of relevant circumstances of one's action. One must know who one is (as we shall see, questions about one's identity arise here), what one is doing, and the proximate outcome of one's action. This knowledge may vary in extent, depth, and difficulty; it includes having a realistic awareness of one's abilities and of what one can do to improve them. But as a rational capacity for action self-knowledge requires both that at appropriate points one reflect on one's immediate purposes in the light of one's more general goals and that one control one's behavior in the light of this reflection. This consideration about control serves to rule out many conceptions of the good life, entirely apart from the limits set by universalist morality. Examples are the alcoholic, the drug addict, the nymphomaniac, and other persons who cannot control their behavior in the light of consequences they do not want. Some of the examples of conceptions of the good life listed above, such as the militarist, would also be excluded on such grounds insofar as they involve violations of human rights.

[3] See Aristotle, *Nicomachean Ethics*, 3. 5.

[4] Cf. the extensive emphasis on "control" of one's actions and "psychic energy" as an essential part of "optimal experience," in Mihaly Csikszentmihalyi, *Flow: The Psychology of Optimal Experience* (New York: Harper Perennial, 1991), chap. 1. See also Samuel Z. Klausner, ed., *The Quest for Self-Control* (New York: Free Press, 1965).

This general freedom is complemented by the capacity for personal autonomy. Autonomy extends the control one has in freedom because it involves that one sets for oneself the rules of one's conduct and acts according to those rules. It thus includes both desire-autonomy and behavior-autonomy (2.2). The connection with self-imposed rules gives autonomy a generality that freedom, even in its long-range aspects, may lack. It involves that one's purposes and actions are one's own, made and accepted by and for oneself, as against being externally imposed; thus it includes both volitional and intellectual elements. Such autonomy helps one in obvious ways to make the best of oneself. One is not buffeted by desires over which one has no control; instead, one understands one's desires and can shape them in the light of fuller rational understanding of oneself; and one can act accordingly. The attainment and maintenance of such autonomy is thus an important part of capacity-fulfillment. It contributes to one's having a strong self-disciplined ego.

As I noted earlier, it may be objected that autonomy cannot be a necessary part of capacity-fulfillment because some persons are made fearful or anxious by the prospect or actuality of being in control of their own lives (2.2).[5] While this phenomenon does indeed occur, it does not remove the point that autonomy is among the best of human capacities. That some persons fear or reject it is usually the result of antecedent circumstances that have sapped their self-esteem or self-confidence: circumstances of severe deprivation or insecurity. But such conditions reflect violations of the universalist moral principle of human rights. Hence, they cannot be used to invalidate that principle or its foundation in the necessary goods of action.

The place of freedom and autonomy among one's best capacities of action yields certain prudential precepts of personalist morality regarding relevant virtues that contribute to successful agency. Although the prudential value of many of these virtues may seem obvious, it is worth spelling them out a bit because of their positive relation to capacity-fulfillment through the necessary goods of action. The virtues include developing and having a sense of personal responsibility, self-control, and self-reliance. Thereby one can control one's emotions so that they do not propel one into self-defeating actions. One should avoid regarding oneself solely as a victim, even if one's external circumstances, genetic or environmental, may warrant such a description. One should, so far as possible, try to take hold of one's own life and to guide it in the

---

[5] See James Griffin, *Well-Being* (Oxford: Clarendon Press, 1986), pp. 54, 58, 70. For older versions of this point, see Erich Fromm, *Escape from Freedom* (New York: Rinehart, 1941), and E. R. Dodds, *The Greeks and the Irrational* (Berkeley: University of California Press, 1970), chap. 8.

light of one's best knowledge. Insofar as external social conditions operate to prevent such use or development of one's freedom, there is abundant justification for uniting with others to try to change them. Such
efforts would themselves help to exercise and develop one's sense of personal responsibility. The development of these virtues is an important
part of self-fulfillment as capacity-fulfillment and thus of a good life.

4.3. IDENTITY AND ALIENATION

It has not often been noted that autonomy includes having a secure
sense of one's own identity. The word "identity" in philosophy has various interrelated uses, ranging from a thing's numerical sameness with
itself to the sameness of mind and brain. The complex meaning of
"identity" in psychology and ethics does not completely depart from the
general philosophical usage, but it specifies that usage by focusing both
on certain relations within the self and on the relation between the self
and various of its important social ties and roles. These roles may be
delineated according to certain life stages (such as where a girl "identifies with" her mother) or according to one's membership in some
broader social or other group demarcated according to gender, religion,
ethnicity, economic class, or other variables. In such cases one attains or
secures one's identity as a boy or a woman or a Muslim or a Pole, and so
forth, where "identity" signifies the self-accepted unity of one's self and
one's role or membership. To have such a secure sense of one's own
identity helps one to make the best of oneself because the complexities
of one's self are thereby molded into a unity of self-regard. One can
thereby marshal one's forces for action more fully and effectively.

The connection of identity with autonomy is that if one is to set one's
rules for oneself in ways that make the best of oneself, one must know
who is this self amid the various roles and connections that surround it.
To have a secure sense of one's identity thus enables one to choose,
from among those environing conditions, those one deems most salient
and important.[6]

We must distinguish between necessary and contingent aspects of
identity. The necessary aspect consists in roles or connections that so
define the person that he cannot be without them; as Erikson put it,
"membership in a nation, in a class, or in a caste is one of those elements
of an individual's identity which at the very minimum comprise *what one
is never not*, as does membership in one of the two sexes or in a given

---

[6] There is an etymological connection between autonomy and identity: *auto* in Greek is
a near synonym of *idem* in Latin.

race."[7] But such identity may also be contingent in that one may lose or find, or choose, or reinforce one's awareness of it. When you think of yourself as being the same as a member of some group, and this membership is important to you, then you may be said to find your identity when you become aware of this membership as being thus important to you. But you may have this identity even if you and others do not acknowledge it. This applies especially, but not solely, to members of previously oppressed groups. Thus you may affirm your identity as black or Jewish or Armenian or female, but also as an American or an intellectual or as a plumber and so forth. One's various identities, however, may also conflict with one another, as where one is both a career lawyer and a mother, or a Pakistani and a Briton, or a homosexual and a Catholic. In such cases one may lack a secure sense of one's identity, and the conflicts may raise poignant problems, whose resolution may be helped by moral arrangements of a society that protects human rights. The fallibilities of the operational aspect of reason are here painfully evident.

One's identity may also have a strong individualist component. It may consist in one's core self that underlies and issues in one's personal capacities or other characteristics that one regards as important in defining who one is. Usually this importance is positive rather than negative; one does not define oneself as cowardly or careless or unintelligent or improvident—although a realistic assessment of oneself may justify such descriptions—but rather in terms of characteristics that one wants to have and to guide one's life by. In this way, again, one's identity is valuable to oneself, and one wants it to receive due recognition from others.

This intra-personal aspect of one's identity has strong implications for one's psychological development. It involves choosing, among various of one's characteristics, which one is to be dominant as constituting one's "real self." Consider, for example, Jones, who is a physician by profession but also the child of a domineering father. Jones acts in a highly effective, self-confident manner in his medical practice, but he finds that outside this role, when he deals not only with his siblings and other relatives but also with persons outside his profession, he acts like a wimp. He tends to "underwhelm" people, giving them a distinct impression of being unsure of himself, diffident, and so forth. He recog-

[7] Erik H. Erikson, *Gandhi's Truth* (New York: W. W. Norton, 1969), p. 266 (emphasis in original). The inclusion of "class" in this list raises questions about class mobility. See also Erikson, *Identity, Youth and Crisis* (New York: W. W. Norton, 1968); Augusto Blasi, "Identity and the Development of the Self," in Daniel K. Lapsley and F. Clark Power, eds., *Self, Ego, and Identity: Integrative Approaches* (New York: Springer Verlag, 1988), pp. 226–42. For a profound development of this point, see Isaiah Berlin, "Benjamin Disraeli, Karl Marx and the Search for Identity," in Berlin, *Against the Current* (New York, Viking Press, 1980), pp. 252–86.

nizes that his upbringing is a strong contributing factor. But he also recognizes that in his interpersonal relations he is partly comfortable with his wimpish self, although he also regrets being this way. But suppose there comes a time in his personal relations—such as when he is courting some woman—when he realizes that he has to make a choice. To act like a wimp with her would be disastrous; but he finds it extraordinarily difficult to marshal with her the same self-assurance he displays in his profession. So at that time he has to decide who he really is, i.e., what is (or is to be) his "psychological" identity. This is also a challenge to his capacity-fulfillment: how to make the best of himself.

It may help to clarify this point if we consider the traditional reflexive injunction, "Be yourself." Taken literally, this raises the question, how can one be anything *other* than oneself? A similar question may apply to Nietzsche's command, "Become who you are!"[8] If, tautologously, you already are who you are, then what is the point of telling you to *become* who you are?

These questions overlook the complex structure of the self, including its dynamic, developmental character (2.3). To get at this requires again that we distinguish between different orders or levels of the self. This may be put initially in temporal terms: there is a difference between what you now are and what you aspire to become or what you have the capacity to become. What you now are may be further differentiated into your first-order ongoing self and your second-order ability to reflect on that self, including your ability to evaluate it in the light of your aspirations or further capacities. This differentiation may include the distinction between what you now desire and what you desire to desire, and so between first-order and second-order desires. But even more, as my example of Jones shows, the very identification of the "you" is at stake here. What is it that Jones now is and desires: his wimpish self or his confident self? To what extent can he control which self he is to be? Here the quest for one's identity becomes most acute. So the injunction to be oneself or to become what one is may involve that, at a second level, one accepts oneself as what one is at the first level, including one's present desires, as against seeking to deny those desires or other traits of oneself.[9] In this way one has the capacity to bring one's unfulfilled self into line with one's fulfilled self. But also, in being oneself, one may try to strengthen

---

[8] *Thus Spake Zarathustra*, Fourth Part (in Walter Kaufmann, ed. and trans., *The Portable Nietzsche* [New York: Viking Press, 1960], p. 351). On this, see also Alexander Nehamas, *Nietzshe: Life as Literature* (Cambridge, Mass.: Harvard University Press, 1985), chap. 6: "How One Becomes What One Is" (pp. 170–99).

[9] See Carl C. Rogers, *On Becoming A Person* (Boston: Houghton Mifflin, 1961), pp. 108–11; A. H. Maslow, *Toward a Psychology of Being*, 2nd ed. (New York: Van Nostrand Reinhold, 1962), p. 141.

or confirm one aspect of oneself that, on reflection, one favors, and to deny or suppress other aspects of oneself that one disfavors. So the injunction to be oneself requires choosing which identity one is to have.

The temporal distinctions here indicated also bear more broadly on how one deals with one's life stages. At their best these stages are processes of growth in which one both develops one's freedom and well-being at each stage and also prepares for the next stages. In this process one must accept oneself for what one is; in this way one can age gracefully, as against a neurotic longing for one's past youth.[10]

These considerations enable us to specify further the connection of autonomy with identity. The autonomy whereby one governs oneself presupposes a sense of one's own identity as being both the subject and the object of this governance. In this way one brings one's second-order desires about one's identity to bear on one's first-order desires. A further connection is that whatever a person's identity (within the limits set by the PGC), it involves certain rights: it must be respected by other persons; at least, it must not be an object of discrimination or harm on the part of other persons, where "harm" is defined in terms of the PGC's requirements. Persons must be permitted and enabled to have a secure sense of their own identity, of their selves as being defined in significant respects by the personal conceptions or the social roles or memberships that are important determinants of whom they conceive themselves to be. In this way persons maintain their autonomy as setting for themselves the rules of their own conduct, where they set these rules in accordance with personal conceptions or social roles or memberships they consider important for themselves. The attainment of such identity is a significant part of capacity-fulfillment because the importance one attaches to it ties it to a central part of what is best in oneself, or at least to what one regards as best. It is also closely related to aspiration-fulfillment because the self's aspirations are deeply rooted in one's conception of who one is (2.1).

These positive contributions of autonomy and identity are confronted by the problems of alienation. Identity and alienation are contrary opposites: the former signifies the "same" (*idem*) while the latter signifies the "other" (*alius*). Where one's identity betokens a unity of one's self-conception and one's roles or membership in some group, alienation involves a disruption of this unity. Standard discussions of this phenomenon go back to Hegel and Marx, carrying on to the present day. Thus in capitalist and other societies workers are alienated from the process and the product of their work, in that they are separated from control

---

[10] See especially Erikson, *Identity, Youth and Crisis, and Childhood and Society*, 2nd ed. (New York: W. W. Norton, 1963), chap. 7. For an ancient empirical parallel, see Aristotle, *Rhetoric* 2. 12–14.

over the process; they are dominated by it; they find it meaningless, exhausting, and brutalizing, and they share inadequately in its rewards. Far from normatively identifying with their work and their roles as workers, they regard it as alienating in that they are, and conceive themselves as, separated from control over it and its fruits. Alienation involves this separation of the self from control over some of its most important activities. So alienation is antithetical not only to the self's identification with its important roles but also to the freedom and autonomy that constitute necessary goods of action.

Alienation can also be found in many other areas of life and action. Persons are alienated from the political process when they find that they cannot control its strong impact on their lives. Even more, they are alienated from one another when the economic and political systems under which they live set them in competition with one another or reduce them to means for another's ends, as against maintaining bonds of cooperation, friendship, and comity. And what is perhaps most serious, each person experiences self-alienation. This includes that one has very little self-esteem and suffers from anxiety, feelings of frustration, and despair. But self-alienation can also involve that one loses major parts of one's self-awareness. "It is the remoteness of the neurotic from his own feelings, wishes, beliefs, and energies. It is the loss of the feeling of being an active determining force in his own life. It is the loss of feeling himself as an organic whole."[11] In such a case one is alienated from that part of oneself that, through its freedom and autonomy, can control how one feels and acts in major parts of one's life.

The word "alienation" is not merely a privative term signifying lack of something. If this is all it is, it would be as universal as nonbeing, since all of existence can be characterized in terms of lacked predicates. But alienation is a normative concept; it signifies a loss or lack of the freedom, autonomy, and identity that contribute in important ways to the self's capacities for successful action. That persons suffer from alienation can nevertheless be an empirical fact: that something valuable has been lost. So alienation presents a serious challenge to capacity-fulfillment. It is one thing to specify that freedom, autonomy, and identity are important components of capacity-fulfillment; it is quite another to hold that most persons can attain such fulfillment in the actual conditions of modern life.

Nevertheless, the fact that many persons undergo the losses and separations of alienation does not remove the value I have attributed to freedom, autonomy, and identity. Such removal would obtain only if

---

[11] Karen Horney, *Neurosis and Human Growth* (London: Routledge and Kegan Paul, 1951), p. 157. See also Otto Fenichel, *The Psychoanalytic Theory of Neurosis* (New York: W. W. Norton, 1945), pp. 18–22, 129–40.

alienation were so pervasive and inevitable that the contrary values were thereby beyond reach, on the principle that 'ought' implies 'can' (so that if one cannot attain freedom and the other necessary goods of action, then there is no point in saying that one ought to have or strive for them). But on the contrary, there are at least three mitigating circumstances that can reduce the impact of alienation. First, alienation is not equally distributed among all groups. If workers on an assembly line are alienated from their work, their supervisors and employers are not thus alienated: they may be, and feel themselves to be, in control of their economic activities and identify themselves with those activities. So this suggests, secondly, that greater democratization of the workplace may reduce alienation, by giving workers greater control over both the process and the product of their work activities. In the political sphere, similarly, provisions for more direct participation of ordinary citizens in the governance of their communities can contribute strongly to the reduction of alienation. More generally, a social order that stresses cooperation and compassion, as against the competitiveness of zero-sum games, can help markedly to reduce the alienation of persons from one another.

A third point bears especially on the neurotic self-alienation whereby one loses control of one's feelings and beliefs and no longer identifies oneself with them. Psychotherapy, amid all its fallibilities, can strive to reduce such loss (see below, 4.7). Even more, the spread of enlightenment among parents, by various means including public education, can help to alert them to the deleterious effects of their undermining of children's self-confidence and the resulting psychic disorders. In these ways alienation can be reduced and the contributions of freedom, autonomy, and identity to capacity-fulfillment can be strengthened. More generally, it must be recognized that many kinds of alienation, especially in social spheres, result from violations of the human rights upheld by the PGC. A social order in which the reasonableness of the principle of human rights is recognized and effectuated can go far toward removing the negativities and separation of alienation.

4.4. PERSONALIST MORALITY AS BASED UPON WELL-BEING

Let us now turn to well-being as the other necessary generic good of action and generally successful action. It will be recalled that well-being, as derivative from the purposiveness that figures in all action, consists in having the various substantive conditions and abilities that are proximately required either for acting at all or for having general chances of success in achieving one's purposes through one's action (3.4). In inquiring into what constitutes the fullest development of well-being, we must also recall its segmentation into three parts: basic, nonsubtractive, and additive. In each of these parts, well-being is a matter of capacities not only for bare action but also for successful action. Since each part is among the best of human capacities within the general purpose of successful agency, the fullest development of each part makes a significant contribution to self-fulfillment as capacity-fulfillment.

It is important to see why well-being, as derivative from the purposiveness of action, is required in addition to freedom and autonomy for filling in the contents of capacity-fulfillment. Freedom and autonomy are not sufficient for a good life because they do not, as such, specify the purposes for which they are to be used. An approach to such specification was provided by the second-order reflection on first-order desires that I presented as part of desire-autonomy (2.2). But, important as such reflection and desire are, there are independent rational criteria for the worth of purposes that serve to demarcate further what constitutes a good life. These criteria derive especially from additive well-being as the generic feature of generally successful action that consists in developing and exercising one's capacity for increasing and improving one's level of purpose-fulfillment. But the other parts of well-being also make their contribution to the criteria.

It may be objected that your autonomy is violated if there is imposed a separate requirement that autonomy be used for good purposes. A strong libertarian thesis holds that, except for preventing force and fraud, no limitations should be imposed on personal autonomy (see also 2.4). This thesis disregards the necessity of pooling resources to help relieve the needs of impoverished persons. It also overlooks that there are rational criteria that serve to determine the justifiability both of purposes and of uses of one's autonomy. Autonomy is rational when the rules one sets for oneself have been arrived at by a correct use of reason, or at least are in accord with rules so derived. Included among these rules are the PGC and its derivatives. So rational autonomy requires respect for the universalist morality of human rights. But there are also other rational criteria that help to show how the various parts of well-being, to which one also has rights, serve to further the purposes of personalist morality concerned with the fullest development of the good life. I shall now present the stages of this development according to the three parts of well-being. Some of the criteria, especially as regards basic well-being, are rather prosaic and obvious. But this does not derogate from their importance; and realism requires that they be recognized.

The fullest development of basic well-being requires that there be adequate protections of life, health, mental equilibrium, and other preconditions of successful action. The purposes of action must provide, at least implicitly, for these preconditions. The emphasis here must be not on the barest modicum of these conditions but on their relation to capacities for successful action. Persons who have sufficient behavioral autonomy can provide and protect these capacities for themselves. But this requires a social, economic, and political background that enables persons to develop the capacities. Millions of persons in many parts of the world live in conditions of severe deprivation that prevent them from attaining such development. This point bears directly on the universalist moral principle of human rights; it indicates one of the many ways in which that principle underlies the very possibility of capacity-fulfillment.

Persons must also, as far as possible, contribute to the protection of their own basic well-being as part of the purposes that enter into their capacity-fulfillment. Here the familiar but often contravened precepts about personal health and hygiene find a proper place. Personalist morality requires that persons develop certain relevant virtues, including healthy habits or life-styles, eschewing addictive drugs and other threats to physical or mental well-being, and avoiding excesses of food or drink. Here again one's emotions must be so moderated that they do not lead one into impediments to successful action. This point marks an important intersection between positive freedom and basic well-being.

Let us now consider nonsubtractive well-being. Since this consists in having the abilities and conditions needed for maintaining undiminished one's level of purpose-fulfillment, the achievement of such well-being requires protections against force, fraud, betrayal, and other conditions that operate to decrease persons' capacities for successful action. Here again the institutional background of human rights has an important determinative role. This includes protection against both political conditions whereby tyrannical regimes oppress their subjects and social conditions whereby some groups are invidiously discriminated against. It also includes economic protections that enable persons to earn a livelihood and to prevent a lowering of their standard of living. For example, losing one's job or suffering a severe decrease of one's wages is often a disaster that calls for a protective political response.

Personalist morality offers precepts for the development of virtues that enable persons to ward off such threats to their nonsubtractive well-being. These include various capacities for self-protection. For example, you must, as far as possible, learn to protect yourself against fraud, lies, and similar kinds of misconduct. You must also avoid self-defeating behaviors; this involves learning from experience about when your well-meant purposes or actions result in frustration. Disappointments in love, other personal relationships, or career are examples of lowered purpose-fulfillment amid insufficiently grounded expectations. Such disappointments often result in alienation from one's purposes in life; one regards one's life as not worth living because it drastically lowers rather than raises one's happiness and sense of fulfillment. As these examples suggest, nonsubtractive well-being has an important psychological dimension. To cease to care about one's projects, to become affectless and without aspirations, are ways of lowering one's capacity for purpose-fulfillment. Avoidance of such adverse states thus provides an important contribution to making the best of oneself. In all these contexts personalist morality prescribes developing certain virtues: that one try to be aware of such contra-purposive conditions and that one avoid, so far as possible, the situations that tend to cause them. This requires, as also in other contexts, heightened self-knowledge and its application to the factors opposed to nonsubtractive well-being (see also 5.3).

In the present context of personalist morality, additive well-being is the most important of practical capacities. You will recall that it consists in having the abilities and conditions needed for increasing one's level of purpose-fulfillment and one's capabilities for particular actions. Viewed more fully, additive well-being may be divided into four parts which progressively expand its relation to capacity-fulfillment. First, it consists in the ability to achieve one's purposes, especially those one considers most important. Second, it is the state or condition of actually having achieved one's purposes. But third, because purposes may be misguided or self-defeating, additive well-being also comprises the ability to reflect critically on one's purposes and to learn from experience, as well as the exercise of this ability. Here there is a close connection with the second-order knowledge that is an important part of freedom and desire-autonomy (2.2). And fourth, as a partial result of such reflection and learning, additive well-being also involves acting on purposes that expand and deepen one's horizons of values and that not only reflect more authentically who one is but also transform who one is. It includes such virtues as being open to new experiences, new challenges, and new values, both personal and social. It also involves taking pleasure in these ranges of experience and value. In these ways one's self-fulfillment is also a self-expansion, but with all the risks inherent in the operational aspect of reason.

It may be thought that additive well-being is close to or even the same as utilitarianism with its emphasis on the maximization of preference-satisfaction. There is indeed a concern for maximization in additive well-being. But there are some significant differences. The most important is that additive well-being is limited by the universalist moral principle of human rights. This involves three points. First, additive well-being does not permit the fulfillment of purposes that violate persons' human rights. Accordingly, additive well-being, unlike utilitarianism, has a distributive as well as an aggregative emphasis; it takes account of the differential impact of purpose-fulfillment on equality of goods. Second, the purposes that enter into additive well-being are not a miscellaneous assortment of preferences or "utilities"; instead, they are articulated in ways epitomized by the criterion of degrees of needfulness for action. This articulation is qualitative as well as quantitative; but the qualitative differences are themselves objective. They are not measured, as in Mill, by the preferences of experienced agents; instead, they are weighed according to their varying impacts on the needs of agency. Nevertheless, third, the direct purview of additive well-being is not that of maximizing total or average utility for society as a whole; rather, it concerns the individual agent's pursuit of his rationally criticized purposes.

In this regard, additive well-being consists in doing something with one's life that goes beyond a miscellaneous assortment of achieved purposes. It involves a sequential pattern of major goals, including, for example, pursuing a career, providing for one's loved ones, supporting a worthy cause, and in other ways immersing oneself in plans or projects that contribute both to one's own development and to goals one regards as valuable. Such modes of purposive activity are obviously related to the aspiration-fulfillment discussed in chapter 2. They go beyond it, however, because now purposes or aspirations are not taken as independent variables; instead, they are critically evaluated by operational reason and by one's other capacities. They are therefore purged of the weaknesses attendant upon aspiration-fulfillment as such. This does not involve that desires are left behind; they could not be actions and omit purposes and desires. But because of the aspect of "best" in capacity-fulfillment, the activities of additive well-being encompass not only a wider but also a deeper range of values, bearing on such components of character as dignity and self-respect.[12]

Much additive well-being is the practical best that it is in one to become because of the deepened reflection and evaluation that it incorporates. We may here again invoke the Purposive Ranking Thesis. Given (a) the context of action with (b) the purpose of being as successful as possible in one's actions, this success including the effects of reflection and learning, it follows that (c) additive well-being as delineated above is the best capacity for this purpose. Unlike some of the other "bests"

---

[12] From Plato and Aristotle on, philosophers have discussed such well-being. It may be instructive to compare these discussions with recent empirical analyses of "perceptual indicators of well-being" (some of which are more directly related to what I have called "aspirations."). See, e.g. Norman M. Bradburn, *The Structure of Psychological Well-Being* (Chicago: Aldine, 1969); Frank M. Andrews and Stephen B. Withey, *Social Indications of Well-Being: Americans' Perceptions of Life Quality* (New York: Plenum Press, 1976). See also James Griffin, *Well-Being* (Oxford: Clarendon Press, 1986); Martha C. Nussbaum and Amartya Sen, eds., *The Quality of Life* (Oxford: Clarendon Press, 1993).

that figure in the Purposive Ranking Thesis, the present one is less a means-end relation and more a relation of constituent part and whole. But this still leaves it open that additive well-being has many parts that contribute collectively as well as distributively to the overall purpose of successful action.

It is especially in the area of additive well-being that the "best" of capacity-fulfillment finds it prime basis. As we have seen, because action is purposive, the agent regards his purposes as good according to whatever criterion enters into his purposes. So in one respect what is best for each agent will be determined by her own ranking of her purposes, and thus by her general preference structure. But this determination can also be strongly affected by the kind of education, including self-education, that one receives or brings about as part of one's additive well-being. Education can acquaint one with a whole range of values—intellectual, moral, aesthetic, economic, political, and others—and this can bring much enlightenment to one's criteria of what is best both in oneself and in the diverse objects of study. The education in question may be informal as well as formal; at its best, it sharpens one's perception of various envisaged goods and enables one to rank them on an informed basis—all this with due recognition of the individual differences reflected in the consideration of scope (3.2).

Much education both develops and uses one's epistemic capacity of operational reason. So here we rejoin the earlier discussion of reason as the best of human epistemic capacities (3.3). In these ways persons can fulfill themselves by developing the personal virtues that correspond to freedom and well-being as the necessary goods of action. I shall go into this development more fully in the following sections.

4.5. VIRTUES AND CULTURE

In the three preceding sections I tried to show how various prudential virtues are required by personalist morality as direct adjuncts of one's attainment and maintenance of freedom and well-being as constituting one's capacity-fulfillment. Other, more traditional virtues can also be shown to be parts of additive well-being. Although some of them are implicit in the virtues outlined in the previous section, it is worth considering them more explicitly for their further contributions to additive well-being in its relation to capacity-fulfillment.

Central to additive well-being viewed as capacities or dispositions is the prospective agent's sense of his own worth. We have seen that every agent, to the extent that he avoids alienation, regards his particular purposes as worth pursuing and hence attributes value to them. When such evaluative purposiveness is more than incidental and transient, the agent has an abiding self-esteem in that he views the worth of his goals as reflecting his own worth as a rational person. He may indeed be self-critical in that he unfavorably estimates his performance in relation to specific objectives. But amid such particular variations he must have a general acceptance of himself as a person whose life, freedom, and well-being are worthy of protection and development. In this way he has a secure sense of his own identity. As was noted above, without such self-esteem, his ability to achieve further goals becomes problematic, and with it his prospects of taking satisfaction in what he accomplishes thereby (3.6).

Closely related to the agent's sense of self-esteem are various prudential virtues of character. These are parts of additive well-being both because they serve to ground and reinforce the agent's self-esteem and because, as deep-seated enduring dispositions that underlie and help to motivate actions, they contribute to his effectiveness in acting to fulfill his purposes. They may be summarized under three of the traditional four cardinal virtues. Courage is the disposition to have and to act from a sound estimation of what is and is not to be feared; it includes the ability to appraise and confront dangers, fortitude and perseverance in the face of adversity, determination in overcoming obstacles as against taking the easy way out. Temperance is the state of character whereby one guides one's conduct judiciously with regard to controlling one's appetites and inclinations; it enables the agent to maintain a proper balance between lust or gluttony and abstemiousness or asceticism in matters bearing on his physical and mental health, and to uphold his self-esteem as a rational person in contrast to being only an animal. Prudence is the proximate ability not only to calculate the most efficient means for achieving one's particular ends but also to distinguish among both particular and more general ends themselves, to ascertain which of one's possible ends are most worth pursuing in light of one's overall capacities and aspirations; it therefore includes both self-knowledge and knowledge of one's natural and social environment, as well as the proximate ability and tendency to bring these to bear on one's actions and projects. Just as all three of these virtues (or groups of virtues) are acquired by regular performance of the corresponding actions, so they contribute to a certain practical stability on the part of the agent whereby he is not deflected from his actions and projects by each new stimulus or by passing, temporary fancies or by insufficiently sifted fears or inclinations. A person who has these virtues is not a mere passive recipient or victim of external causes but rather, as a regular matter, controls his own behavior by his informed, unforced choices and plans.

As so far depicted, these self-regarding virtues are not moral but prudential. To be moral virtues, in the sense in which 'moral' is based on the universalist morality of human rights, they must be guided by or at least be subordinate to the other-regarding virtue of justice as this is embodied in the PGC. To paraphrase Kant, none of the prudential virtues is unqualifiedly good, for a person who acts according to them may use them for immoral purposes. It cannot directly be said, then, that the agent has a (universalist) moral duty to develop these virtues in himself. His moral duty in this regard, rather, is in large part to refrain from actions which hinder the development of the prudential virtues in other persons. Such actions may take a variety of forms: promoting a climate of fear and oppression; encouraging the spread of physically or mentally harmful practices such as excessive use of alcohol, tobacco, drugs, or pornography; contributing to misinformation, ignorance, and superstition, especially as these bear on persons' ability to act effectively in pursuit of their purposes. By such actions the agent violates his recipients' rights to additive well-being as this is found in their having the prudential virtues. He also has the positive duty to assist, so far as he can, the development of these virtues in other persons, while respecting their freedom. This assistance, as provided by individual agents, takes such forms as setting an example of the practice of the virtues in his own actions and supporting a social and educational milieu in which these virtues are respected and fostered.

It must also be recognized, however, that the prudential virtues are cardinal parts of what I have called personalist morality. They contribute to making the best of oneself as an effective, enlightened agent. I shall return to this in discussing duties to oneself later in this chapter.

The virtues I have cited as parts of additive well-being are obviously related to Aristotle's much fuller list of "moral" virtues. It may be helpful here to note how his argument that virtue is the "best"[13] among states of character can be elucidated according to the Purposive Ranking Thesis. To put it formally once again, we have as to (a) the context, states of character; and as to (b) the purpose for whose fulfillment they are being considered, Aristotle sets this forth in his statement that "every virtue both brings into good condition the thing of which it is the excellence and makes the work of that thing be done well."[14] Given this purpose of benefiting or improving both persons and their works, Aristotle proceeds to show that it is best achieved by the moderating of actions and feelings, on the model of art which "does its work well by looking to the intermediate and judging its work by this standard."

---

[13] *Nicomachean Ethics,* 2. 6. 1106b23, 1107a9.
[14] Ibid., 2. 6. 1006a15.

Thus, on the pattern of capacity-fulfillment as achieving the best that it is in one to become, Aristotle's "moral" virtues, and the prudential virtues I have modeled on them, are important parts of such fulfillment.

Let us now consider culture as another context of capacity-fulfillment. "Culture" has many meanings, but the one that is most directly relevant here, at least at the outset, is what may be called its "humanist" sense, which Matthew Arnold famously defined as "a pursuit of our total perfection by means of getting to know, on all the matters which most concern us, the best which has been thought and said in the world."[15] This normative reference to "the best" suggests a connection with capacity-fulfillment as achieving the best in oneself by "getting to know . . . the best which has been thought and said in the world."

There are, of course, severe limitations here. Even if we can agree on the criteria of this "best," getting to know it could still leave one far short of "total perfection" on moral and other criteria. In the intellectual sphere one could attain, for example, scientific or historical knowledge without becoming an excellent scientist or historian; and one could know and appreciate the arts without being an excellent artist oneself.

Within these limitations, there is much to be said for the idea that an appreciation of high culture, in the arts and in humanist education generally, is an important part of capacity-fulfillment. In such appreciation it is difficult to distinguish intrinsic from instrumental values. One can derive keen enjoyment from various of the arts and sciences; informed contact with them can ennoble one, and many works of music, literature, and other arts can provide emotional release that helps one to go on living and improves one's abilities of agency. To foster the development of such appreciation should be a prime aim of education as contributing to capacity-fulfillment.

Questions arise about the criteria of "the best" in humanist culture. If we appeal to the Purposive Ranking Thesis, and if the relevant purposes are such as were mentioned in the preceding paragraph, we find that they can be fulfilled by a large variety of cultural products. Hence the purposes would not yield a single set of rankings. Moreover, insofar as the purposes are themselves diverse, this would involve a diversity of rankings of humanistic cultures.

To deal with this, it will be helpful to note that besides the humanist concept of culture there is another, which may be called the "anthropological." In this sense, a culture is a way of life as it is understood, symbolized, and evaluated by the group that lives it; it is a set both of group

---

[15] Matthew Arnold, *Culture and Anarchy* (Cambridge: Cambridge University Press, 1960), p. 6.

practices and of related beliefs.[16] Two differences between the humanist and the anthropological concepts emerge at once. First, the humanist concept, with its reference to "the best," is normative, while the anthropological concept is positive: it involves or presupposes no value judgments of better and worse between cultures as ways of life. Second, the humanist concept is monistic and absolutist; it seems to assume that there is only one, or only one kind of, cultural "best." The anthropological concept, on the other hand, is pluralistic and relativist: it allows for a large variety of ways of life, so that group practices and beliefs are to be assessed only within given cultures, but not between or apart from them. Some anthropologists have indeed argued that there are "cultural universals," general sets of practices and beliefs that obtain in all cultures.[17] But this view has been criticized on the ground that the practices and beliefs thus delineated are excessively vague and indeterminate.[18]

Despite the differences between the humanist and anthropological concepts, there is an important connection between them. The normative idea of "the best" that figures in the humanist concept is strongly affected by the diversities of the anthropological concept. What persons consider to be "best" in humanist culture, especially in the areas of aesthetic products, varies with the different ways of life and systems of belief and evaluation that figure in the anthropological concept of culture. This variation suggests a severe diminution of the monistic and absolutist pretensions of the humanist concept. The impact of the anthropological concept is further increased by the "culture wars" in which different systems of belief about the principles of right living come into conflict with one another.[19] Here the humanist idea of "the best" is subjected to vehement disagreements rooted in divergent ways of life and values.

To deal with these issues, we should consider how the anthropological cultures are individuated, both historically and geographically. Just

[16] On the transition from the "humanist" to the "anthropological" conception of culture, see George W. Stocking, Jr., "Matthew Arnold and the Uses of Invention," *American Anthropologist* 65, no. 4 (August 1963): 783–99. See also Raymond Williams, *Culture and Society 1780–1950* (New York: Doubleday and Co., 1959), pp. xiv–xv, and Ralph Linton, *The Cultural Basis of Personality* (London: Routledge and Kegan Paul, 1947), pp. 19–25.

[17] See, e.g., Bronislaw Malinowski, *A Scientific Theory of Culture and Other Essays* (Chapel Hill, N.C.: University of North Carolina Press, 1944), chaps. 4, 8–10; and Clyde Kluckhohn, "Universal Categories of Culture," in *Anthropology Today*, ed. A. L. Kroeber (Chicago: University of Chicago Press, 1983), p. 516.

[18] See Clifford Geertz, *The Interpretation of Cultures* (New York: Basic Books, 1973), pp. 37–43, and A. L. Kroeber, *Anthropology: Culture Patterns and Processes* (San Diego, Calif.: Harcourt Brace Jovanovich, 1963), p. 120.

[19] See James Davison Hunter, *Culture Wars: The Struggle to Define America* (New York: Basic Books, 1991).

as the culture that embraced Rembrandt was different from the culture
that upheld Jackson Pollock, so both of these are different from the cultures that took up graffiti and "gangsta rap." It is important to avoid
circularity at this point, as would occur if each of these variant anthropological cultures were defined in terms of their respective humanist cultural products. But the various anthropological cultures or ways of life
can be delineated by criteria that are independent of the humanist cultures that figure in them.

The upshot of these considerations is that when an appreciation of
humanist culture is upheld as a vital part of capacity-fulfillment, the
question arises of which humanist culture figures in this relation. Is capacity-fulfillment achieved as well by an appreciation of Norman Rock-
well as of Picasso, of Edgar Guest as of W. H. Auden, of Danielle Steel
as of Virginia Woolf? The crude utilitarian answer, that it all depends on
the quantity of pleasure one gets from each work, is not much helped
by J. S. Mill's qualitative amendment that an appeal must be made to
the preferences of critics who have experienced both kinds of pleasure.
But a main point of the latter answer is captured by the idea that humanist appreciation is a "minority culture" to which only an elite few
can aspire; as F. R. Leavis wrote, "In any period it is upon a very small
minority that the discerning appreciation of art and literature depends;
it is (apart from cases of the simple and familiar) only a few who are
capable of unprompted, first-hand judgments. . . . Upon this minority
depends our power of profiting by the finest human experience of the
past; they keep alive the subtlest and most perishable parts of tradition.
Upon them depend the implicit standards that order the fine living of
an age."[20]

We must here distinguish between the objects and the subjects of critical evaluation, between the cultural products that are judged to be "the
finest human experience of the past" and the numbers and kinds of
persons who can make appreciative informed judgments about these
products. With the spread of liberal education to all classes of society,
workers and farmers as well as professional aesthetes and intellectuals
can develop a critical appreciation of humanist culture. While the criteria
of such appreciation may vary widely, the normative element, the attainment of the beauty of the aesthetically "best," can be increased for all
persons. To this end they should be helped to develop not only famil-
iarity and technical expertise but also modes of response that emphasize reflective insight as well as emotional involvement. By such means

[20] F. R. Leavis, *Mass Civilization and Minority Culture* (Cambridge: Cambridge University Press, 1930), pp. 3–5 (quoted in Raymond Williams, *Culture and Society 1780–
1950*, p. 271). For the wider diffusion of critical appreciation referred to below, see Williams, *Culture and Society*, p. 344.

cultural appreciation can contribute to capacity-fulfillment, including strong components of enjoyment and fun.

The ability to make informed discriminations between various aesthetic products comprises what may be called "cultural virtues." They involve taking an active role in understanding, interpreting, and reacting emotionally as well as intellectually to the sights and sounds that enter into the arts. This point can be brought out if we consider, for example, whether watching soap operas or violence on television is as good a use of one's time and attention as reading literature that broadens one's horizons by giving deeper insights into the human condition. Both freedom and well-being enter into the development of the cultural virtues. Education, while rejecting cultural dictatorship or coercion, can respect persons' freedom and autonomy by providing opportunities for familiarizing them with cultural products and enabling them to make informed discriminations based on evolving standards. Such aesthetic education can also enhance persons' capacities for purpose-fulfillment.

In their relation to humanist culture as so far considered, persons may be largely passive. Although active efforts at discriminative understanding enhance critical appreciation, persons are nonetheless envisaged as recipients of the cultural productivity of other persons; they are at best aesthetes, not artists. This raises the question of whether a more active role is not also required for persons who are to achieve capacity-fulfillment. In order to make the best of themselves they should not only be able to appreciate the artistic products of other persons; they should also develop their talents by bringing to fruition their own best capacities. In other words, they have certain duties to themselves (4.6). This involves that capacity-fulfillment is an active process of self-development; and the aspects of the self that are thus developed consist in the various virtues that accompany the necessary goods of freedom and well-being. These virtues have two kinds of application. One is general: they assist in all one's projects of purpose-fulfillment. The other is particular: one uses the virtues to make the best of oneself in one or a few lines of activity that are especially appropriate to one's preferences and aptitudes. In this way, one may become a professional athlete or an electrician or an engineer or a philosopher or a journalist, and so forth. At its best, this can be a life of creativity and achievement.[21] Here the idea of "best" must take account of the different applications of "best" distinguished above (3.3).

These distinctions, in the present context, bear especially on the sense of one's identity that we saw above (4.3) is an important contributor to

[21] Cf. Mihaly Csikszentmihalyi, *Creativity* (New York: Harper Collins, 1996); Howard Gardner, *Frames of Mind: The Theory of Multiple Intelligences* (New York: Basic Books, 1993).

one's capacity-fulfillment. The various artistic products of humanist culture, including literature, music, and the visual arts, can have a strong bearing on one's feelings about one's identity. If certain art products are disparaged or denigrated by representatives of the dominant culture (in both senses of "culture") this can have a deleterious effect on the morale and self-esteem of submerged groups, with corresponding diminutions of their capacity-fulfillment. Such persons may hesitate to affirm or even recognize their identities as black or female or working class, out of fear that the cultural products that have emerged from persons bearing their respective identities, or to which their own identities have inclined them, will be ridiculed as inferior and even as ugly. Thus a kind of "cultural imperialism" may obtain, with effects that are as psychologically damaging as other modes of imperialism. Persons have moral rights not to be subjected to such conditions, as parts of their rights to freedom and well-being.

Such considerations serve to bring out again the complex structure of capacity-fulfillment with its contributing factors of freedom, autonomy, identity, and the three levels of well-being. Just as the various products of humanist culture can embrace these factors, so too, especially in societies divided by economic and social forces, the products can operate to exacerbate the divisions. Any realistic account of capacity-fulfillment must take account of such obstacles.

There remains, in any case, the strong emphasis of personalist morality that if you want to fulfill yourself, you should dedicate yourself to a worthy cause which exemplifies as full a development as possible of such rationally ascertained values as human rights, truth, beauty, or expertise in some profession or calling, including skilled craftsmanship and making a loving and happy home. You can rightly regard such values as the best in their respective spheres, and by your active pursuit of some one or more of them you will gradually assimilate it into your own self, so that you will thereby develop what is best in yourself. In this way the subject or self fulfills its best capacity through its own reflection of or assimilation to the object that is best because of its eminent value—all this within the limits set by universalist morality and by the enduring distinction between the self and its objects.

Let us consider how this conception stands in relation to two difficulties that I canvassed above in connection with self-fulfillment in general and aspiration-fulfillment in particular: egoism and elitism (1.1, 2.1). The charge of egoism may seem plausible because in personalist morality one seeks to develop one's own abilities and excellences. But it must be emphasized that this endeavor is not exclusively one of self-regard; as I noted earlier in connection with aspiration-fulfillment, one's self-fulfillment emerges as a "by-product" of one's pursuit of other values (2.4).

Because it is these objective values that one seeks to further, the personalist morality that upholds such modes of life is not egoistic; it is object-oriented, not self-oriented (2.4).

This conclusion may be challenged on the ground that it takes too idealistic or starry-eyed a view of values-pursuit as it actually occurs in many societies, including ours. Many even eminent scientists, physicians, lawyers, activists, scholars, artists, and other professionals engage in vehement drives for recognition and renown—a far cry from the exalted picture of the modest, self-effacing pursuer of independent values. So in this context personalist morality would emerge as egoistic after all.

There is, nonetheless, an important respect in which this thesis must be sharply modified. Regardless of the contingent motivations of some professionals, the fact remains that there are objective criteria for the soundness of the values they pursue and for the assessment of their success in achieving them. You may blow your own horn as loudly as you wish, but if your experiments fail or your accomplishments leave your relevant peers entirely unimpressed, your concomitant pursuit of self-aggrandizement will probably not get you very far. It is at least on this ground of the objectivity of the relevant criteria that the value-pursuits upheld by personalist morality have an important non-egoistic basis.

What of elitism? Since in capacity-fulfillment you seek to achieve the best that it is in you to become, this "best" may involve invidious discriminations both in yourself and in others against abilities and performances that fail to measure up to this "best." It must be recalled, however, that what is "best" must take account of different levels of ability and other qualities (3.2). Within these limitations, including those set by the operational aspect of reason, the capacity-fulfillment upheld by personalist morality can be at least partially attained or approximated by very many persons.[22] This is not to overlook the elements of mediocrity and even viciousness that characterize many persons as they are, including the various effects of alienation (4.3). But self-fulfillment as capacity-fulfillment, while a demanding ideal, can still be within the reach of persons as they are. The elitist impulse can be further reduced by the humbling realization that there are always further reaches of perfection toward which one can strive.

We must here again distinguish between the values pursued or achieved and the selves or agents who pursue or achieve them. An important element of elitism, of very high merit or worth, can indeed be

<hr/>

[22] With regard to Aristotle's conception of happiness, which is in some respects far more demanding than the capacity-fulfillment I have here attributed to personalist morality, he wrote that happiness as he portrays it can be "very generally shared; for all who are not deformed with regard to virtue may win it by a certain kind of study and care" (*Nicomachean Ethics*, 1. 9. 1099b19).

attributed to the objects of one's pursuits when they exemplify high standards of adequacy, of what is best in their respective spheres. But from this it does not follow that the persons who pursue these values are likewise justified in making elitist claims for themselves. There should be a sobering realization of the contributions of luck and of familial and societal upbringing. This realization need not dispense with one's personal responsibility to try to make the best of oneself and to deserve credit for one's efforts and accomplishments (see 5.4). But this does not justify drawing invidious comparisons to other persons who are less fortunate or successful. On the contrary, the requirements of self-respect as based on the human rights of universalist morality call for an awareness both of one's own limitations and of the dignity of others.

It will be recalled that, so far in this chapter, I have been developing various phases of personalist morality, concerned with attaining good lives for individual persons. Even my discussion of the anthropological sense of "culture" has had this individualist perspective as its primary focus. But as we have also seen, the interplay between the humanist and anthropological cultures has also had a strong bearing on the groups to which various individuals belong. To deal further with the problems just canvassed about the clashes of artistic cultures that compete for diverse persons' allegiance, we shall have to go on to the further kind of morality that I have called "particularist" (4.8), in its bearing on such cultural pluralism. Before taking this up, another important phase of personalist morality must be considered.

4.6. DUTIES TO ONESELF

The qualities so far discussed in connection with freedom and well-being as parts of personalist morality are not only virtues of the agent; he also has duties to himself to attain and maintain them as parts of his self-fulfillment. The basis of these duties is related to that of the generic rights that figured in the argument for the PGC (3.4). Just as the freedom and well-being that are the objects of these rights are needed for the agent's actions and generally successful actions, so the virtues are needed in order to make more effective the agent's use of these necessary goods of action. To have these virtues is a duty to the agent for his own sake from within his own standpoint as an agent. But this duty is owed not only to oneself as an individual agent but also to the moral, intellectual, and aesthetic values that are embodied in one's self at one's best. The person owes it to herself to pursue these values because they are important parts of her capacity-fulfillment; because of the goods they embody they set requirements for her choices and actions.

There is a difference, however, between one's having a duty to act from a virtue and one's having a duty to try to develop a virtue. It is the latter that is required for capacity-fulfillment. The reason for this is that the virtues, being long-range dispositions acquired in part by the habitual performance of right actions, cannot be had in the same direct way in which actions are performed, so that a command to have them is not directly fulfillable. On the other hand, the PGC shows that these virtues are good to have precisely because persons who have them are much more likely to do what the PGC requires and to make more effective use of their freedom and well-being as parts of a good life.

Let us now look more closely at the idea of duties to oneself. An initial basis for considering these is that it seems anomalous for someone's duties to be grounded only on the freedom and well-being of other persons but not also on his own freedom and well-being. If A has a duty to refrain from harming B, then why doesn't B also have a duty to refrain from harming B, and A from harming A? The point of this question is not removed by the PGC's provision that the agent is to act in accord with his own generic rights as well as those of his recipients. For there is no distinct requirement or duty here that the agent act in accord with his own generic rights since, as have seen, this is something he necessarily does in his particular actions. But for the agent to do this means that he necessarily sees to it that other persons do not interfere with his freedom and well-being without his consent. Thus the bearing of the agent's generic rights is here other-directed: it is a matter of other persons' not violating his rights without his consent, and thus of other persons' fulfilling their duties to him. This, however, is distinct from duties the agent may have to himself with regard to his own freedom and well-being.

The very idea of there being duties to oneself incurs important objections. (1) If there are such duties and they are strict ones, then, like other strict duties, the person who upholds them believes that strong pressure and even coercion is justified to enforce them. Applied to duties to oneself, this would justify a large degree of paternalism; and when the coercion is applied by the person who has the correlative right, it would entail self-coercion. But this seems odd.[23] (2) If a person has duties to himself, then, because of the correlativity of duties and rights, he also has rights against himself. But any right-holder can always give up his right and thereby release the respondent of the right from his duty. Hence, the notion of duties to oneself is contradictory, since it implies that a person both can and cannot release himself from his duties to

---

[23] For part of this argument, see Kurt Baier, *The Moral Point of View* (Ithaca, N.Y.: Cornell University Press, 1958), chap. 9.

himself.[24] (3) If someone violates a duty to himself, then, if this is like other violations of duty, it follows that a person both gains and loses the same thing by the very same action. For insofar as he is the person to whom the duty is owed, he loses something; but insofar as he is the violator of the duty, he gains that something.[25] (4) A duty to not harm oneself or to act for one's own interest or happiness would be nugatory; for the point of a duty is to curb what one is naturally inclined to do, but one's natural inclinations are already against self-harm and for one's own interest or happiness.[26] (5) If there is a duty to develop prudential virtues bearing on one's freedom and well-being, then, since persons also have rights to freedom and well-being, it follows that the duty and the rights have the same objects. But since the objects of rights are benefits or goods to the right-holder while the objects of duties are burdens to the duty-bearer, it would follow from the idea of duties to oneself that the same objects are both benefits and burdens to the same person. (6) If one has duties to oneself to attain or develop whatever is conducive to one's self-interest, then there would be no limit to such duties, and they would include whatever is instrumental to purely selfish ends.

Despite these arguments, there are at least two ways in which duties to oneself, including the duty to inculcate in oneself various self-regarding virtues, can be derived from the PGC. The first way, which was briefly indicated above in connection with the prudential virtues (4.5), may be further developed as follows. If A has a duty to do X, and if his doing Y is highly conducive to his doing X, then A has a duty to do Y if doing Y is in his power and if it does not involve his violating any of his other duties. Now since every agent has the moral duty to obey the PGC, if there are any personal, self-regarding qualities or prudential virtues which he can inculcate in himself and which are such that his having them is necessary or highly conducive to his obeying the PGC, then it is his duty to inculcate in himself such qualities. For if the agent leads a personally intemperate, fearful, self-brutalizing, dissolute, and unintelligent life, if he is slothful, ignorant, improvident, and lacking in self-respect, then he is less likely to respect other persons and to be able to fulfill adequately his strict duties to them. Hence, he has a duty to

---

[24] See Marcus G. Singer, *Generalization in Ethics* (New York: Alfred A. Knopf, 1961), pp. 311ff.

[25] Cf. Aristotle, *Nicomachean Ethics*, 5. 11. 1138a17–20.

[26] See Leonard Nelson, *System of Ethics*, trans. N. Guterman (New Haven: Yale University Press, 1956), pp. 134–35; also Kant, *Metaphysics of Morals, Doctrine of Virtue* (Akad ed., pp. 384–85 [trans. Mary J. Gregor (Cambridge: Cambridge University Press, 1991), p. 189]), although Kant uses the argument not against duties to oneself but against a duty to pursue one's own happiness.

CAPACITY-FULLFILLMENT, GOOD LIFE

avoid such a life and to inculcate in himself the opposite qualities that are conducive to his fulfilling the PGC's requirements: such prudential qualities as being self-respecting, self-aware, temperate, courageous, provident, and well-informed.

Are these duties of the agent to himself? It may be argued that they are only duties regarding himself but not duties to himself, since their point is to enable the agent to fulfill his duties to his recipients. Even if this is the case, it still shows that the moral meritoriousness of various self-regarding virtues can be justified by the PGC as important parts of one's capacity-fulfillment. In this connection, the fourth argument given above against duties to oneself, that persons are naturally inclined to do what is for their self-interest, is not true if the 'what' refers to means as well as ends. The various good qualities that enable a person to fulfill his duties to others are also advantageous for certain aspects of his own self-interest; but their self-inculcation often goes counter to his immediate natural inclinations. Hence, the agent's inculcating such qualities in himself remains his duty despite its advancing certain aspects of his own self-interest.

That he should try to attain such qualities is also a duty to himself. For his duty to obey the PGC is not only a duty to his recipients; it is also a duty to which he is rationally committed insofar as he is a rational agent and person. As we saw above in connection with the agent's autonomy (3.4), the PGC is not merely an "alien" requirement imposed on the rational agent from without; it is also imposed on him by himself, since he recognizes that it fulfills the same standards or criteria by virtue of which he himself is rational and attains capacity-fulfillment. Hence, the agent's obedience to the PGC is a duty to himself qua rational agent. Since this is a strict duty, it follows that qua rational agent he also has a right against himself: a right that the PGC be obeyed by himself. But, in contrast to the second argument given above against duties to oneself, the rational agent cannot give up this right and thereby release himself from his duty to obey the PGC. For his having both the duty and the right does not derive from some contingent or optional decision, desire, or transaction of his; it derives rather from the rational aspect of himself whose criteria are central to his capacity-fulfillment and are independent of his decisions or desires. And the necessity of his accepting these criteria is similarly independent. It is because of these independent, necessary criteria of rationality that the rational agent has the duties to himself both to obey the PGC and to try to inculcate in himself the self-regarding virtues that are necessary or strongly conducive to this obedience. And it is also because of these criteria that the rational agent cannot, while remaining rational, give up either his rights or his duties in this area.

These considerations show how the other objections listed above can be answered. Insofar as the rational agent recognizes that the personal virtues bearing on freedom and well-being are for his benefit in terms of his capacity-fulfillment, he does not regard them as burdens but as beneficial requirements he accepts for himself. Since these requirements are restricted to the necessary goods of action, the argument for them does not justify duties bearing on contingent selfish ends. His violating the requirements of virtues bearing on freedom and well-being would, accordingly, not be a gain for him.

Let us now look at a second, more analogical way in which duties to oneself may be justified by the PGC. This way is derived from the unity of criteria that can be found in other-regarding and self-regarding virtues and vices and the corresponding actions. The PGC as the principle of universalist morality is directly concerned with other-regarding actions whereby a person is unjust or unfair to others, failing to respect them or degrading and demeaning them; it prescribes the opposite actions and, as we have seen, the inculcation of the corresponding virtues. Now the criteria underlying such moral virtues and vices, or closely similar criteria, are also applied in the sphere of the personalist morality of self-regarding actions and qualities. Examples of these criteria can be found in expressions where it is said that a person who wastes his life on drugs or drink is being 'unfair to himself'; a person who squanders his talents 'does not do himself justice'; a person who is excessively timid 'demeans himself'; a girl who exposes her naked body to leering males 'degrades herself.' These expressions, with their reflexive structure, suggest that there is a certain unity in the criteria for being unjust to oneself and to others, for degrading oneself and degrading others. If there were not such unity of criteria, it is difficult to see how such specific expressions as those just cited could be used in both the personal and the interpersonal spheres.

The application of these criteria to the sphere of personalist morality may occur in at least two different ways. According to each, when it is said that a person demeans himself or is unfair to himself, it is assumed that he is acting on himself, that he is both agent and recipient. One way such self-action may embody this combination is through the temporal distinction invoked above (2.3) between the self as immediate agent and the same self as long-term recipient. Qua agent, he is the person directly acting at that moment; but qua recipient, he is not only this momentary person but also the person who will undergo various effects of that present action. This distinction is a familiar one. The man who, guzzling his fifth martini, says to himself, "I'll regret this later," views himself as recipient of his own action and implicitly (qua subsequent recipient) criticizes himself (qua present agent). Now the PGC requires of every agent that he act in accord with his recipients' rights to freedom and well-being as important parts of his capacity-fulfillment. Applied to the case of action on oneself, this becomes the requirement that the immediate agent take favorable account of his own freedom and well-being as the long-term recipient of his actions. He must, then, be fair to himself in this longer-range perspective. His present self has these duties to his future self; hence, he has duties to himself.

This argument may be construed so far as having only a quantitative reference, involving the distinction between short-range and long-range desires. But what if a person's long-range desires are as wanton, gluttonous, and otherwise degraded as his short-range ones? The question of personalist morality concerns quality as well as quantity. When it is said that someone degrades himself, the reference is not primarily to his acting against his long-range interests but rather to the quality of the interests exhibited by his action, whether short-range or long-range. This qualitative consideration may be elucidated according to two familiar further models, each of which views the person not as divided between present and future selves but as differentiated among diverse interests, aspects, or 'parts' of his total self.

One model is egalitarian: it holds that there should be an equilibrium among such of a person's interests or aspects as his desire for physical pleasure, his intellectual powers, his mingling sociably with his fellows, and the like. In this equilibrium, each of these aspects is in harmony with the others, no one of them dominating to the detriment of the rest. The other model is hierarchic: it holds that one of these aspects should control and organize the others, as 'lower' selves. This controlling aspect is often 'reason,' but it may be the will to power, religious faith, or some one of the many other interests or concerns that have figured among the various substantive criteria of moral rightness and as competitors of reason (3.3). According to the first of these models, a person is unfair to himself when one of his parts or aspects disturbs the equilibrium by dominating the others in his conduct; according to the second model, it is when his lower self controls his higher self. When it is said that a person degrades himself, however, only the second model is usually invoked.

Although these attempts to split up the self incur well-known difficulties, they have an important point in calling attention to the various aspects of an individual's overall personality and to the impact of one of these aspects on the others. The PGC applies analogically, though not literally, to such impacts. According to the first model, it says to any aspect that is acting on the others that it should take due account of these others' generic rights, so that the freedom and well-being of the intellect should not overpower, for example, one's physical well-being, and conversely. According to the second model, the PGC requires that reason, in the sense of the capacity of the person to recognize and act according to the criteria of deductive and inductive rationality, should acquire relevant knowledge about the total self, and that this knowledge should be decisive in organizing the self. From Plato to Freud, philosophers and psychologists have in different ways elaborated on and endorsed this model. And it is this model that figures most directly in self-fulfillment as I have analyzed it here.

According to each model, the PGC sets for each person duties to himself, since it holds that he ought to arrange the various parts of his total self in the ways required by the respective models. Each of these kinds of requirement uses analogically the same criteria as are used to criticize interpersonal relations where one person is said to be unfair or unjust to another or to degrade or demean him. For just as in such social relations the agent acts on his recipients in ways that fail to take considerate account of their freedom and well-being, so too when duties to oneself are violated according to each of the above models, one aspect of the self acts on other phases in ways which fail to take due account of the freedom and well-being of these others. In these ways, self-fulfillment as capacity-fulfillment, by requiring the effective use of one's freedom and well-being as the best of one's practical capacities, incorporates duties to oneself as essential phases of this requirement.

4.7. PARTICULARIST MORALITY: FAMILY, LOVE, FRIENDSHIP

So far in this chapter I have discussed personalist morality as deriving from the freedom and well-being that are the substantive components of the PGC and that contribute to the capacity-fulfillment of individuals. This was contrasted with the interpersonal universalist morality that sets rationally necessary, overriding universally beneficial requirements for actions and institutions. We have seen that the universalist morality provides strong disjustifications of such interpersonal particularist moralities as are epitomized in the actions and institutions of Nazism and Stalinism. But we must now consider the PGC's bearing on other particularist moralities that do not have such obvious viciousness, that indeed are at the opposite extreme, and that contribute strongly to self-fulfillment. Prime examples are the requirements set by one's love for some special person or persons, and by devotion to one's family, friends, and country. Such requirements are particularist, not universalist, for according to them one ought to give preferential consideration to the interests of some persons as against others. This preferential consideration

CAPACITY-FULLFILLMENT, GOOD LIFE **141**

does not involve murder and other violations of human rights whereby the interests of some persons are furthered at the expense of others. But it does nevertheless seem to conflict with the egalitarian universalist morality according to which all persons ought to be treated with equal and impartial positive consideration for their respective goods or interests. If capacity-fulfillment requires practical adherence to the rationally necessary norms of egalitarian universalist morality, then how can one justify the requirements of particularist morality like those just cited? This question is especially pressing because these requirements will themselves be seen to make valuable contributions to capacity-fulfillment. So the question arises of whether self-fulfillment as capacity-fulfillment is self-contradictory because it involves adherence both to universalist morality and to an apparently opposed particularist morality.

This question is important for both modes of self-fulfillment. Love, as one of the strongest objects of human aspirations, would seem to be a prime example of the autonomy of aspiration-fulfillment as neither needing nor allowing any justification by universalist morality (2.4). This would also apply to the aspirations of friendship and familial loyalty. So this also puts into question the claims of capacity-fulfillment as represented by the epistemic primacy of reason with its justification of the overridingness of egalitarian universalist morality.

Let us put this issue into the broader framework of capacity-fulfillment as so far developed. This framework has two components. One is the procedural component of the use of reason, both canonic and operational. The other is the substantive component of the context or subject-matter to which reason is applied to ascertain what is best in that context. We have so far seen that, as applied to the substantive context of how one ought to treat other persons, the use of reason has ascertained that what is best in one is to act in accord with the generic rights of one's recipients as well as of oneself; i.e., what is best in one in this vital context is to adhere to the requirements of egalitarian universalist morality. We are now taking up a distinct context, the particularist one of strongly personal relations of affection as well as other restrictive relations. The questions now are: what does reason ascertain about what is best in one in this context, how is this best consistent with the requirements about what is best in one as set by egalitarian universalist morality, and are there any corresponding rights to the relations of particularist morality? These questions will thus involve the issue of the compatibility of particularist morality and universalist morality in their respective relations to capacity-fulfillment.

The questions are also pressing for another reason. It has been contended, echoing one phase of Nietzsche's thought, that humans can achieve "perfection" while harming other persons and being cruel to them and even being "consumed by hatred." The ground presented for this bizarre thesis is that persons may find "intrinsic value in actions outrageous to others" and may exercise rationality therein.[27] So there remains the question of whether the preferential position of love and friendship among interpersonal relations can be vindicated not only against egalitarian universalist morality but also against particularist moralities that have contents diametrically opposed to love and friendship.

To deal with these questions, we must note the fuller contexts of self-fulfillment as capacity-fulfillment. In one context, that of universalist morality, persons stand to one another in relations that require impartial fulfillment of one another's equal rights. In another context, that of personalist morality, which is both limited and advanced by universalist morality, persons are pursuers of their own purposes, including their self-development. Now in a third context, that of particularist morality, persons are members of smaller groups to whose fellow-members they owe special loyalty and devotion. Persons can fulfill themselves in each of these moralities by recognizing and coordinating their respective requirements. We have seen, for example, how personalist morality must refrain from violating universalist morality (3.7; 4.5). In particularist morality persons can fulfill themselves by recognizing and effectuating their special obligations to help foster the important values of the smaller groups to which they belong. One fulfills oneself through one's communal or associative identification with one's family, one's friends, one's college or coworkers, one's country, and other restricted groups. In solidifying one's place in such groups with their values, one helps also to make the best of oneself. But it is essential to examine whether and how much particularist morality is compatible with universalist morality. Just as universalist morality was seen to clash in certain ways with personalist morality, so it may also seem now with particularist morality.

To deal with this question, we must note that the PGC, as the universalist moral principle of human rights, has two kinds of applications: direct and indirect. In the direct applications, its requirements are imposed in the first instance on the actions of individuals: they must act in accord with the rights of their recipients to freedom and well-being. In the indirect application, on the other hand, the PGC's requirements are imposed in the first instance on the rules of social institutions: to be morally justified they must express or protect persons' equal freedom and well-being. The requirements of these rules are then in turn imposed on the actions of individuals. Thus the actions of a baseball umpire who declares a batter out or a judge who sentences a criminal to prison are morally justified even though they contravene the persons' freedom and well-being, because they operate according to rules, respectively, that have been freely accepted by the participants or that protect all persons' rights to basic well-being. Both applications of the PGC, the indirect as well as the direct, involve further epistemic uses of the capacity of reason and hence further components of capacity-fulfillment.

Now the particularist, preferential status of familial devotion is justified in the indirect application of the PGC. For a marital couple is a kind of voluntary association or grouping that, like other voluntary associations, is justified by the universal right to freedom. But, unlike baseball teams and other voluntary associations, it is formed, as reflecting the partners' mutual love, for purposes of deeply intimate union and extensive mutual concern and support for the participants, purposes that enhance the partners' general abilities of agency and thus contribute to their capacity-fulfillment. Such couples are families, and with their children they are simply larger families, which are also characterized by the parents' special love, concern, and support for their children. These particularist purposes for which families are formed justify the preferential status whereby their members give priority to one another's interests. Although the children have not themselves voluntarily participated in setting up the family, their special concern for their parents and siblings is appropriately viewed as derivative, both morally and psychologically, from the parents' special concern both for one another and for each of their children and, in this way, for the family as a whole.

Thus we have here a reason-based justification of particularist morality through universalist morality. The justification may be summarized in three steps. First, the universalist moral principle of human rights, in its freedom component, justifies the general moral subprinciple that voluntary associations, as defined above, may be established. Second, this subprinciple justifies the formation of families with their special purposes. Third, these purposes, in turn, justify the particularistic, preferential concern that family members have for one another's interests. Thus, through the universal right to freedom, persons have rights to form families and to have the concomitant preferential concerns. This justification does not extend to violations of other persons' rights as upheld by universalist morality, and it also prohibits the nepotism whereby a family member who holds an official position, such as judge or teacher, uses it to favor another family member by giving him a lighter sentence or a higher grade than the rules of his position require. For in such cases to act against the impartiality required by the respective rules is to violate the moral rights of other persons as upheld by universalist morality.

The special preferential purposes embodied in the love of marital couples for one another and for their children reflect fulfillments both of aspirations and of capacities. In producing offspring the parents fulfill their aspirations to give palpable expression and continuity to their mutual love. They make the best of themselves by fulfilling their capacities for such genuine and effective love.

We must here take note of the objection presented above that hatred and cruelty are compatible with human "perfection." If this thesis is correct, it casts doubt on my implicit claim that what is best in the context of personal relationships as part of capacity-fulfillment is love and friendship, not hatred and cruelty. Since the purposes of love and hatred are mutually opposed, a direct invocation of the Purposive Ranking Thesis will not yield a determinate result about which is better. The superiority of love and friendship emerges instead from the justificatory framework of universalist morality with its foundation in the epistemic capacity of reason and consequent mutuality of rights. It is because hatred and cruelty are antithetical to universalist morality's positive concern for the equal freedom and well-being of all persons that hatred and cruelty cannot be parts of what is best in human selves, and hence cannot be parts of capacity-fulfillment. On the other hand, the purposes implicit in love and friendship, because they further the purposes of universalist morality, do reflect what is best in the self in the context of personal relationships; they are therefore intrinsic parts of self-fulfillment as capacity-fulfillment. The personal, emotional capacity that motivates these relationships is, of course, distinct from the rational capacity that serves both to justify them through the PGC and to trace their impacts on other parts of the participants' lives. The argument for the PGC is not intended to remove or subordinate the felt compellingness of these aspirations, if for no other reason than that psychological motivation is distinct from rational justification.

The justification I have given for familial preferences also applies to friendship and love, and, by natural extensions, to wider communities. The relationships of family, love, and friendship, at their best, are marked by freedom or voluntariness of commitment and caring and the great strength of the desire for the other person's good for her own sake. The emphasis on freedom is not antithetical to the recognition of the eminent value of such relationships in a good life, but it points rather to the selectivity or choice as well as the spontaneity that enter into the focus on the persons whom one loves. The selectivity of the relationships makes them prime examples of the capacity-fulfillment whereby one achieves the best that it is in one to become. This best also fits closely the pattern whereby aspiration-fulfillment was seen to require not an "internal" concentration on the satisfaction of one's own desires but rather an "external" concentration on the objects of the desires (2.4).

Doubt may be felt about the need for the kind of argument I have just given. Aren't the particularist preferential values of love, family, and friendship obvious enough without having to be justified through universalist morality?[28] There are at least two replies. First, the argument serves to bring out the essential unity and coherence of moral rightness. To maintain particularist and universalist moralities as two entirely independent sets of norms would leave open the questions of how each can be justified and of how conflicts between them can be resolved. Second, since, as we have seen, there are morally wrong as well as morally right kinds of particularist moralities, the subjecting of particularism to justificatory scrutiny by universalist morality serves to ascertain which modes of particularism are morally right and which wrong.

This conciliation of universalism and particularism may be criticized on the somewhat traditional ground (upheld, for example, by Plato and Rousseau) that families' particularistic concerns exert a divisive influence on the wider society, leading them to ignore the vital needs and indeed the rights of other persons, concern for which is central to universalist morality.[29] While this is indeed a danger, giving priority to the interests of one's spouse and children need not prevent one from being concerned also with the needs and indeed the rights of other persons. Priority does not entail exclusivity, save in such dire and exceptional circumstances as where one can rescue only one of two or more drowning persons, and one of them is one's own child. When the needs in question are extensive and recurrent, and especially when they have sociological roots, provision for them requires state rather than individual action, and family members are rightly called upon through taxation and other means to support such action. But none of this is antithetical to the universalist principle's justification of having primary concern for the members of one's own family.

A related objection may take the following form. The demands of universalist morality are categorically obligatory because rationally mandatory. But I seem to be saying that these stringent demands may be overridden whenever someone has sufficiently strong personal likes for

---

[28] For this objection, see Bernard Williams, *Moral Luck* (Cambridge: Cambridge University Press, 1981), p. 18; Andrew Oldenquist, "Loyalties," *Journal of Philosophy* 79 (April 1982): 186–87.

[29] See Plato, *Republic*, 5. 462Aff.; Rousseau, *Emile*, Book 5; *Social Contract*, Book 3, chap. 15. For a good discussion of this and related points, see Susan Moller Okin, *Women and Western Political Thought* (Princeton: Princeton University Press, 1979), chaps. 2, 8. See also the discussion of "amoral familism" in Edward G. Banfield, *The Moral Basis of a Backward Society* (New York: Free Press, 1958), chap. 5.

friends and other close ties. Such overriding, however, would wreak havoc with justice and other impartial moral requirements. The answer to this objection must recur to the argument against nepotism presented above. In addition, whenever objects of distribution (such as academic grades, prison sentences, and so forth) are sufficiently important, their distribution should be determined by general official or institutional rules that prescribe corresponding rights and duties, and these set limits to justified, particularistically preferential actions.

Let us now look further at love, with its special preferential particularist requirements. The "love" that was referred to above in the examples of Bovary, Karenina, and Hurstwood (2.1), although it involved intense, deep desires to be unified with the beloved, was nonetheless defective because it lacked the external concentration on the objects of its aspirations. The respective love-seekers were so obsessed with the gratification of their own desires that they gave little or no thought to the desires or needs of their respective love-objects (this requires qualification in the much more complex case of Karenina); they did not wish them well for their beloveds' own sakes. Their capacity to love was stunted; the love-seekers did not make the best of themselves because they were too inadequately aware of the external orientation that genuine love requires.

There is a further factor in the inadequacy of such love-relationships. Because the love-seekers were so obsessed with self-gratification, they did not reflect back on themselves with regard to their own possession of qualities that would make them worthy of their beloveds' love. This was especially true of Bovary and Hurstwood: they were too little concerned with making the best of themselves as would-be recipients of the others' love. These considerations have an important bearing on the failure of such persons to achieve either aspiration-fulfillment or capacity-fulfillment.

At its best, love is a deep desire to be unified with the beloved; it includes intense pleasure both in the other's company and in the hope for its continuation and perpetuation. It is strongly concerned with the other's happiness; it is wishing of good for her for her own sake, in a way that goes far beyond general benevolence, for it includes a special feeling of responsibility for the other's fate as linked with your own. In loving, you care for the other person and effectively consider her point of view. The capacity for such love is one of the best of human qualities, and its fulfillment conduces powerfully to achieving the best that it is in one to become.

Love contributes in two ways to capacity-fulfillment, one from the standpoint of one's being the lover, the agent or giver of love; the other from the standpoint of one's being the beloved, the recipient of love. As a giver of love you ennoble yourself, for you focus on the good of a special other for whom you especially wish goodness of life. In seeking to benefit that other you also benefit yourself, for you bring to bear an altruistic capacity that moves in the same direction as the securing of rights but goes far beyond it because of the extent and intensity of your feelings toward your beloved. Correspondingly, as the recipient of love you are made to feel that you are worthy of love, and this not only bolsters your self-esteem but also intensifies your own capacity to love. It is in this context of mutuality that the sexual capacity finds much of its fulfillment.

It must be emphasized that the external orientation required for love does not mean that in focusing on your beloved's good for the latter's sake you must sacrifice your own. Love does not require the extreme kind of altruism parallel to the "moral saints" considered above (3.5). Instead, it corresponds to the moderate altruism upheld by the PGC. Just as that principle requires that you act in accord with the rights of your recipients as well as of yourself, so love requires not that you surrender all concern for your own good but rather that you love the other person as well as yourself. Far from destroying or minimizing yourself, the love relation enriches the lover as well as the beloved by fulfilling one of the best of your moral capacities. In this way the lover maintains her own integrity while also respecting that of her beloved.

The partial analysis of love in terms of capacity-fulfillment may be questioned on the ground that it derogates from the unconditional nature of love. Since capacity-fulfillment involves making the best of oneself, this may be thought to entail that when you love someone you operate according to criteria of optimal development which you impose on someone you potentially love as tests of that person's fitness to be loved. This would suggest a kind of calculatingness that is antithetical to the warmth and the fierce devotion of genuine love. In such a case you would still wish her well for her own sake, but only because she has qualities that correspond to what is best in yourself.[30] So love as capacity-fulfillment would impose conditions about her fitness to be the object of your love.

But can love be unconditional in the sense that the beloved fulfills no conditions at all? Surely, if we are talking about personal romantic erotic love, she must be human to begin with. But also surely one does not love all humans indiscriminately. There is indeed a love of all humankind, what the Greeks called *philanthropia*. But this is not the erotic romantic personal love that singles out one individual as the object of one's ardor. It is also true that you may not be able to enumerate the

---

[30] For extensive discussion of this issue, see Aristotle, *Nicomachean Ethics*, 9. 4–8.

various particular mental and/or physical qualities that make you love her, or that you love in her. ("Let me count the ways"). Nevertheless, it seems clear that there are such qualities; love does not arise or exist in a vacuum. "It is a fact that much erotic attachment, perhaps most of it, is not directed to an individual in the proper sense of the word—to the integral and irreplaceable existent that bears that person's name—but to a complex of qualities, answering to the lover's sense of beauty, that he locates for a time truly or falsely in that person."[31] Let us call this *quality-centered love*. Such love can be a part of capacity-fulfillment, because in loving the qualities in her that answer to your sense of beauty you make the best of yourself as having that sense and as the individual who personifies it.

Can such love be unconditional? A temporal distinction should be drawn here. In the time before you came to love her (what is sometimes referred to as "falling in love"), your love does not exist apart from the qualities in her that make you love her. But once you do love her, your love may well be unconditional: you wish her well for her own sake and want to possess her as such, while setting no requirements abut her continuing to have the qualities that led you to fall in love with her in the first place. The requirements, if any, are now on you: to feel and act toward her with care, tenderness, compassion, empathy, understanding, constancy of affection, and tolerance of her faults. Such features are not, of course, antithetical to the sexual desire, action, and companionship that are among the manifestations of your love.

Such unconditionalness of love sets a very high standard. It is analogous to the love that a parent has for his or her child, where the child's specific merits or demerits have no bearing on the parent's continued love.[32] But whether or not existing love-relationships measure up to this standard, it is not antithetical to love's being an important part of capacity-fulfillment.[33]

These considerations may perhaps be further clarified as follows: Love, like action, has an intrinsic normative component. What you love seems to you to be good, to have value, as meriting being loved. In loving her, in wishing her good for her own sake, you recognize and reinforce the goodness you see in her. Indeed, you wish the best for her.

[31] Gregory Vlastos, *Platonic Studies* (Princeton: Princeton University Press, 1981), p. 28.

[32] See Gregory Vlastos, "Justice and Equality," in R. B. Brandt, ed., *Social Justice* (Englewood Cliffs, N.J.: Prentice-Hall, 1962), pp. 43–45. Vlastos also holds that such unconditionalness also characterizes "our political community" with its egalitarian constitutional protection of citizenship rights (ibid., pp. 45ff.).

[33] For a critique of unconditional love from a feminist standpoint, see Sarah Lucia Hoagland, "Some Thoughts About Caring," in Claudia Card, ed., *Feminist Ethics* (Lawrence, Kansas: University Press of Kansas, 1991), pp. 257–59.

To the extent that your wishing for her has this superlative quality, your capacity to love takes on a corresponding superlativeness; the content of your love reflects back on you, and in this way your love contributes to achieving the best that it is in you to become.

The conditions on which your love is based raise considerations about yourself that go back to the involvement of the self that we noted in aspiration-fulfillment (2.1). Your love, like your aspirations, reflects features of yourself, actual or desired. As philosophers from Plato's *Symposium* on have recognized, love has many varieties that correspond to the varieties of persons, and these in turn are reflected in the conditions or criteria on which your love for your beloved is based. If, for example, you have low self-esteem, the person to whom you direct your love may well reflect this by having characteristics that are inferior to what you might otherwise value. You may value physical beauty more than intelligence or soundness of character or equableness of temperament, because her physical beauty may appeal more to your immaturity then would other, worthier qualities. There is a kind of self-alienation here: you lack effective contact with more valuable possibilities that you might otherwise achieve (see 4.3). Moreover, as in Freud's "compulsion to repeat," you may find it impossible to learn your lesson from one relationship to the next because your own immature impulses or control by your "pleasure principle" leave you powerless to change.[34] So here your operational reason is insufficient in its development or effectiveness, and you lack an important part of freedom. The self-knowledge and emotional control that are needed to overcome such problems are often enormously difficult to acquire; various kinds of psychotherapy are intended to provide help.

In a line that can be traced back at least to Spinoza, such psychotherapy can take the form of enabling you to see how you came to have the emotions you have, what in particular these emotions are in their variety of felt kinds, how they are related to various objects with which you associate them or which you believe to be their causes, how you can improve or change these beliefs in the light of new evidence and thereby redirect your emotions to different objects, how you can motivate and control yourself to accept the new beliefs and to act on them, and so forth.[35] At least part of this repertoire of abilities also involves your

[34] See Sigmund Freud, *Beyond the Pleasure Principle*, trans. James Strachey (London: Hogarth Press, 1950), pp. 19–26. See also Fenichel, *The Psychoanalytic Theory of Neurosis*, pp. 120–21, 541–46.

[35] See Spinoza, *Ethics*, Part V, Prop. 2. For an excellent discussion, see Edwin Curley, *Behind the Geometrical Method: A Reading of Spinoza's Ethics* (Princeton: Princeton University Press, 1988), pp. 128–35. Also relevant here is William James's famous analysis of habit: *Principles of Psychology* (New York: Dover Publications, 1950), vol. 1, chap. 8. For some of the variety of recent psychotherapeutic analyses and approaches, see Heinz Kohut,

relations to other persons: understanding and at least in part empathizing with their own emotions and motivations, being aware of their impacts on yourself, and reacting to them in ways that reinforce your own self-understanding and self-control. These abilities help you to make the best of yourself and they contribute both to personalist morality and to particularist morality.

If we pass over the various deficiencies of love and look at the love that meets the standards of the best considered above, there arises the question of whether persons have rights to such love as they do to familial relations and preferences. They do have the negative rights associated with the right to freedom. But consider the following objection about a positive right to receive love, based on the grounding of human rights in the needs of agency: in order to be successful agents, persons have a great need for love and indeed for a loving spouse. Hence, on the aforementioned ground, persons have claim-rights to receive love and to have a loving spouse.[36] But this is absurd.

This objection seems to construe the claim-right in question as a legal one, so that it trades on the contrast between the external or 'objective' mandates of law and the internal feelings of love and intimacy. But if the right is interpreted as a moral one, having a moral justification, the picture is more complex. For one thing, on some interpretations of 'love' the objection can be denied; love as a deeply spiritual rapport and commitment, while highly valuable, is not a necessary condition of successful action, although it can be very helpful. On the other hand, love as a protective, nurturing parental feeling and corresponding conduct may well be a necessary condition for the growth of children into successful agency, and at least some modicum of this is a right of each child, although its legal enforceability raises many problems. Nevertheless, the state has an appropriate concern to prevent the kind of neglect that signals the absence of such effective love. Even with regard to adults, persons have a right to an effective appreciation for their human dignity, and a corresponding right not to be subjected to the kinds of contempt

---

How Does Analysis Cure? (Chicago: University of Chicago Press, 1984); James E. Maddux, ed., *Self-Efficacy, Adaption, and Adjustment: Theory, Research, and Application* (New York: Plenum Press, 1995); Robert J. Sternberg, *The Triangle of Love* (New York: Basic Books, 1988); Fritz Heider, *The Psychology of Interpersonal Relations* (New York: John Wiley, 1958); Howard Gardner, *Frames of Mind*, chap. 10; Daniel Goleman, *Emotional Intelligence* (New York: Bantam Books, 1995); W. Robert Nay, *Behavioral Intervention: Contemporary Approaches* (New York: Gardner Press, 1976).

[36] For this objection, see Jon Elster, "Is There (or Should There Be) a Right to Work?," in Amy Gutmann, ed., *Democracy and the Welfare State* (Princeton: Princeton University Press, 1988), pp. 62, 74; David Braybrooke, *Meeting Needs* (Princeton: Princeton University Press, 1988), pp. 48, 135.

or blazing hatred that signals the absence of such appreciation. None of this, however, entails the positive legal claim-right to a loving spouse, because, among other things, the condition in question is too deeply spiritual and personal to be an object of legislation (see also 5.7).

The context of family, friendship, and love brings out in an especially poignant form the fallibilism involved in the operational aspect of reason, as it is applied in making generalizations in this area of particularist morality. Families as they actually exist may vary greatly in the kinds and degrees of love and support they provide for their members. Love and friendship may go sour, partly because they may be based on superficial or unworthy features of the persons involved. The applications of reason in this context must take sober account of these empirical possibilities; the ideal must not be confused with the actual. Nevertheless, family, love, and friendship at their best can make powerful contributions to self-fulfillment; and this best provides a worthy target at which to aim.

4.8. PARTICULARIST MORALITY: COMMUNITY, COUNTRY, CULTURE

Particularist morality extends beyond the strongly interpersonal affectional relations of family, friendship, and romantic love. It also involves loyalties to broader groups ranging from neighborhoods to cities and whole countries. Several questions arise here: Can such particularist loyalties be justified in view of the overriding obligatoriness of the universalist morality of equal human rights? If so, how does the justification proceed? A related question concerns the cultural pluralism that was considered above in connection with the diversities of humanist cultures (4.5): How should this pluralism be related to both universalist and particularist moralities? All these questions will be considered here primarily for their bearing on capacity-fulfillment.

To begin with, we must note that a sense of belonging, of being part of a larger nurturing whole, is a valuable component of additive well-being and self-fulfillment. To be a member of a supportive community or country can give one a rootedness and protection that overcome the effects of alienation and solitude. One may thereby identify oneself not only with one's family but also with larger cultural groupings of neighborhood as well as of race, class, gender, ethnicity, nationality, religion, occupation, and other partly interpenetrating variables. All such memberships can be beneficial to the self, giving it a concrete base from which to develop its best capacities.

In order to be justified, however, these loyalties must be in accord with the requirements of the universalist principle of human rights. This accordance must take not only the negative form of refraining from interfering with other persons' freedom and well-being; it must also take the positive form of helping other persons to secure their freedom and well-being insofar as they cannot do so by their own efforts. While various cautions must be observed here, the particularistic groupings to which persons may have specific loyalties must also recognize the overriding importance of universal human rights, economic and social as well as political and civil, and they must be prepared to help other persons and groups to fulfill these rights insofar as they cannot do so by their own efforts. This help will take various forms, from supplying food or rescuing from tyrannical regimes to enabling persons to develop their own productive and political capacities.

It is pertinent here to indicate how the justification of particularist loyalty to one's country differs from the justification presented above for particularist loyalty to one's family and close friends. The latter justification proceeded through the particularist purposes of love and mutual concern and support for which families as voluntary associations are formed. The justification was thus based upon the freedom component of the PGC. But there is a crucial respect in which one's country is not a voluntary association adherence to whose rules is at the option of its members. The respect in question is that one's country, to be morally legitimate and hence deserving of support, must be at least a "minimal state," which is characterized by impartial enforcement of the criminal law and thus equal protection of the freedom and basic well-being of all the inhabitants. The minimal state, then, secures the equal rights to freedom and basic well-being of all persons within its territory and it enforces the mandatory nonviolation of these rights on the part of all such persons. Thus the minimal state with its criminal law is justified by the universalist principle of equal human rights. It is the nonoptionality of observing the criminal law's protections of basic rights and the minimal state's arrangements for its enforcement that most specifically differentiates the state from voluntary associations.

There is a question whether a minimal state will provide the equal protection just referred to unless it is also a constitutional democracy, in that it protects the equal civil liberties of each of its members and allows these to be used in the political processes of determining which persons are to have legislative and executive authority, including but not limited to the specification and enforcement of the criminal law (see 3.6). The civil liberties are vital parts of the overall freedom and additive well-being that are necessary conditions of generally successful actions to which all persons have equal rights, and which are thus important components of capacity-fulfillment. The lack of these liberties severely affects

CAPACITY-FULLFILLMENT, GOOD LIFE

persons' equal dignity and self-esteem; moreover, without them persons are drastically limited in coping with the sociopolitical arrangements that circumscribe their pursuits of their purposes. Thus the democratic state is also justified by the universal principle of human rights through its components of freedom and additive well-being, which bear on the equal protection of the civil liberties.

A further aspect of this justification is that membership in a democratic state can be active through persons' use of their civil liberties, as against the predominantly passive membership that the minimal state provides. Such active membership is an important part of the rights of agency, which are central to capacity-fulfillment, and whose protection is the basis of human rights, because it helps each person to be a self-controlling, self-developing agent who can relate to other persons as a reasonable self, on a basis of mutual respect and cooperation, in contrast to being a dependent, passive recipient of the agency of others.

Given these universalist justifications of the minimal and democratic state, the state's protection of basic and other rights serves, in turn, to justify the particularistic allegiance of its members to its own flourishing in spheres ranging from payment of taxes to military support for repelling unjust aggression. The justification may be summarized in three steps, parallel to the one presented above for familial preferences. First, the universalist principle of human rights, in its component of basic well-being, justifies the general moral subprinciple that minimal states, each operating within a particular territory, may be established. Second, this subprinciple justifies that the state provides equal protection of the basic well-being of all persons within its particular territory. Third, this protection, in turn, justifies the particularistic, preferential concern that each of the state's members has for its particular interests, in recognition of the protection that he or she receives from the state. Thus, through the universal right to basic well-being, each person has a right to belong to a minimal state and to have special concern for its interests. To this extent, nationalism is justified, concomitant with its protection of human rights.

The territorial circumscription of states and their laws is not, then, antithetical to their being justified by the universal principle that all persons' rights to freedom and basic well-being must be equally and impartially secured.[37] That the minimal state secures rights only for persons living within its territory is a practical limitation deriving from the fact

[37] See the discussion of the "particularist requirement" in A. John Simmons, *Moral Principles and Political Obligation* (Princeton: Princeton University Press, 1979), pp. 31ff. I have discussed such requirements in Gewirth, *Human Rights: Essays on Justification and Applications* (Chicago: University of Chicago Press, 1982), pp. 248–50.

that the state's functions must operate in relation to persons who are physically present in a specific physical area. The development of international law, with its provisions for the protection of human rights, provides an important mitigation of this limitation. But the universal principle also justifies that there be a multiplicity of such states so that all persons' rights to agency and capacity-fulfillment are equally secured.

These considerations also have a direct bearing on the cultural pluralism discussed above (4.5). Like the particularism of loyalty to one's state, the diversities of cultures can have their justified adherents so long as they do not violate human rights. The PGC invalidates the kinds of killing and oppression that occur in some cultures. But all those diverse cultural practices and institutions that do not violate the PGC's essential requirements are morally permitted, and indeed are largely encouraged, to exist. In this way a vast array of freedoms and modes of well-being are shown to be morally legitimate. This tolerance is itself an application of the PGC to cultural pluralism: the differences between cultures are to be respected; one must not try to force all cultures into the mold of some dominant culture, for such forcing would violate the rights to freedom and well-being of the members of the various subcultures.

In this context, cultural pluralism is relevant to the rational moral knowledge of the PGC. Detailed awareness of it, as provided especially by cultural anthropology, but also by other empirical disciplines, including history, shows the many different ways of life pursued in different cultures, including their divergent standards of what is permissible and impermissible. This awareness helps to loosen what might otherwise be unduly dogmatic restrictions on the freedom to follow alternative modes of belief and action. But the restrictions imposed by the human rights to freedom and well-being must remain in force.

It may not always be easy to draw the line between the PGC's mandatory-negative and permissive-affirmative applications to various cultural practices. Especially where the practices are controversial the applications require both detailed empirical scrutiny of the practices in question, including their causal backgrounds and effects, and careful analysis of how the PGC's contents bear on these practices. Examples of such controversial practices include various modes of sexual conduct, including premarital sex and polygamy, as well as diverse economic policies and institutions, ranging from entirely "free" markets to modes of governmental regulation. Less controversial, but still quite salient, are such phenomena as the "drug culture" and other practices that adversely affect the well-being of persons. The PGC upholds modes of life that respect the inherent dignity of human beings as having the capacities for rational agency, including the personal virtues that are reflective of such dignity. I have elsewhere discussed the PGC's applications to the economic sphere.[38]

Certain affirmative applications of the PGC to cultural pluralism bear so heavily on the rights to freedom and well-being that they are more mandatory than permissive. These applications deal not with the ways in which cultural groups may treat their individual members by violating their human rights, but rather with the ways in which diverse cultural groups may themselves be treated by the state or the society at large. At issue here is the well-founded contention that the members of various groups—including, within the United States, African Americans, Native Americans (American Indians), Hispanic Americans, women, and others—are markedly inferior to the members of other, dominant groups in their effective rights to freedom and well-being, power, wealth, and status. The members of such submerged groups are discriminated against by the dominant political, economic, educational, and other salient institutions of the wider society. As a result, the persons in question suffer from serious material disadvantages but also from deep feelings of inferiority, envy, and injustice. What the PGC requires here is that cultural pluralism be affirmatively protected: the right to cultural pluralism is an affirmative as well as a negative right. The needs of the members of various subcultures within the dominant culture must be recognized and steps must be taken toward their fulfillment as important parts of capacity-fulfillment. Such respect for cultural pluralism is among the contents of particularist morality.

This issue may be conceptualized in two different ways, with two different upshots for the moral protection of cultural pluralism. One way is to maintain the PGC's direct focus on individual rights. Insofar as the individual members of the submerged cultural groups suffer violations of their generic rights, action must be taken by the state to remove these violations. In this regard, the specific cultural affiliations of the individuals in question would receive no special consideration, except insofar as this was necessary to correct the violations.

Against this approach it has been argued, however, that the members of many submerged groups are so closely linked together by strong ties of group identity—whether in terms of language, history, religion, tradition, race, class, gender, or other variables—that to deal with them only as individuals apart from this identity would fail to respect an essential part of their personhood. On this view, what must be protected is not only individual rights as such but the rights of groups to maintain their own culture within the larger society. An important facet of this

---

[38] See *The Community of Rights*, chaps. 4–7.

distinction bears on the controversial issue of whether, to receive the benefits of affirmative action policies, individuals must be able to show that they have personally been discriminated against, or whether it is sufficient to show that the individuals are members of various hitherto oppressed groups.

Even here, however, the concept of 'group rights' admits of at least two distinct interpretations. On one, more individualist interpretation, the basis of group rights is in their consequences for the rights of individuals: that individual members of a group achieve effective fulfillment of their rights to freedom and well-being requires that the group to which they belong be protected in maintaining its cultural heritage of language, customs, traditions, and so forth. Only so will the autonomy and dignity of the individual members of the group be respected. On another, more collectivist, communitarian, or even organicist interpretation, the group's maintenance of its cultural identity is intrinsically valuable, among other reasons because certain communal goods cannot be parcelled out among the distinct individuals who compose the group but can be had and enjoyed only collectively.

The questions whether it makes sense to talk of 'group rights,' whether they may be classed among human rights, and whether they are reducible to individual rights have been much debated.[39] It is not necessary, however, to take a position on these questions in order to note that the PGC requires emphatic recognition that individuals as members of various suppressed groups have equal rights to freedom and well-being. These rights include acceptance, toleration, and support for diverse cultures so long as these do not transgress the PGC's requirements. So this part of the particularist morality of cultural pluralism is likewise justified by universalist morality.

It is also in this context that the movement for "multicultural education" must be accredited. The promotion of multicultural education is

[39] See Vernon Van Dyke, "The Individual, the State, and Ethnic Communities in Political Theory," in *Human Rights and American Foreign Policy*, ed. D. P. Kommers and G. D. Loescher (Notre Dame, Ind.: University of Notre Dame Press, 1979), pp. 36–62; Jeremy Waldron, "Can Communal Goods be Human Rights?," in Waldron, *Liberal Rights* (Cambridge: Cambridge University Press, 1993), pp. 339–69; Jack Donnelly, *Universal Human Rights in Theory and Practice* (Ithaca, N.Y.: Cornell University Press, 1989), chap. 8. See also Joseph Raz, "Right-Based Moralities," in *Theories of Rights*, ed. Jeremy Waldron (Oxford: Oxford University Press, 1984), pp. 182–200; Will Kymlicka, *Multicultural Citizenship* (Oxford: Clarendon Press, 1995); I. Shapiro and W. Kymlicka, eds., *Nomos XXXIX: Ethnicity and Group Rights* (New York: New York University Press, 1997). The question of the reducibility of "group" rights to individual rights also reflects the debate over "methodological individualism": whether and in what way the facts about social wholes can be reduced to facts about their individual members. On this issue, see the essays collected in *Modes of Individualism and Collectivism*, ed. John O'Neill (London: Heinemann, 1973), parts 3 and 4.

motivated both by directly intellectual concerns and by moral concerns. Knowledge of other cultures serves not only to increase students' awareness of alternative histories and ways of life but also to foster respect for other cultures and the human individuals and groups that comprise them. Such respect falls under the PGC's requirement of equal human rights to freedom and well-being.

There may be conflicts between the intellectual and the moral goals. The diverse epistemic criteria of various cultures raise questions about the intellectual excellence whose promotion must be a prime goal of education. Certain forms of the moral demand for equality may come into opposition with this goal.[40] This difficulty is not, however, insurmountable; but it points up the need for further evaluation of cultural pluralism in the light of rational moral knowledge.

From the above considerations, then, there emerge two general normative relations between cultural pluralism and the moral universalism of human rights. Negatively, moral universalism sets the outer limits of the legitimacy of the various practices of cultural pluralism. Affirmatively, within these limits moral universalism encourages and upholds the diverse practices of cultural pluralism, the differences between human beings with regard to values and ways of life, as diverse paths to capacity-fulfillment.

The diversities of humanist cultures reflected in different artistic products are also to be fitted into these broad protections of cultural pluralism. The identities of persons, and with them their opportunities for capacity-fulfillment, are affected by the appreciative recognition accorded their works of literature, music, and visual arts. Criteria of excellence, including Matthew Arnold's "best that has been thought and said in the world," are indeed relevant here; but one must also be aware of the diverse criteria of excellence and the ways in which the dominant culture may submerge and disparage modes of excellence with which it may not be familiar, especially when they derive from hitherto suppressed groups. Besides broad toleration, the universal principle of human rights may also have more restrictive implications for certain humanist cultural products. These may apply within the dominant Western culture itself. The shocking displays of lustfully injurious conduct found in de Sade, for example, as well as the pornography that depicts the victimization and dehumanization of women, raise serious issues of their impact on the human rights of the persons affected. It must be recognized that serious presentations of human lust and cruelty are found in respected works from the Hebrew Bible and the myth of Gyges in

---

[40] I have discussed some of these issues in "Human Rights and Academic Freedom," in *Morality, Responsibility, and the University: Studies in Academic Ethics*, ed. Steven M. Cahn (Philadelphia: Temple University Press, 1990), pp. 8–31.

Plato's *Republic* to Freud's descriptions of the id and other psychoanalytic writings of the twentieth century. But there is a difference between
such presentations and the exacerbated, graphic clamors found in de
Sade and others. There should probably not be suppression here; but in
any case the principle of human rights cannot be indifferent to the impacts of certain kinds of artistic products on the equal freedom and well-
being of persons and groups who may suffer significant harm from them.

Regardless of one's judgment on this specific vexed issue, two main
points have emerged from this section and the preceding one. First, the
requirements of justified personalist and particularist moralities are not
only compatible with universalist morality but are derivable from it, with
due allowance for the probabilism of the operational aspect of reason.
Second, the various phases of such moralities make important contributions to capacity-fulfillment.

CHAPTER 5

Ultimate Values, Rights, and Reason

5.1. HUMAN DIGNITY AS THE BASIS OF RIGHTS

In the previous chapter I have discussed virtues of personalist and particularist moralities as providing the contents of capacity-fulfillment construed as making the best of oneself. It may be thought that if this superlativeness has been shown to be justified in the spheres of these moralities as well as of universalist morality, as I have tried to do, our task is finished. But at least two questions remain. The first returns us to the connection of capacity-fulfillment with aspiration-fulfillment. Even if capacity-fulfillment consists in attaining the high standards and indeed the perfection that I have discussed, why should persons want to attain it? Why should they be distracted from the comforts of everyday life to take on the challenges posed by achieving a "best" that may demand enormous effort as well as risk on their part?

The answer to this question is that there is ultimately no disconnection between capacity-fulfillment and aspiration-fulfillment. What one aspires to may already represent an ideal for one's full development, and while this is initially grounded in one's actual desires, the failings of those desires can lead one to try to correct them by connecting them to objective parts of the self that have their own standards of excellence and satisfaction. Through all this it must be kept in mind that the criteria of "best" are in important respects relative to the varying capacities of different persons (3.2). The transition from aspiration-fulfillment to capacity-fulfillment is a transition not only from Peter drunk to Peter sober, but also to a Peter who is more aware of the values that are implicit in his strivings and of their constitutive contents. By this sequence, means are made more amenable to desired ends, but in addition the ends themselves undergo a process of learning whereby the criteria that enter into their adoption are derived from a deeper understanding of one's inherent capacities and of the values they can attain at their best. I shall have more to say about this subsequently.

A second remaining question about capacity-fulfillment bears on the objective values that are implicit in the analyses I have given of its various phases. Even if one makes the best of oneself, why is that much of a value? This question bears not on the relation of capacity-fulfillment to one's desires or motivations but rather on its objective validity or overall worth. The "best of oneself" is relative to the self: whatever best it may contain is limited by whatever value the self may embody. But what if this self, viewed objectively, is so mediocre or even evil that its best does not rank high in terms of objective value?

To put it somewhat more specifically: I have derived human rights from the needs of human agency through an argument conducted by reason as the best of human veridical capacities. But are those needs sufficiently important or valuable to serve as an adequate ground for determining what is "best"? The idea underlying this question is that even if agency is the appropriate context for ascertaining this best, there may still be a further requirement: that agency itself be critically evaluated with regard to whether the values I have attributed to capacity-fulfillment on the basis of agency are sufficiently strong that they do not require any validation of their own. After all, what is so great about human agency? I have previously held that agency is the universal context of moral and all other practical precepts (3.4). But this still leaves open the question of whether agency itself is so valuable that it provides a definitive foundation or stopping-point of justification. Or is it the case, instead, that agency requires a grounding in some superior value that would justify the value I have implicitly attributed to agency itself?

A traditional answer to this quest for ultimate justification appeals to the idea of God. The point of this appeal is that human agency is worth supporting because all humans are children of God and hence share to some degree in God's inherent value or goodness. This answer, however, incurs familiar difficulties (see also 5.2).

A different answer, perhaps not so traditional but also pervasively upheld, may be provided by the idea of human dignity. It is because all human beings have dignity that the needs of their agency are eminently worth fulfilling; hence, it is human dignity that provides the ultimate basis of human rights and of the value of self-fulfillment as capacity-fulfillment. Indeed, the close connection between human dignity and human rights has often been remarked. To take a notable example, the Universal Declaration of Human Rights promulgated by the United Nations in 1948 says in its first article: "All human beings are born free and equal in dignity and rights." The monstrous violations of human rights that have disfigured the twentieth century, epitomized by the Nazis' Holocaust and the Stalinist butcheries, have also been attacks against human dignity.

Let us, then, look at human dignity as providing the justification for the value of capacity-fulfillment and human rights. On the view being considered, it is because humans have dignity that they have human rights. This relation is stated explicitly in the preambles to the two international covenants adopted by the United Nations in 1966: "These [human] rights derive from the inherent dignity of the human person."[1] The same relation is emphasized in the Universal Declaration itself when it asserts that "everyone ... is entitled to realization ... of the economic, social and cultural rights indispensable for his dignity," and that these are rights "ensuring ... an existence worthy of human dignity."[2] This grounding of human rights in human dignity can be traced back at least to Kant, who wrote that man "is under obligation to acknowledge, in a practical way, the dignity of humanity in every other man. Hence he is subject to a duty based on the respect which he must show every other man." This duty of respect for human beings because of their dignity entails a correlative right: "Every man has a rightful claim [*rechtmässigen Anspruch*] to respect from his fellow men."[3] Thus it is human dignity that justifies the duty of respect and, with it, human rights.

To understand and evaluate this grounding of human rights, and thus of capacity-fulfillment, in human dignity, we must consider three main questions: First, just what is human dignity? Second, what reasons are there for attributing dignity to all human beings equally? Third, just how does human dignity serve to ground human rights? The attempt to provide adequate answers to these questions requires recognition of some important distinctions.

To get at these distinctions, let us first note a familiar and plausible way of relating human dignity and rights. According to this relation, a person's sense of dignity, of self-worth, is fostered or buttressed when she is in a position to claim rights against other persons. It is the ability or capacity to assert such claims that grounds human dignity. Thus, Joel Feinberg has written: "it is claiming that gives rights their special moral significance. . . . Having rights enables us to 'stand up like men,' to look others in the eye, and to feel in some fundamental way the equal of anyone. . . . What is called 'human dignity' may simply be the recognizable capacity to assert claims. To respect a person, then, or to think of him as possessed of human dignity, simply *is* to think of him as a potential maker of claims."[4]

---

[1] International Covenant on Economic, Social, and Cultural Rights, 1966; International Covenant on Civil and Political Rights, 1966. Both are reprinted in *Basic Documents on Human Rights*, 2d ed., ed. Ian Brownlie (Oxford: Clarendon Press, 1981), pp. 118, 128. See also Declaration on Protection from Torture (p. 35) and Supplementary Convention on the Abolition of Slavery (p. 44).

[2] Universal Declaration of Human Rights, arts. 22, 23 (in Brownlie, ed., *Basic Documents*, p. 25).

[3] Immanuel Kant, *Doctrine of Virtue* (part 2 of *The Metaphysics of Morals*), part 2, chap. 1, sec. 2, para. 38 [Akad. ed., p. 461]; trans. Mary J. Gregor (Cambridge: Cambridge University Press, 1991), p. 255.

[4] Joel Feinberg, "The Nature and Value of Rights," reprinted in his *Rights, Justice, and the Bounds of Liberty* (Princeton: Princeton University Press, 1980), p. 151.

Although this passage may be interpreted in various ways, I shall use it as a means of calling attention to two importantly different concepts of both dignity and rights. First, as to dignity: one concept is, broadly speaking, *empirical*. In this sense, dignity is a characteristic that is often also signified by its corresponding adjective, "dignified"; it is, variously, a kind of gravity or decorum or composure or self-respect or self-confidence together with various good qualities that may justify such attitudes. Thus, we may say of some person, "He behaved with great dignity on that occasion," or "She generally comports herself with dignity." Such dignity is a contingent feature of some human beings as against others; it may be occurrently had, gained, or lost; and, depending on the context, it may or may not have a specifically moral bearing. It is to this empirical concept of dignity that David Hume referred when he emphasized that the "dispute concerning the dignity or meanness of human nature" is to be resolved by taking account of the comparative degrees in which various good or bad qualities are had by different humans.[5] That the passage quoted above from Feinberg also refers to this empirical sense of "dignity" is suggested by his equating dignity with the ability to "stand up like men" and "the recognizable ability to assert claims." Such abilities and capacities are indeed valuable; but, as matters of empirical fact, they are not always had by all human beings, let alone equally.[6] Also, in this sense human dignity is *consequent upon* the having of rights and hence is not the *ground* of rights. For, on this view, one's dignity derives from the ability to make claims, in which the having of rights is said to consist. Hence, this way of relating human dignity and human rights does not meet the condition specified above, according to which rights are grounded in dignity, and not conversely.

Let us now consider a second concept of dignity, which, following one of the United Nations documents cited above, I shall call *inherent*. In this sense, "dignity" signifies a kind of intrinsic worth that belongs equally to all human beings as such , constituted by certain intrinsically valuable aspects of being human. This is a necessary, not a contingent, feature of all humans; it is permanent and unchanging, not transitory or changeable; and, as we shall see, it sets certain limits to how humans may justifiably be treated. When the United Nations Universal Declaration of Human Rights upholds in its preamble "recognition of the inherent dignity and of the equal and inalienable rights of all members of the human family,"[7] it is to this inherent concept of dignity that it appeals.

[5] David Hume, "Of the Dignity or Meanness of Human Nature," in his *Essays, Moral, Political, and Literary* (Indianapolis, Ind.: Liberty Classics, 1985), pp. 80–86.

[6] For an interesting discussion of some important variants in the relation between what I have called "empirical dignity" and the claiming of rights, see Michael J. Meyer, "Dignity, Rights, and Self-Control," *Ethics* 99 (April 1989): 520–34.

[7] Reprinted in Brownlie, *Basic Documents*, p. 21.

This is a concept that sets peculiarly stringent moral requirements. In this sense, dignity is contrasted by Kant with "price."[8] If a thing has a price, then it can be substituted for or replaced by something else of equivalent value, where "value" signifies, as in Thomas Hobbes, a worth that is relative to a persons' desires or opinions. Thus Hobbes recognizes only a certain version of the empirical concept of dignity, which he defines as "the publique worth of a man, which is the value set on him by the Commonwealth."[9] In contrast, inherent dignity cannot be replaced by anything else, and it is not relative to anyone's desires or opinions. It is such inherent dignity that serves as the ground of human rights.

In what, then, does this inherent dignity consist, and just how does it ground human rights? In addition to the relation between dignity and rights considered above, wherein having dignity is the *consequent* of having rights, we must also reject, with a view to our problem, a second relation, wherein having dignity is the *equivalent* of having rights. This relation is suggested in the following passage by Jacques Maritain: "The dignity of the human person? The expression means nothing if it does not signify that by virtue of natural law, the human person has the right to be respected, is the subject of rights, possesses rights."[10] On this view, then, the expression "A has human dignity" simply reduplicates "A has human rights"; to have the dignity just consists in having the rights.

Although this view indicates an important aspect of the relation between dignity and rights, it does not show how human dignity is the *antecedent*, the justificatory basis or ground, of human rights, as against being either their equivalent or their consequent. It is not merely that wherever there are human rights there is human dignity, or that having rights serves to buttress empirical dignity. Even if this is true, the primary relation is that persons have human rights *because* they have inherent human dignity. It is this relation, and its constituent concepts, that we must try to explain and justify.

To move toward this goal, we must note that there are two concepts of rights parallel to the two concepts of dignity. One concept is *empirical* or *positivist*. For some person A to have a right to X in this sense means that there is social recognition and effective legal protection of A's having or doing X. A second concept is normatively moral as based on universalist morality. For A to have a right to X in this sense means that there is normative moral justification for A's being protected in having or doing X, as something that is his personal due or entitlement,

---

[8] Kant, *Foundations of the Metaphysics of Morals*, sec. 2 (Akad ed., pp. 434–35), trans. L. W. Beck (Indianapolis, Ind.: Bobbs-Merrill, 1959), p. 53.

[9] Thomas Hobbes, *Leviathan*, chap. 10.

[10] Jacques Maritain, *The Rights of Man and Natural Law*, trans. D. Anson (New York: Charles Scribner's Sons, 1951), p. 65.

even if such protection is in fact lacking. It is in this sense that we say that all persons have a right to freedom even if some persons, who are legally slaves or subjected to governmentally inflicted torture, are not effectively protected in having the freedom that is the object of this right.

An initial connection between human dignity and human rights, then, is that for each the negation of the empirical mode does not entail the negation of the other, inherent or morally justificatory, mode. That all humans have inherent dignity is not disproved by the fact that some persons behave (or are treated) without empirical dignity, in that they are too raucous or obsequious or servile or lacking in self-control or otherwise "undignified." Similarly, that all persons have human rights is not disproved by the empirical fact that some persons' human rights are violated.

These distinctions also serve to buttress the point emphasized above, that the connection between the claiming of rights and the having of empirical dignity cannot provide the primary basis of human dignity. For, in the inherent sense, human dignity is not a quality that waits for its existence on the empirical fulfillment or claiming of positive legal rights; indeed, it is the ground or antecedent of the rights insofar as they are morally justified, not their consequent.

These points also serve, however, to bring out the difficulties of the questions we are trying to answer here. For a further, especially important similarity between the two pairs of concepts distinguished above is epistemological. It is not especially difficult to find empirical tests for checking whether humans have empirical dignity or socially recognized rights. But it seems to be very difficult (and on some views impossible) to ascertain, or to provide justificatory arguments for the thesis, that all humans equally have inherent dignity: there is an apparent absence of any empirical correlatives for it. Moreover, if inherent human dignity, as the ground of human moral rights, must belong to all humans equally, then it must belong to Hitler and Stalin as well as to Gandhi and Mother Teresa; more generally, it must be a characteristic of criminals as well as saints, of cowards as well as heroes, of fools as well as sages, of mental defectives as well as mentally normal persons, of slaves as well as masters, of subjects as well as lords, of disease-ridden invalids as well as athletes, of drug addicts as well as persons of self-control, of starving proletarians as well as well-fed capitalists, and so forth.[11] There seems, then, to be a

---

[11] On this point, see Kant, *Metaphysics of Morals, Doctrine of Virtue* para. 39: "Nonetheless I cannot deny all respect even to a vicious man as a man . . . even though by his deeds he makes himself unworthy of it" (Akad. ed., p. 463; trans. Mary J. Gregor [Cambridge: Cambridge University Press, 1991], p. 255). See also Thomas E. Hill, Jr., *Dignity and Practical Reason in Kant's Ethical Theory* (Ithaca, N.Y.: Cornell University Press, 1992),

conflict between the high value accorded to inherent dignity and the egalitarian universality of its scope as indiscriminately characteristic of all humans amid their drastically diverse and unequal value. Other values, including life, also characterize all humans; but life is not a normative or possibly differential ideal that can be used to valuationally distinguish some humans from others; nor is it upheld, like dignity, as something to aspire to or strive for. How, then, in view of the vast empirical range of diverse human characteristics, can the ascription of equal inherent dignity to all humans be justified?

We can begin to answer this question if we take note of the ways in which inherent dignity can be empirically instantiated. Let us focus on the related concept of "treating someone with dignity" (where this means to treat her with recognition for her dignity). Negatively, to treat someone with dignity is to exclude certain interrelated kinds of attitudes and actions. Among the excluded attitudes are contempt, blazing hatred that will stop at nothing to inflict injury, discriminatory feelings that totally disregard comparative merits of the person concerned, and so forth. The excluded actions comprise, for example, such cruelties, whether in penal or other contexts, as rape, torture, cutting off of hands, blinding, and so forth. They also include treating persons as if they had only a "price," so that their lives, liberties, or purposive pursuits can be dispensed with through "equivalents" based on political or economic calculations, as in some types of "cost-benefit analysis." Positively, to treat someone with dignity is to accord her certain kinds of consideration; to treat her as an end, not only as a means or an object to be exploited; to treat her with respect for her basic needs, and for herself as worthy of having these needs fulfilled. In this way, as we have seen, the duty to fulfill persons' agency needs would derive from their inherent dignity. More specifically, it would not be difficult to show that the inherent dignity of human beings, because of their intrinsic worth, requires the kinds of protections embodied in the U. S. Bill of Rights and the United Nations Universal Declaration of Human Rights, including within the latter not only political and civil rights but also social and economic rights. All these modes of treatment, negative and positive, are required by the intrinsic worth of human beings in which their inherent dignity consists. But the derivation of rights from dignity must be spelled out if this relation is to be fully understood.

These considerations begin to provide an empirical content for inherent human dignity, for they specify the kinds of empirically ascertainable attitudes and actions that such dignity requires. They also take due

---

pp. 41, 47; Avishai Margalit, *The Decent Society* (Cambridge, Mass.: Harvard University Press, 1996), chaps. 4, 5.

account of the egalitarian universality of inherent dignity for the exclusion of the negative attitudes and actions, and the opposed positive attitudes and treatments, are the moral rights of all humans by virtue of their inherent dignity, regardless of the vast array of empirical differences listed above. At the same time, however, these treatments are not constitutive of inherent human dignity. Humans have such dignity regardless of how they are treated; certain modes of treatment may violate but not remove their dignity. The having of dignity normatively requires certain modes of treatment and prohibits others. Hence, these considerations begin to relate inherent human dignity to human rights, and moral rights to positivist rights, for they show that moral rights can have their effective equivalents in the legal enforcement of certain of the rights. But we are still left with the questions of what is the direct nature of such inherent dignity, what warrant there is for attributing it to all humans equally, and just how it serves to provide the justificatory ground for human rights.

One way of dealing with these questions is to reject any cognitive approach to them and to adopt a kind of emotivist position. Thus, Feinberg says: "'Human worth' itself is best understood to name no property in the way that 'strength' names strength and 'redness' redness. In attributing human worth to everyone, we may be ascribing no property or set of qualities, but rather expressing an attitude—the attitude of respect—toward the humanity in each man's person." This position incurs many of the same difficulties that beset simple emotivist analyses of "good," "right," and other value terms. Since attitudes may vary from person to person and from group to group, the ascription of human worth or dignity would not have the universality that is assumed by the grounding of human rights in human dignity. And if the ascription of dignity to all humans, with its correlative respect, is itself "groundless," as Feinberg also suggests,[12] then no reason can be given that serves to justify the normative necessity that is a basic feature of human rights.

None of this is meant to deny that respect is an attitude and that this attitude is an important requirement for human rights and dignity. But, parallel to our above distinctions between empirical and inherent dignity and between positivist and moral rights, we must also distinguish between two concepts of respect, based directly on their different objects but consequently also on their different contents. Contingent respect consists in a favorable appraisal of variable features of human beings; like the ascription of empirical dignity, it may be justifiably accorded in some cases and withheld in others. Necessary respect, on the other hand, consists in an affirmative, rationally grounded recognition of and regard for

---

[12] Joel Feinberg, *Social Philosophy* (Englewood Cliffs, N.J.: Prentice-Hall, 1973), pp. 94, 93.

a status that all human beings have by virtue of their inherent dignity.[13] It is to such necessary respect that Kant refers when he says that it is "exacted" by human dignity: "man regarded as a person . . . possesses, in other words, a dignity (an absolute inner worth) by which he exacts respect for himself from all other rational beings in the world."[14] But even if such necessary respect is the *ratio cognoscendi* of human dignity, it cannot be its *ratio essendi*. The existence and nature of dignity cannot be constituted by respect; on the contrary, it is because humans have inherent dignity that respect is demanded or required of other persons as the recognition of an antecedently existing worth. This suggests that we must look to the ontological sphere to find human dignity as an inherent, essential characteristic of human beings. But just where should we look?

One famous suggestion, which goes back to the Stoics, is that the universe comprises a moral hierarchy of perfections, in which humans rank just below God. As such, all humans have a certain equal "rank . . . in the universal chain of being";[15] as John Locke put it, they are "Creatures of the same species and rank promiscuously born to the same advantages of Nature, and the use of the same faculties . . . sharing all in one Community of Nature."[16] Human dignity, in such a perspective, is

---

[13] This distinction is indebted to, but is more specific than, Stephen L. Darwall's distinction between "appraisal respect" and "recognition respect," in "Two Kinds of Respect," *Ethics* 88 (October 1977): 36–49. William K. Frankena holds that what he calls "moral consideration respect" (which is close to what I call "necessary respect") is indeterminate with regard to what it morally requires in the treatment of persons: "The principle that we are to respect persons in this sense says only that there are morally right and wrong, good or bad ways of treating and relating to persons, as such or for their own sakes. It does not tell us which ways of treating or relating to them are right or wrong, good or bad." "The Ethics of Respect for Persons," *Philosophical Topics* 14 (fall 1986): 157. This, however, overlooks the kinds of determinate requirements indicated above for "treating someone with dignity." See also the important discussion of "individual human worth" and what it morally requires, by Gregory Vlastos, "Justice and Equality," in *Social Justice*, ed. Richard B. Brandt (Englewood Cliffs, N.J.: Prentice-Hall, 1962), pp. 31–72, at pp. 45–53.

[14] *Doctrine of Virtue*, part 1, book 1, chap. 2, para. 11 (Akad. ed., p. 434–35; Gregor ed., p. 230).

[15] Pico della Mirandola, *Oration on Human Dignity*, trans. Elizabeth L. Forbes, in *The Renaissance Philosophy of Man*, ed. E. Cassirer, P. O. Kristeller, J. H. Randall, Jr. (Chicago: University of Chicago Press, 1948), p. 233. I have rendered Pico's *De hominis dignitate* as "On *Human* Dignity" rather than "On the Dignity *of Man*" because the former is more in keeping with his intentions. It is interesting to note that although Greek and Latin have one word for the generic human being (*anthrōpos, homo*) and a quite different word for the specific male human being (*anēr, vir*), the main modern western languages all have the same word for the generic and the specific (man, *homme, uomo, hombre*, and so forth). German has the generic *Mensch* and the specific *Mann*, but the latter is far closer to *Mensch* than is *Frau*. I have found no explanation for this modern verbal masculinizing of the generic human being.

[16] *Two Treatises of Government*, II, secs. 4, 6.

to be accounted for by this theological-cosmological context, which sets the ontological status of human beings and it consists in or derives from all humans' possession of reason or free will or both.

For various familiar reasons I shall here abstract from this theological-cosmological perspective (despite its immense historical influence). The challenge is to give a purely rational explication or justification of the attribution of equal inherent dignity for all human beings. To this purpose, I shall first focus directly on the alleged connection between human dignity and the possession of reason and free will. At least four objections can be made against this connection. The first three advert to the vast empirical range referred to above. First, since the ability to reason is distributed very unequally among human beings, how can their possession of reason serve to ground or justify the assertion of their *equal* inherent dignity? Second, since both reason and free will can be and are used for bad as well as good purposes, how can humans' possession of them account for the presumed good of human *dignity* or worth? Third, it is to be noted that human dignity is so far viewed not as directly an "objective" or ontological feature or characteristic of human beings but, rather, as supervenient on such features.[17] In this regard, "all humans have inherent dignity" is not a proposition of the same kind as "all humans have reason and free will"; instead, the former is an evaluative statement that is justified on the basis of the latter, descriptive or factual statement. But since supervenience is held to be a contingent relation, in that what supervenes is not entailed or logically necessitated by that on which it supervenes,[18] how is the supervenience of dignity on reason and free will compatible with the alleged *necessity and universality* of inherent human dignity? Fourth, since human dignity is held to be the basis of human rights, which are correlative with duties or "oughts," how does the basing of dignity on *is-statements* about factual characteristics of human beings serve to generate the "oughts" of human dignity and rights?

Despite these objections, I want to suggest that it is in reason and voluntariness or free will as generic features of action that the basis of human dignity is to be found. This involves that dignity is a humanistic characteristic; to find its ground one need not go outside or beyond the nature of human agency itself. The central idea is that just as the needs of agency justify the ascription of human rights (3.4), so it is certain features of agency that serve to ground this justificatory status on the part of the needs of agency and thereby serve as the basis of human dignity. These features of agency ultimately consist in the necessary element

[17] See Feinberg, *Social Philosophy*, p. 90.
[18] See R. M. Hare, *The Language of Morals* (Oxford: Clarendon Press, 1952), pp. 80–89.

of purposiveness that enters into all agency. To be an agent is to have the double capacity to reflect on and control what ends or purposes one sets for oneself and to control one's behavior with a view to attaining these ends. Because of this reflective end-setting, every agent must attribute worth to his purposes. As we have seen (3.4), every agent regards his purposes as good according to whatever criteria enter into his purposes. Hence, he attributes worth to his purposes; he regards them as worth attaining and hence as justifying whatever efforts he makes toward attaining them.

An ineluctable element of agent-estimated worth, then, is involved in the very concept and context of human purposive action. Now there is a direct route from this ascribed worth of the agent's purposes to the worth or dignity of the agent himself. For he is both the general locus of all the particular purposes he wants to attain and also the source of his attribution of worth to them. Because he is this locus and source, he must hold that the worth he attributes to his purposes pertains a fortiori to himself. They are *his* purposes, and they are worth attaining because *he* is worth sustaining and fulfilling, so that he has what for him is a justified sense of his own worth. This attribution of worth to himself derives not only from the goodness he attributes to his particular actions but also from the general purposiveness that characterizes all his actions and himself qua agent. And because of this general context of agency, his attribution of worth also extends to his freedom in controlling his behavior by his unforced choice and to whatever rationality enters into his calculating the means to his ends. For he pursues his purposes not as an uncontrolled reflex response to stimuli, but, rather, because he has chosen them after reflection on alternatives. Even if he does not always reflect, his choice can and does sometimes at least operate in this way. Every human agent, as such, is capable of this. Hence, the agent is, and regards himself as, an entity that, unlike other natural entities, is not, so far as it acts, subject only to external forces of nature; he can and does make his own decisions on the basis of his own reflective understanding. By virtue of these characteristics of his actions, the agent regards himself as having worth or dignity. This attribution of worth must, at least in the first instance, be interpreted neither assertorically nor phenomenologically but, rather, as dialectically necessary, as reflecting a characteristic of human purposive action that every agent must attribute to himself or herself.

This worth or dignity that the agent logically attributes to himself by virtue of the purposiveness of his actions, he must also attribute to all other actual or prospective agents. For their actions have the same general kind of purposiveness that provides the ground for his attribution of dignity to himself. It is not merely that he recognizes that other agents attribute dignity to themselves because of their purposiveness; in addition, he must attribute such dignity to each of them because of their own purposiveness, which is generically similar to his.[19] In this way, the necessary attribution of inherent dignity to all human beings is dialectically established, for, as was indicated above, all humans are actual, prospective, or potential agents.[20]

The further development of this argument shows that every agent logically must hold or accept that she and all other actual or prospective agents have rights to freedom and well-being as the necessary conditions of their action and generally successful action. Since I have presented this argument above (3.4), I shall not repeat it here. The argument indicates how human rights are grounded in human dignity or worth. For it is from the worth that each agent attributes to her purposes and hence, a fortiori, to herself as purposive agent that there necessarily follows the claiming of rights to the necessary conditions of acting in pursuit of those purposes. Since she must acknowledge that the rights are had by all humans equally, this also serves to impose a universalist moral restriction on the purposes she is justified in regarding as worth pursuing, and hence, too, on her ascription of worth or dignity to herself. Thus, although the existence of human rights follows dialectically from the worth or dignity that every agent must attribute to himself, the content of that dignity is in turn morally modified by the universal and equal human rights in which the argument eventuates.

On the present account, the existence of both human dignity and human rights is viewed, not as having an independent ontological status, but, rather, in keeping with the dialectically necessary method, as agent-relative, that is, based on a rational justification that must be accepted by every agent. Since, however, agency or action is the general context of all morality and practice, it follows that the existence of human dignity,

---

[19] The universalization of the agent's dignity-attribution to other agents may be criticized by what I have elsewhere called the "individualizability" and "particularizability" objections. I have set out these objections and shown how they are to be answered in *Reason and Morality*, pp. 115–25. Brian Barry has presented a version of the individualizability objection without noting my fuller refutation of it. See Barry, *Theories of Justice* (Berkeley: University of California Press, 1989), pp. 285–88.

[20] Kant writes: "The ends which a rational being arbitrarily proposes to himself as consequences of his action are material ends and are without exception only relative, for only their relation to a particularly constituted faculty of desire in the subject gives them their worth. And this worth cannot, therefore, afford any universal principles for all rational beings or valid and necessary principles of every volition." *Foundations of the Metaphysics of Morals*, sec. 2 (Akad ed., pp. 427; Beck, pp. 45–46). Kant here overlooks that even though the ends or purposes of particular actions are themselves particular, universality is involved, first, in the fact that all the particular purposes have worth for a single agent, who is therefore their source or locus, and second, that all other agents have the same relation to their respective purposes and the worth they embody.

and with it of human rights, has been shown to be normatively necessary and universal within the whole relevant context.

On the basis of these considerations, I shall now try to show how we are to deal with the four objections presented above against the derivation of human dignity from humans' possession of reason and will. As for the first objection, the unequal abilities of reason among human beings do not refute the argument's conclusion about the equal distribution of human dignity and rights, for two main reasons. First, the primary ground on which every agent logically must hold or accept that he has rights to freedom and well-being is not that he possesses reason or other practical abilities, but rather that he has purposes that he wants to fulfill by acting. For if he had no purposes, he would claim no rights of agency, nor would he act. And this having of purposes is equal and common to all agents, whether wise or foolish. As we have seen, it is this generic purposiveness that underlies the ascription of inherent dignity to all agents.

Second, although it is indeed true that one must use reason to follow the argument (so that in this and other ways the dialectical argument invokes the concept of a rational agent), the use of reason that enters the argument is a minimal deductive and inductive one that is within the reach of all normal human beings. Here, "normal" means having the practical abilities of the generic features of action: the abilities to control one's behavior by one's unforced choice, to have knowledge of relevant circumstances, and to reflect on one's purposes. Where human beings are not normal even in this minimal sense, the attribution of dignity and rights to them must follow what I have elsewhere called the Principle of Proportionality,[21] according to which the having of rights is proportional to the degree to which humans and other entities have the abilities of agency. But this inequality of rights is itself, in turn, based on a more fundamental equality of inherent dignity and human rights, because the unequal extents to which different humans should have the objects of various rights are grounded in an equal concern for the freedom and well-being of all humans. Just as the equality of human dignity and rights is compatible with some humans' being given more food or protection than other humans when the former have a greater need for such objects in order to sustain their basic well-being, so too the lesser freedom allowed to some mentally deficient humans is justified by an equal concern for the basic well-being and dignity of them and of all other humans.[22]

[21] See Alan Gewirth, *Reason and Morality* (Chicago: University of Chicago Press, 1978), pp. 120–28.

[22] For further replies to objections about the equal distribution of human rights, see Gewirth, *Human Rights: Essays on Justification and Applications* (Chicago: University of

We must also note another way of relating human dignity to humans' possession of reason and will. Regardless of the specific extents to which they are developed in different humans, these capacities have certain generic features whose various applications—intellectual, aesthetic, and moral values—bring dignity to human life. But the basis of this dignity is the dignity inherent in all normal human beings as having these general capacities, directly reflected in their purposive actions and resulting judgments of worth. Where humans are so mentally deficient as not to have them even in minimal form, the Principle of Proportionality applies, but again with the egalitarian proviso of equal concern for dignity and rights indicated above.

The second objection concerned the compatibility of human dignity as based on reason and free will with the bad purposes to which these human capacities can be put. The criterion of "bad" here may be prudential or moral; I shall here confine myself to the alternative that this objection incorporates a universalist moral criterion in its judgment of the agents' purposes. Such a criterion, however, does not enter the argument until the agent has universalized his ascriptions of worth and rights to himself so that they must now be attributed to all human brings equally. As was indicated before, this universal and egalitarian attribution serves in turn to modify and restrict the agent's rationally justified assessments of his purposes. Thus, to begin with, whatever the content of his purposes, the agent must attribute worth to himself in the way indicated above; but then, once the argument has established the moral restrictions that he logically must accept, these restrictions must be applied both to his purposes and to his judgments of dignity. The agent's initial ascription of worth or dignity to himself and to all other agents, based on the worth he attributes to his purposes in acting, remains in any case as an inherent and necessary quality.

We must also consider here another variant of the objection about bad purposes. The dialectical argument presented above made human dignity derivative from an agent's valuing his purposes. But may not an agent *dis*value his purposes? If he has been brainwashed or has very low self-esteem from other causes, such as drug addiction or a hopeless outlook on life, he may well feel that what he wants is no good, that his purposes are vile and worthless, so that, far from generating a judgment of his own worth, they may reinforce the opposite judgment.

There are two main answers to this objection. First, if he has been

Chicago Press, 1982), pp. 76–78; also my essays, "On Rational Agency as the Basis of Moral Equality: Reply to Ben-Zeev," *Canadian Journal of Philosophy* 12 (1982): 667–72; "Replies to My Critics," in *Gewirth's Ethical Rationalism*, ed. Edward Regis, Jr. (Chicago: University of Chicago Press, 1984), pp. 225–27; "Why There Are Human Rights," *Social Theory and Practice* 11 (1985): 234–48.

brainwashed or subjected to related kinds of controls over his mental functioning, then he is not an agent in the strict sense intended here, since he does not control his behavior by his unforced choice. In such a case the principle of human rights, based on the necessary conditions of agency, requires that, as far as possible, the deleterious effects of such previously inflicted constraints on his agency be removed, so that his preexisting potentialities for agency may be actualized. Second, insofar as the person in question is indeed an agent, so that he controls his behavior by his own unforced choice, he must, as purposive, regard his purposes in acting as having *some* value for him, since otherwise he would not unforcedly choose to act as he does. It is true that agents function under many kinds of constraints, both internal and external. But these, in cases of action, that is, of voluntary and purposive behavior, do not have the combined aspects of compulsoriness, undesirableness, and threat that cause choices to be forced.[23] Hence, amid the varying degrees to which agents may value their various purposes, there persists an enduring element of valuation and hence of judgment of worth, from which the agent's judgment of his and all other agents' worth has been shown to be logically generated, regardless of possible contingent variations. This worth or dignity, moreover, is inherent because it derives from the very nature of purposive action. And it is intrinsic because, in its primary form, it is not instrumental to any other goods and because it is the basis rather than the effect of the worth that agents attribute to their purposes.

The third objection was about supervenience. It is indeed true that the attribution of dignity to human beings is supervenient on the "natural fact" of their being actual, prospective, or potential purposive agents. This supervenience, however, is not contingent but, rather, logically necessary, by virtue of the necessary connection between (a) acting for a purpose, (b) regarding that purpose as worth achieving, (c) regarding oneself as worth sustaining or preserving, (d) regarding oneself as having worth or dignity, and (e) extending this judgment to all other purposive agents.

Another way to put this point is in terms of moral realism: the doctrine that moral judgments are literally true. Applied to the attribution of dignity to all human beings, this means that such attribution is literally true because it corresponds to the normative structure of action. The attribution logically must be accepted by every even minimally rational agent because it logically follows from factual statements that he logically must accept by virtue of being an agent.[24]

[23] For fuller discussion of this point, see *Reason and Morality*, pp. 31–42, 48–63.

[24] For fuller discussion, see the section "Analytic Truth and Morality" in ibid., pp. 171–87. See also *Essays on Moral Realism*, ed. Geoffrey Sayre-McCord (Ithaca, N.Y.: Cornell

Fourth, the argument for human dignity and rights surmounts the "is-ought" problem because the dialectical attribution of rights, and hence of "oughts," follows logically from the agent's acting for purposes he wants to fulfill.[25]

The upshot of this section is that the idea of human dignity can serve as the justificatory basis for regarding the needs of human agency as sufficiently important or compelling that they can provide, in turn, an adequate justificatory basis for human rights. Since respect for those rights is a central part of self-fulfillment as capacity-fulfillment, the claim of the latter to be a worthy, indeed mandatory, ideal for humans' striving to make the best of themselves has been given a further justification. If the argument has been sound, it has shown that the dignity associated with human agency, without the help of extra-human factors, can account for the mandatory value of capacity-fulfillment as making the best of oneself.

5.2. SPIRITUALITY AS SELF-TRANSCENDENT EXCELLENCE

According to the argument of the preceding section, the value of self-fulfillment as capacity-fulfillment is grounded in the human dignity that pertains to all persons as actual or prospective agents. In appealing to purposiveness as the salient feature of agency, with its associated features of reason, freedom, and will, the argument serves further to connect capacity-fulfillment with strivings for aspiration-fulfillment, while taking account of the difficulties associated with the latter. But this raises the further question of whether the capacity for agency on which purpose-fulfillment is based does not comprise or even require other values that give further justification for the goodness of capacity-fulfillment. Don't humans have other capacities that serve to ground this goodness? Despite the arguments given above for distinguishing self-fulfillment from egoism (2.4), it may still be felt that self-fulfillment as so far construed is too greatly focused on the human personal element to deserve the justificatory conclusions I have based on it. What is needed, on this view, is a way of "emancipating man from his present limitations."[26]

University Press, 1988). In the editor's valuable introduction (pp. 1–23), he confines "cognitivist intersubjectivism" to the thesis that spells out "the truth conditions of moral claims in terms of the conventions or practices of groups of people" (p. 18). This overlooks, however, the alternative presented in this section, according to which the truth conditions consist not in such contingent or variable "conventions or practices" but rather in the necessary normative structure of action, including the value-claims that must be made or accepted by all humans qua agents.

[25] See my essay "The 'Is-Ought' Problem Resolved," in *Human Rights*, pp. 100–127.

[26] George Santayana, "Reason in Religion," in *The Life of Reason*, one-volume edition

I have partly dealt with this question above in discussing love and the moral, cultural, and other virtues that enter into various phases of capacity-fulfillment. But all of these goods are humanly centered; whatever goodness they may have is derivative from the human needs and ideals in which human agency variously expresses itself. It may be held that if capacity-fulfillment is to be vindicated as a sufficiently deep, secure, and mandatory value, it must in some way be buttressed by another value: spirituality. On this view, only if humans can be shown to be spiritual beings, or to attain spirituality, can their capacity-fulfillment pass muster as a worthy ideal.

Throughout human history, but especially perhaps since medieval Christendom, there have been many different conceptions of spirituality. In the present context the idea has two main interrelated components. One is self-transcendence: a spiritual person is one who in some sense transcends himself.[27] The other component is excellence: to transcend oneself is in some way to excel, to be superior to what is transcended.[28]

The reflexive relation of self-transcendence may incur all the difficulties discussed earlier in connection with self-fulfillment (3.1). If we look at "transcendence" by itself, these difficulties may be avoided; thus, for example, if God transcends the world then God excels, or is better than, the world. But how would this apply to human self-transcendence? How can you go beyond yourself and be better than yourself?

One answer would tie self-transcendence to capacity-fulfillment as making the best of oneself. On this view, you transcend yourself when your better or more developed self supersedes or triumphs over your worse or less developed self. Capacity-fulfillment would here involve a process of self-improvement whereby one goes beyond one's present self to become a better self. This is, indeed, a plausible view of self-transcendence. But it would not, as such, take account of the objection about spirituality: that for self-fulfillment as capacity-fulfillment to be a worthy ideal, it must in some way comprise a self-transcendence whereby the limitations and imperfections of the human condition are overcome.

We may distinguish two extreme conceptions of self-transcendence. One is occurrent or episodic: to endure as a person, or indeed as a thing, is to move from existing at time t_1 to existing at time t_2. At t_2 one transcends what one was at t_1 in that, simply by having different temporal

---

(New York: Charles Scribner's Sons, 1954), p. 181. See also the insightful essay by Martha C. Nussbaum, "Transcending Humanity," in her book *Love's Knowledge* (New York: Oxford University Press, 1990), chap. 15.

[27] See Reinhold Niebuhr, *The Nature and Destiny of Man* (London: Nisbet and Co., 1941, 1943), vol. 1, pp. 2–4, 14–18; vol. 2, pp. 3–6.

[28] See Charles Hartshorne, "Transcendence and Immanence," in Mircea Eliade, ed., *Encyclopedia of Religion* (New York: Macmillan, 1987), vol. 15, pp. 16–21.

predicates, one goes beyond what one was at that earlier moment. This assumes the nonsymmetricalness of time's arrow; as time moves on one does not return to one's earlier state. The normative element of excellence may also be found here: for if to survive, to persist in being, is a good for the entity in question, then at t_2 it excels what it was at t_1.[29] Because, however, this conception applies indiscriminately to all persisting things, it makes only the most meagre contact with spirituality conceived as a differential value.

At the opposite extreme from this conception is a theological, extraterrestrial conception: for humans to transcend themselves is for them to move beyond their earthly selves by putting their faith in an eternal transcendent God.[30] To have such faith is to excel oneself, to go beyond oneself in excellence, because one moves from a purely naturalistic, human-centered focus to one that invokes an absolutely perfect being, a being, moreover, that not only created the world but also has a providential, loving concern for all its human inhabitants. It might be held that such self-transcendence attains the kind of spirituality that was invoked in criticism of the purely humanistic conception of capacity-fulfillment. To believe in God, on this view, is to have a more realistic idea of the limitations of the human condition, including the values that the unaided human reason and will can attain.

A traditional, and crucial, question for this conception is whether humans, in invoking it, really do transcend themselves. If the idea of God is a human construct, then it does not, as such, enable humans to go beyond themselves, no matter how sincere their faith. On this view, far from man's being created in the image of God, the reverse relation is the true one: God is created by man in the image of man, by conceiving a being that has all the perfections that humans can imagine, and that thus escapes the limitations of the human condition through having perfect justice, perfect mercy and love, perfect knowledge, and eternal existence.

The great power of this religious conception is attested by its persistence throughout the ages. To humans who internalize it, it can bring a serenity, a feeling of security, the enormous comfort that comes from a belief that one's earthly existence does not circumscribe oneself because, after physical death, there is eternal life. In certain circumstances, religion has also been a powerful force for justice because of its doctrine of the equal worth of all humans as children of God. But history also attests to the conception's limitations and dangers. It requires an act of faith for

---

[29] Cf. Spinoza, *Ethics*, 3, Prop. 6: "Each thing, as far as it can by its own power, strives to persevere in its being" (trans. Edwin Curley, *The Collected Works of Spinoza* [Princeton: Princeton University Press, 1985], vol. 1, p. 498.)

[30] See Niebuhr, *The Nature and Destiny of Man*, vol. 2, pp. 3–6.

which there is no rational evidence; it can lead to self-righteousness, fear, quietistic acceptance of oppression, fanaticism, intolerance, divisiveness, hatred, war. To invoke these empirical consequences of religion is at least as legitimate as to cite the vast beneficial psychological and moral effects it has had for so many persons.

In what follows I shall neither accept not reject the contribution that religion can make to the understanding and appreciation of human spirituality. One may, indeed, welcome a certain "inclusivist" ideal whereby the religious contribution is accepted so long as it is consistent with the universalist moral principle of human rights.[31] The moral primacy of human rights must, indeed, be pressed, as must also the veridical primacy of reason. In the present context, without invoking religion, I shall offer a conception of spirituality that can serve as a helpful rational complement to capacity-fulfillment as so far discussed. If self-transcendence and excellence cannot be appealed to as moving from the human to the divine, they can still be invoked within the human sphere itself.

One way of getting at this is by the distinction between "spiritual" and "material" values. In this contrast, spiritual values consist in ideals of moral, intellectual, and aesthetic excellence. They involve that one goes beyond one's narrow personal concerns of self-aggrandizement, that one in effect surrenders oneself to the pursuit of goodness, truth, beauty as these are embodied in justice, rights, and compassion; in scientific inquiry; in artistic accomplishment and aesthetic appreciation; and in other realms of value. The ground for calling such pursuits "spiritual" is precisely that one goes beyond oneself, i.e. beyond concerns focused solely on oneself; one recognizes the demands of a broader moral, intellectual, and aesthetic culture. These demands are experienced as objective because they embody criteria of excellence that one does not make or invent but rather discovers, and that are felt to make demands of acknowledgment on one based on the cogency of those criteria. This returns us to the "externalist" view of aspiration-fulfillment discussed earlier (2.4).

One segment of such self-transcendence is epistemological. But here the factor of excellence must be present before the cognitive activity in question can be called spiritual. On the one hand, whenever one knows something about the external world, one may be said to transcend oneself in that one moves beyond the limitations set by one's own body or frame of reference.[32] According to some skeptical views, such epistemic

---

[31] See the judicious discussion of this issue in Philip L. Quinn, "Political Liberalisms and Their Exclusions of the Religious," *Proceedings and Addresses of the American Philosophical Association* 69, no. 2 (November 1995): 35–56.

[32] Cf. Thomas Nagel, *The View from Nowhere* (New York: Oxford University Press, 1986), pp. 74–77.

self-transcendence is impossible precisely because there is no way of getting out of, or going beyond, one's own cognitive framework. But here factors of excellence emerge that make an important difference. Regardless of how humanly centered one's cognitive formulations may be, there are criteria such as control of nature, explanatory and predictive power, and generality that enable us to differentiate degrees of cognitive excellence and thereby to transcend the limitations set by the restrictive purview of ordinary sense experience. When heights of extraordinary excellence are reached in this epistemic sphere by giants like Newton, Darwin, and Einstein, there is abundant ground for calling their achievements spiritual.

The arts provide comparable vehicles of self-transcendence. When Picasso offers a new way of seeing things in the disjointed context of anomic modernity, when Bach and Mozart evoke profound serenity with their harmonies and variations, when Dickens and George Eliot give insights into the struggles and tragedies of nineteenth-century England, they enable us to move outside our narrow sphere of direct experience through compelling modes of artistic disclosure. Such encounters are profound bases of spirituality.

An especially eminent area of self-transcendence is found in the universalist moral saints and heroes who risk their lives in times of mortal danger to rescue innocent persons threatened with torture or death by evil regimes or other disasters. The Christians who sheltered and otherwise protected the Jews during the Nazi genocide are twentieth-century examples.[33] What these persons transcended was their self-protective selves, characterized by the almost instinctual motivation of self-preservation. What they transcended to was an ideal of universalist moral excellence that they exemplified, and perhaps also strove to fulfill, in their own actions.

Such actions are supererogatory in the literal sense of going beyond strict duty. This going beyond is a form of transcendence; one goes beyond strict moral requirements, and one thereby transcends oneself as a person who is ordinarily limited by those requirements. But not all supererogatory actions are heroic or saintly; acts of simple courtesy, for example, may go beyond one's strict duties and the correlative rights of their recipients.[34] Nevertheless, the primary supererogatory actions are

---

[33] See Philip Hallie, *Lest Innocent Blood Be Shed* (New York: Harper and Row, 1980); Samuel P. Oliner, *The Altruistic Personality: The Rescuers of Jews in Nazi Europe* (New York: Free Press, 1988); Lawrence A. Blum, "Moral Exemplars: Reflections on Schindler, the Trocmes, and Others," *Midwest Studies in Philosophy* 13 (1988): 196–221.

[34] Cf. Joel Feinberg, "Supererogation and Rules," in Feinberg, *Doing and Deserving* (Princeton: Princeton University Press, 1970), and J. O. Urmson, "Saints and Heroes," in A. I. Melden, ed., *Essays in Moral Philosophy* (Seattle: University of Washington Press, 1958), pp. 198–216.

those that put their agents at great risk; such agents perform exceptionally valuable actions of saving lives or rescuing from other serious dangers. It is to such agents that self-transcendence applies.

As we have seen, the PGC, as the universalist moral principle of
human rights, requires that one act in accord with the generic rights of
one's recipients as well as of oneself (3.4). Unlike utilitarianism, the
principle does not require an unlimited maximizing of goodness with no
recognition of differential rights and duties. While the classification of
certain actions as supererogatory disappears in a utilitarian framework, it
persists in the framework of the PGC because of the latter's requirement
of moral reasonableness whereby the self has rights against other persons
as well as duties toward them. The rights involve that one's freedom and
well-being are to be protected against other persons, as well as that
other persons also have these rights (3.4).

It will be recalled that the PGC requires a certain generic consistency
between one's upholding one's own rights and one's respecting the
rights of other persons. In the present context of heroic or saintly supererogatory actions, it may be thought that such actions commit the agent
to inconsistency in that he favors other persons over himself. Consider,
for example, the saint or hero who subordinates or even sacrifices his
own freedom and well-being to those of other persons: "I'll risk my life
in order to save yours," or "You shall have the last seat in the life-boat
rather than I." Here, insofar as the agent and his recipients are prospective purposive agents and he grounds his judgments on this quality, he
may be thought to be contradicting himself. For he seems to be saying
that his recipients have rights to freedom and well-being that he does
not have even though he is relevantly similar to them with regard to the
quality which grounds the having of these rights; or at least he seems to
hold that he should act in accord with their generic rights but not in
accord with his own. His inconsistency here, however, it may be
thought, is in the reverse direction from the usual self-interested kind,
for he distributes freedom or well-being or both in a way which is dis-
advantageous to himself and advantageous to his recipients. But such
inconsistency, with its accompanying actions, is surely not immoral;
on the contrary, it represents the highest form of supererogatory morality. Doesn't this refute the thesis of the argument for the PGC, that an
interpersonal inconsistent distribution of goods or rights is a morally
wrong one?

To deal with this question, we must look more closely at the relation
between the saint's or hero's supererogatory principle and the PGC. As
we have seen in developing the PGC, it is inconsistent for the agent to
act in accord with his own generic rights and not in accord with his recipients' generic rights. Now it might be thought that the supererogatory principle is the reverse of this and is hence equally inconsistent.

Nevertheless, the saint or hero cannot be rationally interpreted as holding that he should act in accord with his recipients' generic rights and not in accord with his own generic rights. For him not to act in accord with his own generic rights, i.e., for him to act in disaccord with or in violation of these rights of his, would mean that in acting he allows other persons to interfere with his freedom and well-being without his consent. Such a nonconsensual abdication of one's generic rights, however, would be not only pointless but also impossible. For since his action is voluntary and purposive, this would mean that in some particular action he voluntarily permits himself to be treated involuntarily, or consents to have the necessary conditions of his action removed without his consent. But when a person performs heroic actions like those just mentioned, he consents to these threats to or deprivations of his life and liberty, so that they are not cases of his acting in violation of his own generic rights. On the contrary, he still acts in accord with his generic rights, for he still sees to it that there is no interference with his freedom and well-being without his consent.

The saint or hero is also not saying that in acting as he does he acts in accord with his recipients' generic rights. It is indeed the case that he does not violate their generic rights and in this sense he acts in accord with them. But he also acts beyond what their rights require of him, which is why his action is supererogatory. For when the hero sacrifices his life or liberty for his recipients' sakes, it is not a question of their rights nor hence of his duties in the strict sense. The recipients do indeed have rights to life and liberty, but only in the sense that other persons ought to refrain from interfering with their life and liberty, or ought to assist them to preserve these if this can be done at no comparable cost to themselves; but not in the sense that another person ought to sacrifice his own life and liberty for the sake of theirs (see 3.4). Such sacrifice would involve that the agent sets up a disparity or inequality between himself and his recipients with regard to freedom and well-being in favor of his recipients; but what the PGC requires as a matter of strict duty is that the agent not set up such a disparity in favor of himself. The case of the saint or hero is thus different from that where a person can save someone else's life at no risk of his own. His self-sacrifice is an act of grace on his part, but not of strict duty, unlike what is required by the PGC and its derived rules and judgments. Hence, the agent is not here being generically inconsistent.

Does the PGC, then, provide any basis for either approving or disapproving such supererogatory actions or for recognizing their moral merit? This basis is found in the fact that the PGC requires at least that the agent not distribute freedom or well-being in a way that is to his recipients' disadvantage by giving them less of it in some transaction than he takes for himself. For since it is necessarily true of the agent, so long as he is an agent, that he acts in accord with his own generic rights, the PGC's concern is that he should maintain the conditions of just distribution by not violating his recipients' generic rights. Since supererogatory actions provide overabundant assurance of this result, they are to this extent in conformity with the PGC. The saint or hero acts in the direction indicated by his recipients' generic rights, and he also acts in accord with their generic rights since he both does not interfere with their freedom and well-being without their consent and helps them to have freedom and well-being. But his action goes considerably beyond such non-interference and beyond their strict rights, because he helps them at the risk of losing his own freedom and well-being.

As I have suggested, to call such actions supererogatory assumes a certain base-line of ordinary motivations. There are, however, moral philosophies besides utilitarianism that do not assume such a baseline. Aristotle's "great-souled" man, for example, does not regard his actions as supererogatory when he sacrifices his life for his country or his friends or for some other noble cause. Such actions are just what he expects, and demands, of himself.[35] A similar exaltation of human motivations may be found in Kant's doctrine that it is a moral (though "imperfect") duty to seek one's own perfection and the happiness of others.[36] The classification of some actions as supererogatory assumes as its baseline the more ordinary limits of most ordinary persons. But it must also be noted that the ordinary people who risked their lives to save Jews from the Nazi murderers did not envisage themselves as being exceptionally virtuous. They did what they felt had to be done, out of caring and compassion, but with no thought of a more moderate motivational baseline that was exceeded by their actions.[37] Nor did they follow the economists' model of "rational," strategic calculation of how rescuing others may probably help one to receive such help oneself when one needs it or may otherwise benefit oneself. The ground is not primarily one of reciprocity but rather a recognition of persons' common humanity as purposive agents.[38] This involved an overriding of the racial, ethnic, religious, and other categories that operate to divide humans from one another and that figure in the perspectives of many ordinary people.

[35] Aristotle, *Nicomachean Ethics*, 9. 8. 1169a18–27; also 3. 1. 1110a26–28; 4. 3. 1124b7–9.

[36] See Kant, *Metaphysics of Morals, Doctrine of Virtue*, Introduction, secs. 4–8 (Akad. ed., 385–94; trans. Gregor, pp. 190–97). See also David Heyd, *Supererogation* (Cambridge: Cambridge University Press, 1982).

[37] See above, n. 33.

[38] See Kristen R. Monroe, Michael C. Barton, and Ute Klingmann, "Altruism and the Theory of Rational Action: Rescuers of Jews in Nazi Europe," *Ethics* 101 (October 1990): 103–22; Kristen R. Monroe, *The Heart of Altruism: Perceptions of a Common Humanity* (Princeton: Princeton University Press, 1996).

What is the relation between the moral supererogatoriness of heroic and saintly actions and the "best" that figures in capacity-fulfillment? The latter, unlike the former, is within the reach of most persons; yet each is in a way a superlative. Can it be that the supererogatory is somehow better than the best? To put the question otherwise: Is self-transcendence compatible with self-fulfillment? It might seem not. For in self-transcendence one somehow goes beyond oneself, while in self-fulfillment, by bringing to fruition what is implicit in oneself, one remains securely anchored within oneself. This contrast is not right, however. In self-fulfillment, as already indicated, one goes beyond one's present, unimproved self to a self whose best capacities are developed and exercised as fully as possible. And in moral self-transcendence, it is still one's self that acts, but on the basis of motivations and risks that go beyond those of most persons.

The more specific answer to these questions requires that we recall the different scopes of the three "bests" that we took over from Aristotle's analysis of the "best constitution" (3.2). The "best" of capacity-fulfillment corresponds to what is best in most persons on average, while the heights of the supererogatory correspond to what is the absolutely best morally. That the latter is attained by relatively few persons who are "moral exemplars" is not antithetical to the former's being attainable by most persons. The superlativeness of aspiration-fulfillment and capacity-fulfillment is exceeded by the supererogatory because the best achieved by the former modes of fulfillment reflects desires and abilities of more ordinary persons, as against the achievements of which extraordinary persons are capable. This contrast does not, however, detract from the great value of capacity-fulfillment. The Purposive Ranking Thesis in its application to this comparison involves as the relevant context the moral exertions that go beyond the satisfactions of ordinary life.

The excellence and self-transcendence that constitute spirituality are, then, within the reach of extraordinary human beings so that they do not have to move to a nonhuman sphere in order to achieve it. Human selves have available to them modes of excellence that enable them to make the best of themselves, or at least to recognize the criteria of this "best" and to be motivated to conform to them.

5.3. THE MEANING OF LIFE

The improvement and exaltation of human life found in capacity-fulfillment and spirituality are perhaps sufficient bases for that self-fulfillment which has been the object of our quest. One fulfills oneself by making the best of oneself through developing one's best capacities; and some humans can approach even closer to perfection by transcending the limitations that characterize most persons. It may be thought that such bringing to fruition of one's worthiest capacities can serve as an adequate and even final answer to the question of the ultimate values of human life.

Doubt may be cast on this finality if we recur to the ideal of aspiration-fulfillment. It may be felt that it is not enough to invoke the objective ends of capacity-fulfillment; for, after all, if these ends are to be salient ideals for which persons are to strive, they must somehow be connected to human motivations, especially as these are evinced in one's aspirations. But once one tries to make this connection, the question may arise of what is the point or purpose of all these strivings. Why should one exert oneself to achieve all these excellences? In final analysis, what good does it do? Where does it get one in the end? Such questions all point in various ways to the ultimate question of the meaning of life. (Here and throughout I confine myself to human life.)

We may distinguish two opposite extreme attitudes that have been taken on this question, with many intermediates. One attitude is indifference. For many persons the question of what is the meaning of life simply does not arise. They go about the business of living their lives without ever raising the question of its "meaning." For other persons the question is momentous; it is, indeed, the most weighty and important of all questions. Persons in the former group, if they ever encounter the question, may associate it with effete, world-weary aesthetes who have nothing better to do with their time and who are so far removed from the struggles of everyday living that they can adopt a supercilious or perhaps even querulous attitude toward it. Persons in the latter group often embrace a holistic attitude wherein those struggles are evaluated in terms of their overall significance; they wish to rise above the minutiae of ordinary living in order to evaluate them with regard to their ultimate point or purpose. A partial ancestor of this outlook is found in Aristotle's thesis, at the beginning of the *Nicomachean Ethics*, that unless there is some ultimate purpose or goal of human practical activities, the desires that motivate them will be "empty and vain."[39] In a somewhat parallel way, it is thought that unless human life as a whole has some ultimate meaning, human strivings are inconsequential and meaningless. On this view, the concerns of capacity-fulfillment and even of the self-transcendence of spirituality are of no definitive value unless they are tied to an affirmative answer to this ultimate question.

There are, however, several ways in which this idea can be related to the everyday strivings of the ordinary people who are generally indif-

---

[39] Aristotle, *Nicomachean Ethics*, 1. 2. 1094a17–21.

ferent to the question of the meaning of life. When one's everyday life is bitter and stressful under the impact of disease, poverty, slavery, or other extreme afflictions, when it becomes an arduous struggle simply to survive, one may well ask whether the struggle is worth it, what good can come of it.

Apart from these normative issues, some philosophers have been suspicious of the very concept of the meaning of life. Their thesis can be summarized briefly as follows: only linguistic or ideational signs have meaning; life is not such a sign; therefore, life has no meaning. On this basis it is also held that the very question of the meaning of life is itself meaningless.

This thesis can be attacked on the ground that it unduly restricts the notions of "sign" and "meaning." Signs may be other than linguistic or ideational; they may, for example, be causal, as when smoke is a sign of fire. We can, nevertheless, take account of the conceptual issue and use it to come to fuller grips with the question of the meaning of life. As was suggested above, persons who raise the question of the meaning of life interpret it as asking what is the purpose or point of life. What, then, is the relation between "meaning" and "purpose"? We can approach this question by noting the contention just mentioned, that meaning is a property of signs.

Is there, then, any relevant sense in which life itself is a sign? In general, a sign is something that mediately takes account of something else.[40] For example, where Socrates would be immediately (i.e., non-mediatedly) taken account of if he were directly encountered in the marketplace or were manhandled by someone else, he is mediately taken account of by the name-sign "Socrates" or the description-sign "teacher of Plato." In a parallel way, where fire would be immediately (i.e., non-mediatedly) taken account of if it were directly observed by someone or if he were burned by it, it is mediately taken account of by smoke as a sign of fire. In these and other cases, besides the sign and its object or designatum (what it takes account of), there is a third factor: the interpreter who uses the sign to take account of the object.

Let us now repeat the question: Is there any relevant sense in which life can be regarded as a sign? One might say that if there is life there is certain brain activity, so that life is a sign of such activity. But this would put the cart before the horse; brain activity is a sign of life, rather than conversely. Brain activity when observed enables the observer or interpreter to take account of the presence of life in the entity that has or

[40] See Charles W. Morris, *Foundations of the Theory of Signs* (Chicago: University of Chicago Press, 1938), pp. 3–6. Cf. the discussion of "modes of meaning" in relation to the meaning of life, in Robert Nozick, *Philosophical Explanations* (Cambridge, Mass.: Harvard University Press, 1981), pp. 574–79.

undergoes the activity, so that life is mediately taken account of through such activity.

One of the salient ways in which life itself can be regarded as a sign proceeds through the interpretation one makes of it. If the interpreter takes account of certain values or purposes through the mediation of life, in that he takes life to exist for the sake of, or to be justified by, these purposes, then he interprets life as a sign of those purposes. This would involve that, for the interpreter, those values or purposes are mediately taken account of by the process or activity of life. In this relation are found not only the "semantical" dimension of the sign, its reference to a designatum, but also, and especially, its "pragmatic" dimension, the sign's relation to its interpreter, who interprets life as existing for the sake of certain values or purposes. And since a sign is, or has, meaning, those purposes would constitute the meaning of life. So in this way the question of the meaning of life comes down to the question of the purpose of life.

It will have been noted that this analysis makes the meaning of life relative to the evaluations of interpreters who are agents engaged in purposive action. On this view, life has meaning insofar as one interprets it as a valuational sign whereby it betokens certain purposes or values as being striven for or fulfilled. In the absence of the agent-interpreters, life is not a sign and has no meaning.

The interpreters may vary in many different ways, which are partly the same as the different conceptions of the good life noted earlier (4.1). There may be religious and secular interpreters, theoretic and practical interpreters, economic and romantic interpreters, and so forth. More generally, we can distinguish two opposite extreme kinds of interpreters. One kind is pluralistic. On this view there is not life, but only many different lives which have many different meanings depending upon the values or purposes that different agent-interpreters pursue. Thus Aristotle, after positing happiness as the highest end or purpose in human life, went on at once to recognize that different persons have widely divergent conceptions of happiness, including pleasure, wealth, and honor or public recognition, so that for these groups life would have different kinds of meaning. Aristotle then went on to give an interpretation of happiness based not on the varying subjective desires or aspirations of different persons but rather on the specific objective "function" of human beings.[41] I have tried to do something parallel to this in moving from aspiration-fulfillment to capacity-fulfillment, but with a variation soon to be noted.

At the opposite extreme from the pluralistic kind of interpreters is a global or holistic kind. This purports to set a single valuable end or

[41] *Nicomachean Ethics*, 1. 5, 7.

purpose for all human life and action. Aristotle was such an interpreter when he held that theoretic contemplation is the sole ultimate end or "best" for all humans who are capable of it.[42] The religionists who hold that union with God alone gives meaning to life also belong to this group, as do thinkers who uphold the will to power, the quest for beauty or love, the pursuit of freedom or justice, and so forth.

Just as the pluralistic view can eventuate in an anarchic chaos of interpretations of the meaning of life, so the holistic or global view can lead to an authoritarian dogmatism wherein rival conceptions are condemned as at best shortsighted and even evil, and made objects of scorn as well as persecution.

I want to suggest an intermediate interpretation along the following lines. From the pluralistic interpretation it takes over the initial validity of the great variety of purposes and values pursued by various agents. But from the holistic interpretation it takes over the idea that those purposes can be evaluated according to objective criteria. The application of these criteria, however, does not yield a single kind of value or purpose as supremely valuable in contradistinction to its rivals, as in Aristotle's exaltation of theoretic contemplation. Rather, the application recognizes the many different capacities of different persons and the ways in which these can be adapted to their different purposes. In this way, the meaning of life comes down to the many aspects of capacity-fulfillment that I have discussed in the preceding chapters.

It will be recalled that the analysis of capacity-fulfillment was based on the values and virtues that were found in the effective development of freedom and well-being as the generic features of successful purposive action. In this perspective, the meaning of human life is constituted by the pursuit of these values and virtues. The meaning of life consists in the values that the agent who lives the life regards as most worth pursuing. It comprises not only the attainment of those values but also the pursuit itself. In briefest compass, it consists in the best kinds of purposive action, where the purposes may consist not only in various objects outside the action but also in the actions themselves when they are performed for their own sakes; and the criteria of "best" are found in the considerations of capacity-fulfillment discussed above.

Three restrictions on this generalization must be noted at once. First, in contrast to the pluralistic kind of interpretation, the pursued values must not be a miscellaneous assortment of purposes; they should be organized according to some general plan that is intelligible and indeed compelling to the agent. This organization will take account of different levels of value as interpreted by the agent. This need not involve some

---

[42] Ibid., 10. 7.

sort of supreme value, but rather a general hierarchic ordering in which some values are deemed superior to others, and without the infinite regress in which each order of values or desires requires validation by a further order (see 2.1). I have tried above to suggest some of the relevant criteria that can help to determine this ordering, including the Purposive Ranking Thesis.

Second, the purposes must be, and be regarded as, attainable by the agent. Empirical evidence, of some degree of substantiality, can be very helpful here. On the other hand, for the religionist who holds the meaning of life to consist in union with God, the absence of such evidence may not remove her pursuit of this goal. But at least she must regard it as attainable.

It is this point about attainability that makes the famous "myth of Sisyphus"[43] at once so dramatic and, in large part, so uncompelling. It is dramatic because it gives a brilliant exemplification of the idea that human life is ultimately meaningless and futile because it can be assimilated to a person's being condemned by the gods eternally to push a large rock to the top of a hill from which it rolls down on the other side, from which it is to be pushed up again, and so ad infinitum. What the myth implies, then, is that human life can attain no worthy purposes and hence is meaningless: Sisyphus has no sound basis for interpreting his life as consisting in, or being justified by, or as mediately taking account of any sound values. The myth is largely uncompelling, however, because it overlooks the vital, attainable values and purposes that give zest and meaning to human lives as they are ordinarily lived. As was suggested earlier, the myth may be relevant to persons who live lives that are mean, brutal, desperate, disorganized, full of anguish and despair. Yet even for Thomas Hobbes' persons in the "state of nature," whose lives were "solitary, poor, nasty, brutish, and short,"[44] there was a drive toward the values of purpose-fulfillment, a drive sufficiently strong to lead them to try to extricate themselves from their predicament. That Hobbes' authoritarian solution is not the only feasible one is indicated by Locke's way of moving from a very similar state of nature to a solution based on limited constitutional government.

Besides the poignancies of unrelieved human suffering, the myth of Sisyphus may also have a point when human life is viewed from the global or holistic perspective of the millennia of the whole universe. In that perspective human life is a mere dot amid the happenings of time;

---

[43] See Albert Camus, *The Myth of Sisyphus*, trans. Justin O'Brien (London: Hamish Hamilton, 1955), esp. pp. 96–99; Richard Taylor, *Good and Evil* (London: Macmillan, 1970), chap. 18; Joel Feinberg, *Freedom and Fulfillment* (Princeton: Princeton University Press, 1992), chap. 13.

[44] Hobbes, *Leviathan*, chap. 13.

the successes of human purposive strivings are not only extremely temporary but totally swallowed up in and disregarded by an inexorably changing cosmos. But there remains the question of why one should regard this perspective as the only relevant one. Its assumptions are contradicted by the very persons who uphold it; they pursue their own purposes of trying to understand human life, and they regard these purposes as sufficiently worthwhile to freely expend their energies in pursuit of them.[45] To regard the global perspective, with its conclusion about the ultimate meaninglessness of life, as the sole decisive basis for evaluating life, is thus analogous to the self-defeatingness of philosophers who reject the principle of noncontradiction while implicitly invoking it in their very rejection. More specifically, persons confronted with extreme adversities can strive not merely to adjust to them but also to seek ways to overcome them or at least to limit their impacts. Such attitudes are different from the utter hopelessness encapsulated in the myth of Sisyphus.

A third restriction on the idea that the meaning of life is to be found in important purposive action is that the purposes must themselves meet certain valuational criteria. To begin with, they must not violate the principle of universalist morality with its focus on human rights. The Nazis, Stalinists, and others who found the meaning of their lives in their advocacy of and obedience to the policies of bloody tyrants may indeed have led what for them were meaningful lives, including the restriction about systematization included above. But their ideals of a perfect society lacked the corroboration of universalist moral principle and empirical and other rational evidence that would have prohibited the murders of Jews, "kulaks," and others of their victims. The present restriction about universalist morality sets a further requirement, the reasons for whose overriding importance were discussed above (3.4). In addition, the purposes that constitute the meaning of life must take account of the relative rankings of better and worse that enter into the various components of capacity-fulfillment along some such lines as those that have figured in the above analyses of it.

According to the conception of the meaning of life presented here, meaning is supplied by agents who interpret their lives as striving for highly important purposes they make their own. It may be felt that this is too fragile a basis for the meaning of life, that it makes this meaning too "subjective," too relative to individual human agent-interpreters. What may be sought, instead, is a kind of objective and universal basis, such as is found in God's plan for the universe or in the march of history

---

[45] Cf. R. M. Hare, "Nothing Matters," in E. D. Klemke, ed., *The Meaning of Life* (New York: Oxford University Press, 1981), pp. 241–47.

or in the triumph of oppressed classes over their oppressors or in one of the many other holistic ways that have figured in traditional philosophies of history.

I do not think, however, that these ideas are cogent unless they are viewed as providing justifications or motivations for human purposive action. If they are viewed within this framework, they become not mere vehicles for wish-fulfillment but viable bases for action. But apart from this they have no predictive or explanatory cogency.

The answer I have given to the question of the meaning of life reflects the same framework of purposive action as has figured in the analysis of capacity-fulfillment. That analysis applied reason to the generic features of action to derive the PGC as the principle of universalist morality, and it then examined the components of freedom and well-being as the necessary goods of purposive action to derive the various parts of personalist morality as comprising the good life. The meaning of life, similarly, consists in the pursuit and attainment of the values of personalist morality as guided by the rational justification of universalist morality and the analysis of freedom and well-being as central to the highest development of the virtues based upon these necessary goods of action.

5.4. INDIVIDUAL AND SOCIAL CONTEXTS OF SELF-FULFILLMENT

The analyses of self-fulfillment presented above have reflected both individual and social contexts. It is individuals who strive to realize their aspirations and to make the best of themselves. But these purposive strivings occur within various social contexts, including the impacts of familial, economic, political and other conditions that affect what aspirations persons have, how likely they are to fulfill them, to what extent they can make the best of themselves, and what effects these achievements have on other persons. So there is an important sense in which self-fulfillment is also other-fulfillment, or, if not that, is at least conditioned by others and has an impact on others. It will help us to understand self-fulfillment further if we pursue the social context in its relation to individual selves (see also above, 2.2).

Let us begin from the myth of Sisyphus just considered. Imagine that the gods had made one concession to Sisyphus: that his beloved wife would be his companion in the endless task of stone-rolling. Surely the bitterness of his absurd fate would continue to plague him. But it is also likely that, while desperately pitying his wife's shared predicament, he would derive a certain comfort from her presence. And she, because she also loved him, would similarly be comforted by being near him and sharing his life with him. A parallel situation can perhaps be found among prisoners in Nazi concentration camps; they too gained a certain solace from the companionship of their fellow-sufferers.[46] This comparison, while inaccurate in certain respects, at least suggests that both self-fulfillment and its opposite can be strongly affected by the social contexts of their respective modes of persistence. This lends further support to the contribution of particularist morality to capacity-fulfillment (4.7). It also shows how even in the limiting cases of exceptionally adverse circumstances, a minimal social context can condition the possibility of self-fulfillment.

How far does this social impact go? In the circumstances of ordinary life, as against the Sisyphean and Nazi pathologies, to what extent can the individual self control whether it will fulfill itself? There is a long determinist tradition, encapsulated in part in the doctrines of Marx and Freud, that casts doubt on the autonomy whereby persons can control their choices and behaviors. For example, Marx, writing of the capitalist and the landowner, said that "individuals are dealt with here only insofar as they are the personifications of economic categories. . . . My standpoint . . . can less than any other make the individual responsible for relations whose creature he remains, socially speaking, however much he may subjectively raise himself above them."[47] On this view, capitalists and landowners are so completely locked into their social-economic roles that they are not "responsible" for what they do in those roles; and presumably they cannot succeed in fulfilling themselves in ways that go outside the roles. Self-fulfillment would here be at the mercy of economic categories.

A still more far-reaching determinism, biological as well as social, has been upheld by John Rawls, who based one of his principles of justice in part on certain theses about the ultimate causation of human abilities, achievements, and efforts. According to these theses, the economic rewards or income that persons receive from their productive activity are not to be attributed to their own desert, because persons do not deserve either their natural or their socially derived abilities. For these abilities stem from genetic or environmental sources beyond the agent himself, "for which he can claim no credit"; hence, their economic "outcome is arbitrary from a moral perspective."[48] "Even the willingness to make an

---

[46] See Bruno Bettelheim, *Surviving and Other Essays* (New York: Alfred A. Knopf, 1979), pp. 53, 65, 69.

[47] Karl Marx, *Capital*, vol. 1, Preface to the 1st ed., trans. Ben Fowkes (New York: Vintage Books, 1977), p. 92.

[48] John Rawls, *A Theory of Justice* (Cambridge, Mass.: Harvard University Press, 1971), pp. 74, 104.

effort, to try, and so to be deserving in the ordinary sense is itself dependent upon happy family and social circumstances."[49] From this it is held to follow that persons also do not deserve whatever income and wealth they may acquire through these externally generated abilities; and this negative conclusion would also apply to their modes and achievements of self-fulfillment. So on this model, in the generation of self-fulfillment the biological and social context counts for everything, the individual self for nothing.

As has been frequently pointed out, Rawls's argument rests on a kind of transitivity assumption: If A does not deserve X (the abilities he derives from the natural and social conditions of his starting-point in life), and if X is a necessary condition of Y (the income and wealth he acquires through using these abilities), then A does not deserve Y. This assumption, however, overlooks the possibility that A may make an independent contribution to his getting Y, since X is only a necessary, not a sufficient condition of his getting Y. There is a difference between having externally derived abilities and using them; one may deserve what one gets by the latter.[50]

This distinction, however, may not capture the full force of Rawls's thesis. It is to be noted that the causal relations asserted in his thesis are conveyed by rather vague expressions: a person's ability, character, or effort, together with the wealth and income that he may attain thereby, is "determined," "decided," "settled," "affected," "strongly influenced by," "is itself dependent upon," "is the cumulative effect of," "depends in large part upon,"[51] his natural and social conditions, "for which he can claim no credit" and which he therefore does not deserve. These expressions are more general than Marx's assertion, quoted above, that "the individual" is not to be held "responsible for relations whose creature he remains, socially speaking." Rawls's statements raise the question of the extent of such "dependence" or "influence" or being "affected." What Rawls seems to suggest, without saying so explicitly, is a determinism so complete that the person himself contributes nothing either to his own actions or to the development of his own character and abilities. A realistic sense of personal responsibility is thereby rejected, including the individual's control over his own self-fulfillment. The picture given is suggestive of Descartes's view of the motion of material objects: each motion is the result of the impact on it of external objects moving according to natural laws; no object has any independent causal

[49] Ibid., p. 74; see also p. 312.
[50] See Rex Martin, *Rawls on Rights* (Lawrence: University Press of Kansas, 1985), pp. 164–65; Derek L. Phillips, *Toward a Just Social Order* (Princeton: Princeton University Press, 1986), pp. 359–60.
[51] Rawls, *A Theory of Justice*, pp. 72, 74, 104, 312.

influence on its own motions.[52] Applied to Rawls's conception, this raises the question: how can it be that each person's actions, character, and outcome are so completely "determined," "settled," "affected," "influenced by," and "dependent upon" only factors other than the agent himself? Is each of these factors in turn similarly "determined" only by still other factors? If not, then why should independent causal efficacy be attributed to (some of) these other factors and not to the individual agent himself? If, on the other hand, none of these factors has independent causal efficacy, then how does the whole process get started? Is there some Initiating Cause that sets these natural and social forces in motion, imparting to them from without a seemingly exclusive and exhaustive causal efficacy that is not to be attributed to their own powers or behaviors?

Despite such problems, there is indeed plausibility in Rawls's claim that persons' actions and characters are influenced by their external natural and social context. This point precludes unqualified acceptance of the opposed view that blames the plight of poor people on their "laziness" or "stupidity" with no recognition of their debilitating social circumstances, and that attributes the self-fulfilling achievements of the more successful solely to their own intelligence and efforts. Such frequently expressed pejorative and laudatory judgments fail to take account of the diverse causal backgrounds to which Rawls's thesis directs emphatic attention.

What is needed is an intermediate position that views persons' actions and characters, including those that enter into their self-fulfillment, neither as completely determined by external natural and social forces nor as completely independent of those forces. A tenable position of this sort may be outlined in two steps. The first develops the comparative perspective just suggested. It must be kept in mind that Rawls's discussion of desert occurs in the context of various interpretations of equality of opportunity, so that it is on considerations of comparative rights or entitlements that his thesis is focused. Now certain comparative judgments of economic desert and of other attempts at self-fulfillment are plausible and well-founded. For example, if A is born poor and otherwise disadvantaged, then he deserves more credit for his productive and self-fulfilling work than if he had been born rich and otherwise advantaged; and so, concomitantly, he deserves more credit than does "well-born" B. Such comparative judgments have two interrelated grounds. One calls attention to the much greater obstacles A had to overcome in order to become a productive worker, and to the much greater degree of effort he had to exert in this overcoming. The other ground focuses on the

[52] See Descartes, *Principles of Philosophy*, part 2, sec. 37.

goods A produces by his efforts. Even if these goods are modest by comparison with what B produces, A may still deserve more credit for producing them than does B, at least so far as concerns the agent-oriented considerations of obstacles and effort. The case is clearer still if A's and B's products are roughly similar as embodying beneficial effects.

The sense in which A is said to "deserve" credit is that it is fitting or appropriate that A receive appreciation or commendation not only for the good he has personally done but also for the personal qualities of effort and control he has had to exert in overcoming the obstacles to his being capable of such productivity.[53] A is an economically productive agent and the thesis of nondesert does not apply to him (even if it does to B). Such a comparative perspective is more cogent than the blanket assertion that "[e]ven the willingness to make an effort . . . is itself dependent upon happy family and social circumstances."[54] When A exerts his efforts, is none of this "dependent upon" himself, especially in view of his lack of "happy family and social circumstances"?

This brings me to the second step toward the intermediate position mentioned above. Even if happy family and social circumstances may facilitate development of the willingness to make an effort, they are not sufficient conditions of such development. On the contrary, once an at least minimally facilitative upbringing has done its part, what kind of character one develops, including one's willingness to make appropriate efforts toward self-fulfillment, is then up to the individual herself, through her own actions that are under her own control and her own sense of personal responsibility. Education and other conditioning provided by the social context can operate not as exclusively determining actions and character but as laying foundations for autonomous action, so that once these foundations are laid it is then within the person's power to choose to act in one way rather than in another. The foundations in question include training whereby persons learn to control their direct emotions in the light of knowledge about available alternatives and also develop their capacities for productive agency and other phases of self-fulfillment. It is in this context that the comparative considerations referred to above become especially apposite. Thus, for example, if a person born poor is given education and other kinds of socially provided help, the use he makes of them—whether to neglect the opportunities they offer or to pursue them—will depend on his or her own choices or decisions. In this way he can be held to be responsible for what he does and to deserve punishment or rewards. But without such

[53] See Feinberg, *Doing and Deserving*, pp. 56–58, 82; George Sher, *Desert* (Princeton: Princeton University Press, 1987), chaps. 4, 6.
[54] *A Theory of Justice*, p. 74.

upbringing, the extent of his responsibility and desert will be correspondingly much more limited.[55]

This position is a modification of the agent-cause theory of human action, according to which actions are caused by persons themselves through their own free choices, as against being caused by beliefs and desires over which they have no control.[56] If persons themselves are identified with their autonomous choices, then such a view of action is true of persons once they have undergone appropriate habituation. The need for social habituation, education, and training is not thereby denied; on the contrary, it is indispensable for the development of productive agency and self-fulfillment in general. This theory can directly accommodate the freedom that is one of the generic objects of human rights, consisting in control of one's behavior by one's unforced choice while having knowledge of relevant circumstances.

Parallel ideas apply to Marx's assertion that the capitalist or the landowner is not to be held "responsible" for the social relations "whose creature he remains." Despite the pressures of the capitalist's role, it is not so omnipotent that it inevitably prevents him from taking account of other considerations, including moral ones. Although this is a broad issue, the causal factors of the social context can be surmounted by the individual's rationally grounded and emotionally supported awareness of his moral obligations.

The education and other modes of social conditioning referred to in my comments on Rawls are among the objects of human rights. This

---

[55] The double aspect of education and autonomous action can be traced back to Aristotle, who says on the one hand that persons who are to benefit from instruction in ethics "must have been brought up in good habits" (*Nicomachean Ethics*, 1. 4. 1095b4), and on the other hand that persons are responsible for the development of their own characters through the actions they voluntarily perform (ibid. 3. 5. 1113b3 ff.). The implication of these two sets of passages is that a suitable early upbringing is a necessary condition of autonomous action, but that given this upbringing, what persons do, including the characters they form by their actions, are up to them. On the other hand, without such upbringing persons lack the necessary condition of moral understanding and responsibility. A similar double emphasis can be found in John Dewey, *Human Nature and Conduct* (New York: Henry Holt and Co., 1922), part 1, secs. 1, 2; see also Dewey, *Democracy and Education* (New York: Macmillan Co., 1916), chap. 4. For an application of this double consideration in the sphere of social work see Helen Harris Perlman, "Self-Determination: Reality or Illusion?," in F. E. McDermott, ed., *Self-Determination in Social Work* (London: Routledge and Kegan Paul, 1975), pp. 65–80.

[56] See Roderick Chisholm, "Freedom and Action," in Keith Lehrer, ed., *Freedom and Determinism* (New York: Random House, 1966), pp. 11–44; Richard Taylor, *Action and Purpose* (Englewood Cliffs, N.J.: Prentice-Hall, 1966); Alan Donagan, *Choice: The Essential Element in Human Action* (London: Routledge and Kegan Paul, 1987), chaps. 9, 10. For a representative sample of difficulties, see Irving Thalberg, "How Does Agent Causality Work?" in Myles Brand and Douglas Walton, eds., *Action Theory* (Dordrecht, Holland: D. Reidel Publishing Co., 1976), pp. 213–34.

follows from the general point that the human rights are rights to free-dom and well-being as the necessary goods of human action (3.4). To assure that these goods are made available to all persons, the rights must receive political enactment, so that in this way the social context, which in other respects may limit the possibility of self-fulfillment, serves also to promote it. As I noted above, the rights are both negative and posi-tive. Both sets of rights protect basic well-being. The negative rights are embodied in part in the criminal law, which prohibits murder and other basic harms. The positive rights include the provision of health care for all persons; they also secure phases of additive well-being, in-cluding education and other means of developing productive agency whereby persons, by participating in the economic process, can take care of their other needs. So this returns us to the point that self-fulfillment, while being facilitated by the appropriate context of human rights, must be an achievement of the autonomous individual.

It is important, however, to view the social context in a further way in its relation to self-fulfillment. This context operates not only as an effi-cient cause that helps to generate self-fulfillment; it is also constitutive of self-fulfillment. The self-fulfilled person does not live in isolation; an im-portant part of his being fulfilled consists in his having friends and other associates with whom he can share mutually appreciated values (see also 4.7). Persons make the best of themselves in such relationships; their capacities are enhanced by the sharing and affection that their relation-ships embody. Even if it is true, as Aristotle said, that "when men are friends they have no need of justice"[57] and hence of rights, still friends who attain capacity-fulfillment not only have the freedom and well-being that are the objects of human rights but also help one another to have and maintain these necessary goods of action.

As we have seen, persons who attain capacity-fulfillment effectively accept the human rights embodied in the PGC and hence act as reason-able selves (3.4, 5). Even if, as friends, they make no explicit claims or demands on one another, they still have rights against one another. Rights may be understood, recognized, and fulfilled without having to be demanded as rights. What makes them rights in their primary form is that they are important interests whose protection is due or owed to persons for their own sakes, with correlative duties of respondents. If this protection is not contested by other persons, the primary aspect of their being rights is not thereby removed.[58] So in this way the social context of friendship, while an intrinsic part of self-fulfillment, does not remove the contribution of rights to such fulfillment.

[57] *Nicomachean Ethics*, 8. 1. 1155a25.
[58] For fuller discussion of this point, see Alan Gewirth, *The Community of Rights* (Chi-cago: University of Chicago Press, 1996), pp. 88–90.

If the human rights are given legal enforcement, how does this bear on the point stressed above that the universalist morality grounded in reason does not impose "alien" requirements on the self (3.4)? There seems to be a difficulty here which can be illustrated by a *modus tollens* argument. If the requirements of universalist morality are not alien to the self, then they do not need legal enforcement; but if they do need legal enforcement then presumably they are alien to the self, since such enforcement imposes on the self requirements it would otherwise not accept. Also at issue here is the vaunted autonomy of the reasonable self. If this self is autonomous in acting in accord with other persons' rights, then the rights do not need legal enforcement; but if they do need legal enforcement, then when the self acts in accordance with them it is not autonomous. A similar argument can be raised about human dignity: if persons are subjected to legal compulsions this violates their dignity. In all these arguments there is an apparent conflict between individual and social contexts of self-fulfillment, between the autonomous individual's achievement of capacity-fulfillment and the social-legal enforcement of the human rights that are central to such fulfillment.

While these arguments are plausible, they are not conclusive. Legal enforcement of human rights does not make them alien to the self or violate its autonomy. The enforcement need not take the form of coercive threats for noncompliance; it may instead operate as a coordinating device whereby the disparate efforts of individuals are brought into some sort of harmony. Such coordination may be needed even if persons spontaneously respect human rights, for their correlative duties may be fulfilled in many different ways, some of which may be more effective than others or may conflict with one another in the absence of legal coordination. Moreover, where the human rights have such general objects as freedom and well-being, these objects must be specified in ways that make them more amenable to effectuation. These considerations apply not only to such positive rights as health care, education, and property but also to the rights embodied in the criminal law.

Autonomy and dignity are not violated but are respected when the reasonable self is aware of the need for legal enforcement as serving these objectives. So here again the individual and social contexts of capacity-fulfillment are brought together. Autonomy and political obligation, far from being antithetical to one another, are seen to complement one another. The autonomous person, in setting his own law for his conduct, recognizes that the law must be coordinated with the laws of other autonomous persons in order to fulfill the moral rights to which he adheres as a reasonable person. So in this way the individual emphasis on autonomy is brought into harmony with the social context of legal enactment and enforcement. The ways in which each context contributes to self-fulfillment can serve to remove potential conflicts within self-fulfillment.

Viewed in larger perspective, the distinction between individual and social contexts of self-fulfillment provides a broad dividing line between two important traditions of modern political philosophy. The individualist emphasis is found in such thinkers as Hobbes, Locke, and John Stuart Mill, while the social context figures centrally in Rousseau, Hegel, and Marx. Any brief categorization of the two traditions is bound to be misleading. In particular, it would be false to say that the individualists are concerned only with the self-fulfillment of individuals while the communitarian philosophers who emphasize the social context are concerned rather with the value or health of the society at large. Both traditions are concerned with the self-fulfillment of individuals, but the communitarians, unlike the individualists, uphold two complementary theses about such fulfillment. One thesis is ontological: membership in a community is part of the very identity of individuals; such membership makes them who they are; it is constitutive of their beings and hence of their self-fulfillment as bringing to fruition who they are, both in their aspirations and in their best capacities. While identity, as we saw above (4.3), has an important normative aspect, the second thesis makes the normativeness quite central because it embodies a prescription for social policy. This second thesis holds that whatever is valuable in individual self-fulfillment derives from the social context: as I noted above, the social context not only generates individual self-fulfillment but also is constitutive of it. The individualist tradition upholds the opposite of each of these theses.

While I have already to some extent committed myself to each of the communitarian theses, it is important, for the fuller understanding of self-fulfillment, to note some qualifications. Let us begin from the idea, common to both traditions, that the self-fulfillment of individuals is a central value. This idea may be put as a kind of ethical individualism. Such individualism is not to be equated with ethical egoism; it is not a reflexive relation whereby each individual should aim only at his own benefit. It is rather a social relation bearing on the ends of social policies and institutions in relation to individual self-fulfillment. It is the equal goods and rights of individuals, including their rational autonomy, that constitute the primary objects of human rights as concerned with self-fulfillment and hence the primary criterion or end of moral rightness as set forth in the principle of human rights. Thus, in this respect, the state or society itself is to be viewed as valuationally instrumental, not final; in its primary basis as a morally justified kind of association it is a means to protect the equal rights of individuals, including their opportunities for self-fulfillment, rather than an end or good in itself.

This ethical individualism receives a strong communitarian specification, however, in at least three ways. First, what the principle of human rights justifies is not the egoistic drives of some individuals as against others but rather a whole system of equal and mutually supportive rights and duties as contributory to each individual's self-fulfillment. This system comprises a common good in the distributive sense that goods are common to—equally held by—each of the individual members of the community; but it adds the requirement of mutuality whereby persons not only must refrain from removing from others the necessary goods of action and self-fulfillment but must also help others to obtain these goods when they cannot obtain them by their own efforts. This mutuality requires a context of institutional rules that are central to community. Second, these rules require systematic contributions by all persons, so far as possible, to maintain the society that supports the human rights of each. Rewards in the way both of monetary income and of social recognition are allocated in accord with such social contributions. In certain extreme situations the contributions may require heavy sacrifices by individuals to preserve their communities. Third, the individuals can develop a loyalty to their community, a shared social sentiment of support and advocacy that they experience as contributing to their own self-fulfillment. This loyalty stems in the first instance from the community's securing their own equal individual rights. But it is also fostered by the group interests, the social bonds that persons maintain through their participation in cooperative activities and that make them communal as well as individual beings. So in these ways the ethical individualism of self-fulfillment is reconciled with communitarianism.

If this ethical individualism is not made basic to self-fulfillment, the communitarian emphasis on the social context may pose serious dangers. When the communitarian holds the ontological thesis that the self is "constituted" by its roles in the communities to which it belongs,[59] how far does this constitutiveness go? Does the self's membership in its various communities so exhaust its selfhood that it has no independent resources for deciding among them or even for rejecting some of them in favor either of further communities or of aspects of its own individuality that, at least in some degree, fall outside its various communities? Is the self's freedom and rational autonomy exhausted by its membership in communities? A negative answer to these questions is suggested by

[59] See Michael J. Sandel, *Liberalism and the Limits of Justice* (Cambridge: Cambridge University Press, 1982), pp. 150 ff., 161; Alasdair MacIntyre, *After Virtue* (Notre Dame, Ind.: University of Notre Dame Press, 1981), pp. 204–9; Charles Taylor, "Atomism," in his *Philosophical Papers* (Cambridge: Cambridge University Press, 1985), vol. 2, pp. 187–210.

one communitarian's statement that "*certain* of our roles are *partly* constitutive of the persons we are."[60] These restrictions seem, then, to leave an important place for the individual autonomy of thought and action which is central to self-fulfillment.

What are the precise moral bearings of the self's being constituted by the communities to which it belongs? Must the demands or obligations deriving from the communities always be fulfilled, regardless of their impact on one's rationally grounded moral rights? If Nazism, Stalinism, Maoism, and South African apartheid represent kinds of communities, then the duties that stem from them, far from being mandatory, must be rejected because of their violations of human rights. It must not be forgotten that two of the prime kinds of *koinōnia* or "community" in Western thought, those of Plato and Aristotle, sanctioned slavery and other forms of extreme inequality. It is here that the concept of the reasonable self (3.5) must be invoked as a corrective to such communitarian extremes.

The ethical individualism outlined above offers a way of reconciling the idea that self-fulfillment is a value of individuals with the further idea that the social context contributes vitally both to the generation and to the contents of self-fulfillment. This contribution, far from removing the rational autonomy of individual selves, helps to make it possible.

The aspirations and capacities that enter into self-fulfillment have here been analyzed as requiring the use of reason, in a strictly specified sense, to provide their justified grounds. The justificatory argument has held that aspiration-fulfillment can be an essential source of happiness if it is guided by the resources of personalist morality with its prudential uses of freedom and well-being. The argument has also undertaken to show that the capacity-fulfillment whereby one makes the best of oneself requires the rational recognition and acceptance of the universalist morality of human rights, and that this morality serves to ground such important virtues as self-respect as well as cultural development. Particularist moralities of loyalty to family, friends, lovers, and country have also been shown to be justified by universalist morality. The dignity of humans as rational agents and the spirituality whereby they may transcend the ordinary limits of self-concern have also been invoked to provide further support for the inherent value of self-fulfillment. In these and other ways I have tried to show that self-fulfillment is an eminently worthy ideal not only for individuals but for the social context that helps both to generate it and to provide some of its most valuable contents.

[60] Michael Sandel, *Liberalism and Its Critics* (New York: New York University Press, 1984), p. 5, emphasis added.

5.5. ON VARIETIES OF SELF-FULFILLMENT

Of the many questions that may be raised about my analysis of self-fulfillment, a main one concerns its scope: Does the analysis apply to all human selves? I have tried to do some justice to the diversities among human beings, especially with regard to the different criteria of "best," their different applications to human virtues and values, and their different conceptions of the good life. But a pervasive current in modern thought holds that the relevant diversities are far greater. This is parallel to the charges of parochialism and imperialism that are sometimes leveled against the list of human rights in the Universal Declaration of Human Rights promulgated by the United Nations in 1948.[61] But the possible objections about limited applicability and unduly restricted scope are far more extensive in the whole area of self-fulfillment. We may note at least seven foci among variations of human selves that may be invoked to support these objections. The foci are not mutually exclusive; they have significant extensional overlaps as well as some distinctive features. I shall illustrate them by various examples; but it must be emphasized that the examples are only a very limited selection from a vastly greater range.

1. *Time and History.* Human selves have existed throughout human history, but they have varied greatly in their values and purported virtues. Within the Western tradition itself there are the contrasts between the heroic self-aggrandizement glorified in Homer, the self-abnegation and humility upheld in some phases of Christianity, and the rationalist moderation and egalitarianism of moderns like Locke and Kant, and so forth. Because of such varieties, strong doubts may be raised as to whether the selves that have existed in different times have had sufficient similarities to ground as uniform a conception of self-fulfillment as I have tried to develop here.

2. *Space.* Similar doubts may be raised about geographically separated groups within the same historical era, especially between East and West. The quietism of many Hindus, the aristocratic Confucianism still upheld in parts of China and elsewhere, the vehement entrepreneurship of Western capitalists, are among the many examples of diverse selves whose self-fulfillment would presumably take diametrically opposed forms. Especially emphasized in this connection is the ontological contrast between the "Western" view of persons as atomic individuals and

---

[61] See, e.g., Adamantia Pollis and Peter Schwab, *Human Rights: Cultural and Ideological Perspectives* (New York: Praeger, 1979), chap. 1: "Human Rights: A Western Construct with Limited Applicability," pp. 1 ff.; A.J.M. Milne, *Human Rights and Human Diversity* (Albany: State University of New York Press, 1968), pp. 2–4.

the "Eastern" view of them as constituted by their social groups. This contrast, however, is also found in the West itself in the opposed views of liberal individualists and communitarians.

3. *Gender*. It is frequently held, and not only by feminists, that what constitutes self-fulfillment is very different for men and women. It is by now a very familiar thesis that women fulfill themselves, achieve their "best," through feelings and actions of caring and compassion, in contrast to men's invocations of rights, justice, and autonomy.[62] Especially in view of my emphasis on human rights as the basis of universalist morality, it may be held that my analyses of self-fulfillment partly in terms of rights reflect a too one-sided set of concerns, biased in the direction of males as against females.

4. *Religion*. Many religions reflect different conceptions of the human self, with regard to its nature, destiny, and values. Within Western Christianity itself there is the familiar contrast explored by Max Weber between the cooperativeness and quietism of Catholicism and the competitiveness and industriousness of Protestantism. A more bogus contrast has also been drawn between the "justice" and "righteousness" held to be characteristic of Judaism and the "love" and "self-denial" of Christianity. The thesis of the transmigration of souls in Hinduism stands in contrast to the kinds of immortality upheld in Christianity and elsewhere, as well as to the mortalities accepted in other religions. The agonized conflicts over the right to abortion rest in part on religious disagreements over the status of the fetus as a human self, with its diverse implications for the fetus's right to self-fulfillment. Again it would seem that these religious contrasts should yield diametrically opposed conceptions of self-fulfillment.

5. *Class*. For overworked, poorly paid industrial workers and peasants, self-fulfillment may have drastically different contents from those it has for affluent captains of industry, movie stars, professional athletes, and other wealthy members of more fortunate classes. For an outlook that regards the human condition as an effect of class war, with its reflection of exploitation of the very poor by the very rich, what constitutes self-fulfillment may well vary greatly. Revolutionists who live for the overthrow of the oppressors may well construe their self-fulfillment in ways that are very different from the class they regard as their oppressors.

6. *Ideology*. The contrast just noted also applies to differences of ideology, which also bears in part on the differences regarding religion and gender. Ideology is a matter of world outlook and accompanying values, and this can be reflected not only in economic areas but also in political

---

[62] See Carol Gilligan, *In a Different Voice* (Cambridge, Mass.: Harvard University Press, 1982).

conceptions of the role of government, the contrast between governmental assistance and individual self-reliance, and similar centers of
ideological controversy. Upholders of the welfare state may well have
different conceptions of human selves and their fulfillment from those
maintained by libertarians and some conservatives.

7. *Personality and Temperament.* Playboys are temperamentally different from serious scholars, and what constitutes self-fulfillment for
them reflects these differences. Partly this is also a matter of ideology. If
you think life is a lark wherein one should eat, drink, and be merry, this
will yield a quite different idea of self-fulfillment from a life animated by
a religious or intellectual quest for austere values that demand the ut-
most seriousness of purpose.

8. *Nonhuman Beings.* Although self-fulfillment is focused on the for-
tunes of human beings, it may be held that the focus is drastically incomplete if it does not take account of the relations of humans to other
animals as well as to the whole natural environment. On this view, to live
in accordance with the conditions of nature is required not only because
of the obvious impact of animals and plants and the surrounding atmosphere on human flourishing in the way of food, nonpolluted air, and
similar conditions of human well-being, but also because, as parts of the
whole of living creation, animals and plants deserve respect on their own
account.[63]

These are some of the chief possible objections bearing on the scope
of my account of self-fulfillment; there are others, including those based
on race, which cut across some of the ones listed. To do full justice to
them would require many books, each at least the size of this one. In the
following brief reply, I shall try to suggest two main interrelated points,
without pretending to give anything like the full support each would
require. One point is that insofar as the objections rest on valid conceptions of the human self, they can be accommodated by the ideas that
have entered into my analysis of self-fulfillment. "Accommodate" is a
very general word; I use it here to mean either that these other conceptions can be seen to be instances or species of the general conception of
the self and its values that I have presented here, or that these other
conceptions can be added to my general conception without damaging
its validity. The other point is that insofar as the objections cannot be
thus accommodated, they rest on invalid conceptions of the human self.

The first point reflects the aim I have pursued in this book of showing
how self-fulfillment is based on the necessary conditions of human ac-

---

[63] See Paul W. Taylor, *Respect for Nature: A Theory of Environmental Ethics* (Princeton:
Princeton University Press, 1986); John Kleinig, *Valuing Life* (Princeton: Princeton University Press, 1991).

tion. Because these conditions apply universally to all actual or prospective agents, they cut across the various different conceptions of the self that the objections invoke. All humans are actual, prospective, or potential agents, and the conditions of their agency are sufficiently similar that they apply to the many different humans who have existed through diversities of history, geography, and so forth. This may, of course, be denied; it may be held that the desirability of freedom and the contents of well-being, especially additive well-being, have varied too greatly to justify such a generalization. Nevertheless, the animating ideals of women, proletarians, and others can be plausibly interpreted as strivings toward these generic features of successful action.

It must also be kept in mind that my project here is a normative one. Its aim is not simply to describe the operative ideals of self-fulfillment that persons have actually pursued; although it must take account of those ideals, it aims to subject them to critical evaluation based in part on the necessary goodness of freedom and well-being as the generic features of successful action and on the universalist morality, with its mutuality of rights, of which those features provide the contents.

Many of the other conceptions of the self and its values listed above can be viewed not as rivals of the conception developed here but rather as permissible adjuncts to it that do not damage its validity. This applies, for example, to many "heroic" virtues, to the cooperativeness stressed in some varieties of Catholicism, and to respect for nature.

Also to be kept in mind here is the second point mentioned above, that conceptions of the self that cannot be accommodated by the conception developed here are invalid. This is a central aspect of the normative aim of the present account. Consider, for example, the Hindu practice of suttee, where a widow was required to throw herself on her husband's funeral pyre. Concerning this practice it has been written:

> [S]uttee works, for those for whom it works, as a representation and confirmation through heroic action of some of the deepest properties of Hinduism's moral world. In that world existence is imbued with divinity. The gods have descended to earth. . . . A shared cremation absolves sins and guarantees eternal unity between husband and wife, linked to each other as god and goddess through the circle of future rebirths.[64]

Even if one gives the most benign interpretation of the widow's willingness to commit suicide with this justification, there remains the question of whether her conduct is free or voluntary in the sense that she not only controls her behavior by her unforced choice but has knowledge of

[64] Richard A. Shweder, *Thinking Through Cultures* (Cambridge, Mass.: Harvard University Press, 1991), p. 16.

relevant circumstances, and is to this extent rational. If one views the religious beliefs in question as having been instilled through a long process of enculturation, with no opportunity provided for their critical (including empirical) assessment, then suttee and similar practices are egregious violations of the human rights to freedom and well-being. On this ground the conception of self-fulfillment that includes this practice must be regarded as invalid.[65]

A parallel criticism applies to some of the other conceptions listed above. Consider, for example, the communitarian thesis, which I have considered above (5.4), that the self is partly constituted by its roles in the community to which it belongs. This can be acknowledged as an important psychological and sociological truth that applies to persons in both Eastern and Western societies. But the normative conclusions that are sometimes drawn from it may have diverse impacts on human rights. The thesis may be used to justify duties of mutual assistance that persons owe to one another because of the benefits they have derived from their societies. But the thesis may also be used to uphold a totalitarian submerging of the self in its community, with concomitant violations of human rights. In such cases the communitarian conception of the self, viewed as justifying these violations, is invalid. The invocation of this conception does not pose an acceptable challenge to the conception of self-fulfillment presented here.

While any conclusions about the universality of the conception of self-fulfillment developed here must be tentative, the primacy accorded to freedom and well-being as the generic features of human action and to the universalist moral principle of human rights can, I think, be sustained. These considerations provide at least certain limiting criteria for the validity of conceptions of the self and its fulfillment.

5.6. HUMAN RIGHTS AS BASES OF SELF-FULFILLMENT

In view of the primacy accorded to human rights in my analysis of self-fulfillment, it will be helpful to undertake a more detailed scrutiny of the criticisms that have been brought against the whole concept of human rights. The criticisms have borne especially on the conceptions of the self that are found in doctrines of human rights, so that they are directly relevant to the theses about self-fulfillment that I have developed on the basis of these conceptions. Two main interrelated kinds of criticism have

---

[65]I have developed this point more fully in "Is Cultural Pluralism Relevant to Moral Knowledge?," *Social Philosophy and Policy* 11, no. 1 (winter 1994): 22–43.

been brought against human rights as resting on conceptions of the self. One kind is, broadly speaking, empirical; the other kind is moral.

The empirical criticisms have focused on the point that the conception of the self in doctrines of human rights is too abstract, so that it fails to correspond to the realities of human personhood. The abstractness is said to arise because persons as holders or subjects of human rights are conceived to be so very much alike, and are characterized in such a minimal way, that the concrete differences which give them their fuller identities are overlooked. These overlooked differences generate four sorts of empirical objections, which I shall call the individualistic, the ethnocentric, the historical, and the inegalitarian.

The individualistic objection sets itself in opposition to the atomistic separateness of human selves that it finds in theories of human rights. It says that, according to these theories, the holders of human rights are bare, unrelated individuals who have in common only such general traits as rationality and autonomy. This objection has two parts. One is ontological. It contends that such an individualistic conception of the self overlooks that what exist are not rootless, traditionless, unrelated individuals but rather social or communal beings—that is, persons who exist among, and owe their specifically human traits to, various groups or communities that have diverse histories, traditions, and environing bonds of loyalty. The proper conception of the self, then, is provided by the communitarian thesis that individuals are constituted by the different communities to which they belong: they are not bare humans, but rather Frenchmen, Russians, Chinese, and so forth; Jews, Christians, Moslems, and so forth; and similarly with many other groupings.[66] Hence if rights are to be invoked at all, it is groups or communities, rather than the individuals of traditional rights theories, who can properly be held to have rights; this can be seen quite graphically in the civil rights claims of blacks, women, and other submerged groups, as well as in the nationalist demands of Kurds, Basques, and many other claimants of the right to national self-determination, and so forth.[67]

A second part of the individualistic objection is deontological. It bears on the entities to whom moral precepts are addressed, and who hence have moral obligations or duties. These too are not bare, unencumbered individuals but rather persons who are characterized by their

[66] For this criticism, see above, n. 61.

[67] See Vernon Van Dyke, "The Individual, the State, and Ethnic Communities in Political Theory," in *Human Rights and American Foreign Policy*, ed. D. P. Kommers and G. D. Loescher (Notre Dame, Ind.: University of Notre Dame Press, 1979), pp. 36–62; Van Dyke, *Human Rights, Ethnicity, and Discrimination* (Westport, Conn.: Greenwood Press, 1985).

diverse roles in social institutions, including capitalists and laborers, rulers and ruled, husbands and wives, and so forth through myriad other groupings. The true morality is one of "my station and its duties."[68] The general individualistic objection, then, is that human rights as traditionally conceived overlook or falsify the communitarian setting of the human self, the rich diversity of communal contexts in which persons live and from which they derive their most salient characteristics.

A second, closely related objection is the ethnocentric. This holds that the natural or human rights that have been traditionally upheld in Western culture, at least from Hobbes to the United Nations Universal Declaration of Human Rights, have reflected a conception of the self and of self-fulfillment that is unique to that culture, not universal. In this conception the self is a rational, calculating, autonomous, self-seeking individual, and its corresponding institutions are those of industrial capitalism and, for the most part, political democracy. But such a conception is foreign to much of the world; it is not found in Chinese or Hindu cultures, and even in parts of the world influenced by Catholicism the emphasis is far more on cooperation and community than on competitiveness and individuality. Hence, the pretensions of Western doctrines of human rights to universality and impartiality reflect at best sheer ignorance of how selves are conceived and maintained in other parts of the world, and at worst a sinister kind of cultural imperialism.

A third empirical objection is the historical. In large part this simply puts the preceding objections into a longitudinal or temporal frame. But the historical objection also contends that even within Western culture itself the idea of human rights as the normative property of distinct individuals is a recent development, so that it is far from having the universal, transhistorical validity that is claimed for it. The idea is not found among the ancient Greeks or Romans, nor in Roman law or in medieval thought at least up to William of Ockham in the fourteenth century; and even with Ockham the idea of rights is not extended to any universal human rights. During this whole vast era the dominant conception of the human self was organic rather than individualistic: it viewed humans as organically interrelated members of societies, either small-scale, as with the Greeks, or universal, as with the Romans and medievals.[69]

[68] The locus classicus of this position is F. H. Bradley, *Ethical Studies*, 2nd ed. (Oxford: Clarendon Press, 1927; first published 1876), pp. 160 ff. The position can also be found in Hegel and Marx.

[69] See H.L.A. Hart, "Are There Any Natural Rights?," *Philosophical Review* 64 (1955): 176–77, 182; Isaiah Berlin, *Four Essays on Liberty* (Oxford: Oxford University Press, 1969), p. 129; MacIntyre, *After Virtue*, p. 65 ff. For the denial of the concept of rights in Roman law, see Henry Sumner Maine, *Dissertations on Early Law and Custom* (London: John Murray, 1891), pp. 365–66, 390; Michel Villey, *Leçons d'histoire de la philosophie du*

A fourth kind of empirical objection is the inegalitarian. It points out that none of the empirically discriminable qualities that are held to ground human rights belong equally to all human selves. For example, humans are drastically unequal in the degrees to which they have or use such qualities as rationality, self-control, foresight, and other abilities of agency. Hence, the concept of human selves as possessing relevant equalities fails to provide a realistic basis for human rights (see also 5.1).[70]

From these four empirical objections it is concluded that the idea of human rights depends on so empirically deficient and unrealistic a conception of the self that the idea should be either radically changed or completely rejected. It cannot provide an adequate basis of self-fulfillment.

Let us now turn to the moral criticisms. These are especially continuous with the individualistic objection. One moral objection, which goes back at least to Bentham and Marx, I shall call the egoistic. It holds that the self as conceived in human rights doctrines is purely self-interested, self-centered, and amoral. For since a right involves a claim that a person makes for the support of his or her interests, it evinces a preoccupation with fulfillment of one's own desires or needs regardless of broader social goals; hence it operates to submerge the values of community and to obscure or annul the responsibilities that one ought to have to other persons and to society at large.[71]

A closely related moral objection is the adversarial. The claiming of rights is held to thrust persons into combative and potentially coercive relations whereby each seeks to impose burdens on others for his own benefit. But such claiming can be dispensed with when persons maintain the relations of community that make for social harmony.[72] Hence, the conceptions of the self that enter into the idea of human rights are held to be morally as well as empirically deficient. Self-fulfillment as based on these conceptions cannot be a worthy ideal.

---

droit (Paris: Librairie Dalloz, 1957), chaps. 11, 14; W. W. Buckland, *A Textbook of Roman Law from Augustus to Justinian* (Cambridge: Cambridge University Press, 1963), p. 58.

[70] See F. A. Hayek, *The Constitution of Liberty* (Chicago: University of Chicago Press, 1960), pp. 85 ff.

[71] See Jeremy Bentham, *A Critical Examination of the Declaration of Rights*, in B. Parekh, ed., *Bentham's Political Thought* (New York: Barnes and Noble, 1973), pp. 261, 268 ff.; Karl Marx, *On the Jewish Question*, in R. C. Tucker, ed., *The Marx-Engels Reader*, 2nd ed. (New York: W. W. Norton, 1978), p. 43; Tom Campbell, *The Left and Rights* (London: Routledge and Kegan Paul, 1983), pp. 14–15, 22.

[72] See Richard E. Flathman, *The Practice of Rights* (Cambridge: Cambridge University Press, 1976), pp. 183 ff.; Joseph Raz, "Right-Based Moralities," in Jeremy Waldron, ed., *Theories of Rights* (Oxford: Oxford University Press, 1984), pp. 196–97.

To deal with these important criticisms, we must move back several steps. We must ask such questions as the following: What is the point or purpose of human rights? What contents can they justifiably be held to have? How, if at all, can it be known or proved that there are any human rights, i.e., moral rights that belong equally to all humans?

I have already dealt above with many phases of these questions, especially the last, epistemological question, where I presented a rational justification of the PGC as the universalist moral principle of human rights (3.4). I now want to focus on how the justification bears on the conception of the self, especially as it enters into self-fulfillment. According to this conception, the self is a rational agent, in at least two senses of 'rational': first, it can use conceptual analysis to reason that it has rights to the necessary means for its general pursuits of its ends or purposes; second, it can recognize that consistency requires its acceptance of similar rights on the part of all other actual or prospective agents. Thus all the human rights, those of well-being as well as of freedom, have as their aim that each person have rational autonomy in the sense of being a self-controlling, self-developing agent who can relate to other persons on a basis of mutual respect and cooperation, in contrast to being a dependent, passive recipient of the agency of others. Even when the rights require positive assistance from other persons, their point is not to reinforce or increase dependence but rather to give support that enables persons to be rational and reasonable agents, that is, to control their own lives and effectively pursue and sustain their own purposes without being subjected to domination and harm from others while at the same time they recognize the same rights on the part of others. Such agency is both the metaphysical and the moral basis of human dignity.

I now want to show that when the self is viewed in the context of the PGC as the principle of human rights, the criticisms I outlined above can be given adequate answers. To begin with, let us look at the inegalitarian objection, which argued that it is impossible to justify equal human rights because none of the empirically discriminable qualities that are held to ground the rights are had equally by all human beings. It may be contended, in this regard, that the argument for the PGC has not established that all humans have equal rights, because persons are unequal in their abilities of agency.

It is worth stressing the difficulty of this objection by looking briefly at John Rawls's elaborate justificatory framework for his two principles of justice. This framework has earned all of the criticisms that are embodied in the empirical objections I summarized above. For in holding that the principles of a just constitutional order are those that would be chosen by persons who are in an 'original position' characterized by a 'veil of ignorance' whereby they are completely ignorant of all their particular qualities,[73] Rawls bases his theory of human rights and justice on a conception of the self that is completely abstract because deprived of all the particularities of age, sex, race, class, nationality, religion, and so forth. Thus the basis of Rawls's idea of human rights is not humans as they actually are but unreal phantoms, to whom the individualistic, ethnocentric, and historical objections readily apply.

What, however, of the inegalitarian and egoistic objections? Rawls does, indeed, provide for egalitarian and altruistic, or at least beneficent, aspects of selfhood and social policies. But it is precisely here that we find the serious epistemological difficulties that confront any moral and political philosophy that tries to justify equal rights. For Rawls attains his egalitarian conclusion only by the question-begging device of putting equality into his premises through the same contra-rational assumption of the veil of ignorance as we have seen to succumb to the other empirical objections. In Rawls's theory, it is because persons in the original position are assumed to be completely ignorant of all their particular, individualizing characteristics, and in this way equal, that they are held to choose a constitution that enshrines both equal freedom and the difference principle according to which social and economic inequalities are justified only if they serve to maximize the goods of those who are least advantaged.[74] If such an accusation of question-begging is countered by the claim that the veil of ignorance is a guarantee of fairness because it serves to remove self-partiality, the question still remains of how such a result can be relevant to the actual self-interested human selves to whom Rawls wants his principles to apply. Hence, if equal human rights can be justified only by Rawls's kind of argument, then they rest on a flimsy basis indeed, and the inegalitarian and egoistic objections against human-rights conceptions of the self are given seriously inadequate answers.

Is there any other justificatory theory of human rights, then, that can provide a more adequate conception of the self, and thereby also more adequate replies to the various empirical and moral objections listed above? I think there is: I have tried to provide it above (3.4). I think it is important to emphasize the severe intellectual difficulties of the project. The inadequacies of Rawls's basic framework of the original position can be understood if we recognize how difficult it is to ground a theory of equal human rights. Since humans seem to be unequal in all their empirically ascertainable qualities that are relevant to having rights, how can their moral equality be posited except by holding, as with Locke and Kant, that humans' moral equality rests on some

[73] Rawls, *A Theory of Justice*, pp. 12, 19. 136 ff.
[74] Rawls, *A Theory of Justice*, pp. 75–83.

transcendental, non-empirical basis, or by making, like Hobbes, the transparently false assumption that all men by nature are "equal in the faculties of body and mind,"[75] or by entirely dispensing, like Rawls, with the empirical, particularizing characteristics in respect of which humans are unequal?

It might be thought that an egalitarian basis for human rights can be found in the minimal biological needs to which all participants in the human plight are equally subject. All humans do indeed have equal basic needs for some modicum of food, clothing, and shelter, for protection against physical assault, and so forth. But here there arise at least two questions. One is the question of relevance. Why should it be these features in which humans are equal that serve to ground their rights, as against such unequally distributed features as intelligence, self-control, leadership qualities, and so forth? Second, there is the question of justification, which here takes the form of the famous 'is-ought' problem. Even if all humans are equal in their basic needs, how does this generate any rights to the fulfillment of the needs? Why should one person's needs for certain basic goods ground any duties on anyone else's part? If some persons can fulfill their basic needs without the help of various other persons, then how, if at all, do these latter persons have any title or claim to the help of the former persons?

Let us now consider how the conception of the self that enters in the principle of human rights can serve to answer the criticisms outlined above. To begin with, let us look at the inegalitarian objection. It may be contended, in this regard, that the argument for the PGC has not established that all humans have equal rights, because persons are un-equal in their abilities of agency.

There are at least two replies to this contention (see also above, 5.1). First, the abilities of agency that enter into the argument require only a minimal rationality that is within the reach of all normal human adults. The abilities involve that the agent knows who he is and what he is doing and that he can control his behavior for the sake of his purposes and can recognize elementary forms of consistency and empirical connections. Second, the agent's right-claims are directly based not on his rationality or other abilities of agency but rather on his having purposes he wants to fulfill by acting, and this having of purposes pertains to all actual or prospective agents. Hence, the salient aspects of agency on which the PGC bases the having of rights show that all humans, qua actual or prospective agents, have the rights equally.

What, however, of biological humans who are incapable of any kind of action, such as the famous case of Karen Anne Quinlan as well as

---

[75] Thomas Hobbes, *Leviathan*, chap. 13, init.

infants who suffer from various disabling diseases?[76] If human rights are rights to the generic features of agency, then how can any of these humans have such rights, let alone have them equally with normal human agents? The main answer to this question involves what I have elsewhere called the Principle of Proportionality (3.4): where humans lack the minimal rationality and the abilities that enter into normal agency, they have the generic rights to the degree to which they approach having these abilities.[77] Hence, insofar as there is any biological possibility that the humans in question will attain the normal abilities of agency, they have rights to the fostering of these abilities. Even where such attainment seems hopeless, they still have rights to be helped to attain as close an approximation of these abilities as possible. But in all such cases, as we saw above (5.1), there is an important respect in which the humans in question still have rights that are equal to those of normal humans.

Let us now connect this egalitarian consideration with the individualistic objection. It must be admitted that there is a sense in which the conception of the self that enters into the idea of human rights is indeed abstract. This abstractness, however, as part of the conclusion that all humans have equal rights, is not based, as with Rawls, on an arbitrary or artificial stripping away of all particularizing properties of human selves. In keeping with the ethical individualism discussed above, the argument does not involve any denial of the rich communal attachments and diversities of actual human beings. On the contrary, the argument takes humans as they actually are. What is required is that the features of human selves that are permitted to enter the argument be only those that no agent can consistently reject. The reason for this confinement to the generic features of agency, furthermore, is that, as we have seen, action is the universal relevant context of all the otherwise divergent moral principles and other practical precepts. Hence, the restriction to the generic features of agency, far from being arbitrary in the way of Rawls's and other egalitarian conceptions, is instead based upon the necessary connection of morality with action, and thus upon reason in the most stringent sense. Arbitrariness pertains rather to arguments that insist on tying the possession of human rights, or other moral conclusions, to human characteristics that are not in this way necessarily connected with the context of action. For it is this context that logically must be accepted by every actual or prospective agent, so that its generic features and the moral principle implied thereby cannot be rejected by any agent without self-contradiction. From this it follows that all

---

[76] This question is stressed by Douglas N. Husak, "Why There Are No Human Rights," *Social Theory and Practice* 10 (1984): 125–42. I have replied to Husak in "Why There Are Human Rights," *Social Theory and Practice* 11 (1985): 235–48.

[77] On the Principle of Proportionality, see *Reason and Morality*, pp. 121 ff.

humans equally have the generic rights as a matter of moral principle, regardless of the different communities to which they may belong.

This consideration also bears on the deontological part of the individualistic objection, which holds that moral precepts are addressed not to bare, unencumbered individuals, but rather to individuals as members of groups or communities. Even if it is recognized that individuals are strongly influenced and perhaps even constituted to some degree by the communities to which they belong, this does not alter the fact that moral and other precepts require actions and that, in final analysis, it is individuals who act. As is indicated by such famous phrases as Marx's "Man makes his own history" and "Workers of the world, unite!" it is assumed even in 'social-role' moral precepts that, within limits, action is under the control of the persons addressed by the precepts—that they can have knowledge of relevant circumstances and choose to act in one way rather than in another for purposes or reasons they accept. Thus the generic features of action still apply in such cases.

Let us now consider the historical and ethnocentric objections. It is not true that the idea of equal human rights is a modern Western construct; as I have shown elsewhere,[78] the idea can also be found in ancient and medieval sources as well as in non-Western cultures. This is not surprising, in view of the universality of the generic features of action, on which human rights are based. Thus Aristotle's analysis of human action, which focuses on these features, is just as applicable today as it was in ancient Greece or in the late medieval period when Thomas Aquinas took it over with certain qualifications.[79] This does not mean, of course, that the idea of human rights had the same degree of support in all eras or climates; historical factors strongly influenced the idea's acceptance.

There is another respect, however, in which the historical and ethnocentric objections should be considerably discounted. The fact that the idea of human rights has not been accepted in various eras or climes does not prove that the idea is invalid or that it has limited relevance. For human rights are a normative, not an empirically descriptive conception; they provide a moral model for how persons and groups ought to be regarded and treated even if existing systems of interpersonal and political relations depart from it. Even if 'ought' implies 'can,' the obliga-

[78] See *Reason and Morality*, pp. 98–102. See also A.W.H. Adkins, *Moral Values and Political Behaviour in Ancient Greece* (London: Chatto and Windus, 1972), p. 104 and passim; Brian Tierney, "Tuck on Rights: Some Medieval Problems," *History of Political Thought* 4 (1983): 429–41; Fred D. Miller, Jr., *Nature, Justice, and Rights in Aristotle's "Politics"* (Oxford: Clarendon Press, 1995).

[79] Aristotle, *Nicomachean Ethics*, 3. 1–5; Thomas Aquinas, *Summa Theologica*, 1, 2. qu. 6–17. See Alan Donagan, "Thomas Aquinas on Human Action," in Norman Kretzmann et al., eds., *The Cambridge History of Later Medieval Philosophy* (Cambridge: Cambridge University Press, 1982), pp. 642–54.

tions do not entirely lapse when existing social conditions render them difficult or impossible. For such impossibility is not ingrained in the nature of things if it derives not from material conditions of life but from social practices, institutions, and traditions that can be changed by enlightened forms of individual and social action.

Much depends on which kinds of human rights are in question. The rights fall into a hierarchy according to their needfulness for action and successful action, so that when the rights conflict, those must take precedence that are more needed for action (3.4). Thus primacy belongs to the basic rights whose objects are such segments of basic well-being as life and physical integrity, so that they require for their fulfillment food, clothing, and shelter, but also freedom from torture and similar disabling practices. As this consideration already shows, while the distinction between political and civil rights, on the one hand, and social and economic rights, on the other, may be plausible in some contexts, the basic rights include components from both sides of the distinction. A political system which excludes some persons from available food or subjects them to slavery cannot be excused on the ground that its traditions render impossible any other ways of treating the submerged groups.

Closely connected with such basic rights is the institution of the minimal state, which is characterized by the impartial application of the criminal law. Such law is justified by the PGC insofar as it serves to protect all persons equally against basic and other harms.

There are several steps between such basic rights and the kinds of civil and political rights enshrined in constitutional democracy. Such a democracy is justified by the PGC, in the first instance, because its civil liberties are an important application of the right to freedom. But, in addition, a constitutional democratic government derives its legitimacy from the method of consent, which is an institutional application of the right to freedom. This method may, of course, operate in many different ways. But effective civil liberties are not merely a secondary kind of right, to be installed only after basic well-being has been assured. On the contrary, such liberties also function as important protections for the equal basic rights of all the persons in a society, since, without them, the rulers may favor the basic well-being of some groups at the expense of others.

These considerations also provide a basis for answering the egoistic objection against human rights-based conceptions of the self. While rights do involve claims to the fulfillment of individual interests, the human rights also require of each person that he act with due regard for other persons' interests as well as his own. For the PGC shows that all prospective agents are in the position of being the respondents as well as the subjects of the generic or human rights. Every person, qua actual or prospective agent, has rights to freedom and well-being against all other persons, but every other person also has these rights against him, so that he has correlative duties toward them. The concept of the generic or human rights thus entails a reciprocal universality: each person must respect the rights of all the others while having his rights respected by all the others, so that there must be a mutual sharing of the benefits of rights and the burdens of duties. The human rights hence require mutuality of consideration and thus a kind of altruism rather than egoism. By such a reciprocally universal conception of human rights, each individual's personal claim to and protected property in the necessary goods of action is combined with a responsibility for interests shared in common with all other persons.

In the first instance, the duties required by the universality of human rights are negative: each person must refrain from removing or interfering with the freedom and well-being of all other persons, where this well-being ranges from life and physical integrity to such goods as self-esteem. But the duties are also positive, requiring active assistance in circumstances where one person can help another to avoid drowning, starvation, or other threats to his basic well-being without comparable cost to himself. In broader social contexts where basic well-being and equality of opportunity (which involves additive rights) can be fostered only by collective action, the positive duties require appropriate governmental provisions so far as practicable, but they also require individuals' advocacy of other persons' rights to these goods and taking the necessary steps toward their support, including taxation.

These positive requirements, which should be embodied in appropriate laws and institutions, are not violations (i.e., unjustified infringements) of the respondents' own rights to freedom. For basic rights, such as the rights of starving persons to food, as well as additive rights to such goods as education, take precedence over the rights of other persons to make full use of all their wealth, since the objects of the former rights are more needed for agency than are the objects of the latter rights. Because the principle of human rights entails this requirement of mutual aid where needed and practicable, it is a principle of social solidarity, as against exclusive preoccupation with private interest.

This point also bears on the adversarial objection. As we saw above, rights need not be demanded in order to be rights. But when important rights are threatened or violated, forceful insistence on their fulfillment is quite in order. On the other hand, when mutual rights are effectively recognized, and especially when this recognition is stabilized in effective institutions, the adversarial stance can and often does give way to an atmosphere of mutual respect and civility. An example of this contrast is provided by the relations between whites and blacks in the American

South before and after the passage and enforcement of civil rights legislation. Thus the desiderated removal of adversarial relationships may
well depend on the implementation rather than the rejection of rights.

What emerges from the above considerations is that the principle of
human rights can meet the various objections that have been raised
against it. So I submit that human rights provide a secure foundation for
the conception of self-fulfillment as it has been worked out here.

5.7. ARE SELF-FULFILLMENT AND RIGHTS COMPATIBLE?

A central thesis developed in this book is that, in contrast to self-aggrandizement and self-abnegation, self-fulfillment for each person requires
both that he have the effective human rights to freedom and well-being
and that he be a reasonable self who effectively accepts that all other
persons also have these rights (3.4, 5). In addition to the considerations
discussed in the preceding section, a basic conceptual argument may be
advanced against the soundness of this thesis. The argument holds that
the very ideas of self-fulfillment and of rights are so deeply opposed to
one another that the connections I have here sought to establish between them are invalid and indeed incoherent.

The oppositions in question may be listed under four interrelated
headings. First, self-fulfillment is a teleological concept: it is concerned
with advancing persons' pursuits of their purposes. The concept of
rights, on the other hand, is deontological: it is concerned with setting
limits to those pursuits (see also 2.5). Second, self-fulfillment is a maximalist concept: it aims to advance persons' freedom and well-being as
fully as possible. Rights, on the other hand, are a minimalist concept:
their objects are the minimal but indispensable needs of human life and
agency. Third, self-fulfillment is optional in the double sense that its
pursuit is subject to one's choices and that one is not entitled to demand
of other persons that they advance it for oneself. Rights, on the other
hand, are mandatory in that a right-holder is in a justified position to
demand of other persons that they respect her rights, and also in that it
is impermissible for her to alienate certain of her rights. Fourth, in partial summation of the other oppositions, self-fulfillment is an ideal; as
such, it bears not on what is to be immediately had but rather on a
hoped-for attainment at some future time. Rights, on the other hand,
entail duties, compliance with which must be immediately forthcoming.
So for all these reasons it may be insisted that self-fulfillment cannot co-
herently be held to include the having of rights.

In reply to these oppositions, it must first be recalled that the thesis
that the having of rights is included in self-fulfillment was established by

the use of reason as the best of one's veridical capacities. As being this best, reason is a maximalist concept, and so too is self-fulfillment construed as making the best of oneself, with its content ascertained by the use of reason. But from this it does not follow that all the rights included in self-fulfillment, either as constitutive of it or as instrumental to it, must themselves also be maximalist. On the contrary, some of them, such as the right to basic well-being, are the minimal but essential preconditions of agency. More generally, while self-fulfillment as capacity-fulfillment includes that the self has and respects human rights, these rights do not, in turn, extend to the whole of self-fulfillment. Insofar as freedom and well-being are the necessary goods of action and generally successful action, they are indeed the objects of human rights. But self-fulfillment, while being based on these necessary goods, also has contents that go beyond them; these contents include various abilities, virtues, and institutions that help persons to make the best of themselves. So, on the one hand, rights provide vital opportunities for self-fulfillment; without the human rights, self-fulfillment is enormously difficult, and it is indeed impossible because lacking the effective foundation given by reason. On the other hand, rights do not provide the full content of self-fulfillment; this content derives also from other sources, especially in the ways traced in personalist and particularist moralities. These moralities, as we have seen, do indeed have important relations to human rights, but they also have further contents.

Some objects of the human rights, such as education and other phases of additive well-being, are more than minimalist conditions; they contribute to self-fulfillment because they enable persons in various ways to expand their capacities for purpose-fulfillment. But this does not entail that there are human rights to the whole of self-fulfillment, so that there remains part of the contrast between the maximalist nature of self-fulfillment and the less-than-maximalist contents of rights.

As we have seen, the rights that persons have as part of their self-fulfillment are both negative and positive. The negative rights require that obstacles not be put in the way of persons' attaining self-fulfillment. In this way various discriminations such as those based on race and gender are not to be countenanced. The positive rights include that steps are to be taken to remove the handicaps imposed by poverty and illness, and the abilities of productive agency are to be developed. This involves especially the right to education. Because of this positivity, rights are not solely "deontological" in the sense that identified this exclusively with the setting of limits to persons' pursuits of their purposes. As a right of persons, self-fulfillment requires positive actions by respondents, not only refraining from action, so that the right is teleological as well as deontological. In these ways self-fulfillment is already more than an "ideal" in the sense of a mere hope as posited by the above objection. It is, rather, a direct requirement for the actions of persons toward other persons that they both refrain from hindering and that they provide needed assistance with regard to the proximate necessary preconditions of self-fulfillment.

Persons have correlative duties in connection with each of these requirements. Fulfillment of these duties is also a part of persons' self-fulfillment because it involves that, as reasonable selves, they recognize the requirements imposed on them by the use of reason as the best of veridical capacities.

It is indeed true and important that there is not a positive right to self-fulfillment in the sense that other persons have a duty to directly provide fulfillment for each person. As we saw above in the case of aspiration-fulfillment, the primary agent must be the person herself through her own choices, efforts, and knowledge (2.3); and the same holds for capacity-fulfillment. So a person is not in a justified position to demand of other persons that he be fulfilled or that he achieve self-fulfillment. But he is in a justified position to demand of others that they not put obstacles in the way of his self-fulfillment and that they provide certain kinds of needed assistance toward this end. More generally, self-fulfillment includes having all the human rights, economic and social as well as political and civil, for the two interrelated reasons that the universal having of these rights is justified by reason and the effective having of the rights enables persons to have the conditions and abilities of successful agency. In addition, as we have also seen, persons have duties to themselves in connection with self-fulfillment because the optimal values it embodies set objective requirements for their choices and actions (4.6). In these respects and to this extent self-fulfillment is mandatory rather than optional for each person.

5.8. SELF-FULFILLMENT AND RATIONAL AGENCY

The components of self-fulfillment as developed here have all derived in various ways from the root idea of the self as a rational purposive agent. This hoary idea has had a prominent and indeed a central place in much of moral philosophy since the ancient Greeks, as well as in Freud's positing of the ego over the id. My use of the idea has had much in common with dominant parts of the tradition. The rational agent applies reason to his actions by ascertaining the most efficient means to his ends or purposes; thus he uses hypothetical imperatives in what I have called the "operational" aspect of reason (3.3). In this context reason tries to take as veridical account as possible of relevant facts. It is limited and fallible, although it is also self-critical in seeking to overcome its errors. From Plato to the present reason has been conceived as having this veridical capacity.

Such reason, while it can ascertain the means to various ends, cannot ascertain or establish the moral rightness of the ends themselves. On this crucial question, either reason must be given up in favor of desire or some other 'noncognitive' capacity, or else it must have a further use or aspect. If, moreover, the moral ends that are at issue are to set requirements for action that are binding on all persons as actual or prospective agents, they must be categorical and determinate: categorical in that they are normatively mandatory for all persons regardless of their contingent personal preferences or social conventions; determinate, in that the ends must not admit of mutually inconsistent contents. So reason must here be apodictic, in what I have called its "canonic" aspect (3.3). If reason is to justify such moral ends, it must be through its having justified a supreme moral principle that is itself categorical and determinate.

In my use of reason in its canonic aspect to justify the universalist moral principle of human rights as the supreme moral principle, I have followed what I call a *dialectically necessary method*. The method is *dialectical* (as against assertoric) in that it begins not from statements directly made by the speaker or writer but rather from statements or claims represented as being made by a protagonist or interlocutor—a rational purposive agent—and it then examines what these statements or claims logically imply, involving at some point a contradiction of the original statement. But this contradiction cannot be viewed as definitively establishing the truth or falsity of the original statement—which is the aim of the dialectical method—unless the method is also dialectically *necessary*, in a way I shall shortly spell out. It must be kept in mind throughout that the use of the dialectically necessary method is to be attributed not only to the philosopher but also to the rational agent who pursues and reflects on his purposes.

To see the point I am driving at about necessity, we must note that my invocation of the rational agent differs from most members of the tradition because they use a *dialectically contingent method*. Their method is dialectical in the way just indicated. But their method is dialectically *contingent* in that the statements or "maxims" from which they begin are left open to the optional choices of the protagonists; there is no necessity that these statements be made as against any others. Such a dialectically contingent method can be found from Plato's Socratic dialogues through Kant to John Rawls and R. M. Hare in the present day.

Because of this optionality, the dialectically contingent method cannot justify moral principles that are definitively true, or categorical and determinate. While some of the specific grounds of this disability may vary from one philosopher to another, a general point is the following. If two statements are inconsistent with one another, it is indeed logically impossible to accept or act according to both of them simultaneously. But this still leaves open the question of which member of the inconsistent pair is to be accepted and which rejected. For inconsistency can be avoided and consistency maintained or restored by rejecting either of the two mutually inconsistent statements. Consider, for example, Kant's second main version of the categorical imperative: "Act so that you treat humanity, whether in your own person or in that of another, always as an end and never as a means only."[80] This principle is to be assimilated to Kant's fourth example of the categorical imperative, which sets forth the obligation to help persons who are in dire need. He says that the maxim that one should refrain from giving such help cannot be willed to be a universal law, "because such a will would contradict itself."[81] For the universalized maxim that no one in dire need is ever to be helped contradicts the refrainer's own will that he should be helped when he is in dire need.

But Kant's use of a dialectically contingent method severely limits the cogency of his argument. It is indeed true that one cannot consistently accept both (*a*) "No one in dire need should ever be helped" and (*b*) "I, when in dire need, should be helped." In the dialectically contingent method, however, it is open to an interlocutor, depending on the relative strength of various of his contingent inclinations or ideals, to accept either *a* or *b*.[82] The method thus provides no conclusive ground for accepting or rejecting either statement of the inconsistent pair. For this reason, the judgments and principles that can be justified by the dialectically contingent method are not determinate; nor are they categorical, because one can accept or reject one or another principle by consulting or shifting one's personal inclinations or ideals.[83]

[80] Kant, *Foundations of the Metaphysics of Morals*, sec. 2, trans. L. W. Beck (Indianapolis, Ind.: Library of Liberal Arts, 1959), p. 46; Akad. ed., p. 428.

[81] Ibid., p. 42; Akad. ed., p. 424.

[82] See Henry Sidgwick (*The Methods of Ethics*, 7th ed. [London: Macmillan, 1907], p. 389n.), who says that a man might be of such independent spirit "that he would choose to endure any privations rather than receive aid from others." Such an idiosyncratic but empirically possible "choice" is a species of what R. M. Hare has called the "fanatic," a person who is "moved" to adhere to some principle or ideal even if its application to himself goes against his self-interested inclinations. See R. M. Hare, *Freedom and Reason* (Oxford: Clarendon, 1963), pp. 104 ff. I have dealt with the fanatic in *Reason and Morality*, pp. 96–97. In both Sidgwick and Hare these refusals of help even in cases of dire need are presented as being based on contingent or optional choices. For a valuable reply to Sidgwick, see Marcus G. Singer, *Generalization in Ethics* (New York: Alfred A. Knopf, 1961), pp. 272–74.

[83] For a fuller discussion of this point, see *Reason and Morality*, pp. 166–68.

These deficiencies directly apply to Kant's principle that humans should always be treated as ends in themselves, never merely as means. For insofar as the principle is held to be justified on the basis of his first version of the categorical imperative, it has not yet been shown that the principle can avoid the contingency and variability found in the maxims from whose universalization Kant tries to derive a contradiction and thereby to justify the principle that humans should always be treated as ends. By his use of a dialectically contingent method, he cannot definitively justify, by an appeal to statement *b* above, the rejection of statement *a* and thereby the rationally necessary acceptance of the principle that persons must always be treated as ends, never merely as means. For some person, on the basis of principles or maxims to which he may adhere as a matter of optional choice, may reject statement *b*. To put it another way, the "contradiction in the will" that Kant aims to exhibit cannot attain the conclusiveness he intends insofar as the "will" in question is contingent in its content. For this reason, when the "rational agent" is interpreted as using a dialectically contingent method, her rationality cannot securely establish any moral principle, including the connection of self-fulfillment with universalist morality.

In contrast, the rationality I have used in its canonic aspect to establish the supreme moral principle with its intrinsic relation to self-fulfillment is what I have called a dialectically necessary method. This involves that logical necessity attaches to the content as well as to the form of moral argument, including the argument to the supreme principle of morality and other moral principles. The statements from which the argument begins are not left open to the optional choices of protagonists; on the contrary, they are statements that every person logically must accept simply by virtue of being an actual or prospective agent. The argument proceeds to show that, by accepting these agency-necessitated statements, every actual or prospective agent is logically committed to accept a certain supreme principle of morality (3.4). Any agent contradicts herself if she rejects the principle; but this stringent irrationality cannot be evaded, as can arguments using dialectically contingent methods, by shifting or otherwise consulting one's optional inclinations or ideals. On the contrary, because the very contents of the statements that enter into the argument logically must be accepted by any (every) agent, on pain of self-contradiction, the principle that emerges from the argument logically must also be accepted by every agent, so that the principle is apodictically rational and thus categorical and determinate.

An important reason for confining the argument to such logically necessary practical contents is the following. Both in their history and in their contemporary status moral principles are involved in fundamental conflicts about how persons ought to act, especially toward one another.

Now if, amid these competing principles, there are statement contents that every agent logically must accept simply by virtue of being an agent, then this should bring a halt to the conflicts of principles in a rationally required way.

As these considerations indicate, in the dialectically necessary method the formal necessity of consistency must be supplemented by the substantive or material necessity that is to be found in the idea of action or agency. This idea is materially necessary for two main reasons. First, all moral and other practical precepts, amid their varying contents, are concerned, directly or indirectly, with actions, with telling persons how they ought to act, especially toward one another, so that action or agency is the necessary context of all morality, as well as of practice in general. Second, all persons are actual, prospective, or potential agents, and no person can reject from himself the whole context of agency, except, perhaps, by committing suicide; and even then the steps he takes to achieve this purpose would themselves be actions.

The material necessities here indicated do not have the kind of Leibnizian absoluteness of holding in all possible worlds, in the sense in which the "possible" reflects the infinity of logical possibilities. Rather, these necessities reflect the constraints of the whole relevant context in this existing world. But within this context logical necessity obtains when the necessary contents of action are predicated of agents. Now, as we have seen, the necessary contents that are used by the dialectically necessary method consist in the generic features that characterize all action and generally successful action. Because they are such generic features, they logically must be accepted by every actual or prospective agent. If any agent rejects these features, then he rejects the necessary conditions that are proximately involved in his agency, so that he is caught in a contradiction.

These necessary conditions of action are thus on a quite different footing from the contingent, variable attitudes or purposes that may enter into Kant's maxims. For the latter, as "subjective principles of volition," may reflect the subject's "ignorance or inclinations."[84] In contrast to these variable contents, the dialectically necessary method bases the argument for the supreme principle of morality on the necessities of the generic features of action that logically must be accepted by every agent, regardless of his contingent inclinations or ideals. As we have seen, these generic features are freedom and well-being, which are, respectively, the procedural and the substantive necessary conditions of action and generally successful action. It is on the basis of this necessary content that the argument to the supreme principle of morality

[84] Kant, *Foundations*, secs. 1, 2, pp. 17n., 38n.; Akad. ed., pp. 400n., 421n.

establishes that every actual or prospective agent logically must accept the principle. The general line of the argument is that, by virtue of having to accept these logically necessary conditions of agency for himself, every agent is logically committed to accept that he has rights to these conditions and that all other actual or prospective agents also have these rights.

From these considerations it can be seen why the rational agent proceeds by the use of the dialectically necessary method. As rational, he seeks truth and wants to avoid arbitrariness. The surest way to attain these values is by adhering, in the canonic aspect of reason, to what is necessarily connected with the context of action to which, as an agent, he is logically committed. In this way his thinking is restricted to what he, like every other purposive agent, is logically or rationally justified in claiming from within his conative standpoint as seeking to achieve his purposes.[85] It is by the use of a dialectically necessary method that the rational agent in my above argument has derived the components of self-fulfillment, including their various relations to the three types of morality. In this way I have tried to show that self-fulfillment as capacity-fulfillment has a firm rational basis.

The total self that gets fulfilled consists in more than reason alone. As we have seen, for self-fulfillment reason must be applied to action, and action especially involves the conativeness whereby agents pursue purposes they regard as good. This conativeness is not, as such, an intellectual or "cognitive" matter. Without such conativeness or purposiveness, the concepts of goods and rights would not enter the justificatory argument for universalist morality. It is this conativeness that underlies the prescriptiveness whereby rational self-fulfillment sets requirements for action. Because of this conativeness, agents regard their purposes as good and claim rights to the necessary conditions of their fulfillment. Thus both the right-claims and the correlative 'ought'-judgments have prescriptive force for agents, who advocate or endorse the actions to which the 'oughts' are attached. As we have also seen, it is the purposiveness of human action that underlies the ascription of dignity to human agents and that provides the general answer to the question of the meaning of life (5.1, 3).

There is, however, a basic unification of this purposiveness with reason, in at least three ways. First, operational reason seeks out the means to the fulfillment of purposes. Second, reason in its canonic aspect justifies the universalist moral principle, which serves as an ultimate criterion of the rightness of ends or purposes themselves. Third, the awareness of

[85] For fuller discussion of these points, see *Reason and Morality*, pp. 42–47, 158–61.

the purposiveness of action and of its normative implications becomes available to the rational agent both empirically and through the conceptual analysis of action, which analysis is a form of deductive reasoning. Hence the prescriptive and other 'noncognitive' elements of value and morality are subsumed under and are used by the cognitive elements of deductive and inductive rationality, including especially reason in its canonic aspect.

An important feature of the dialectically necessary method as developed here is that it uses the veridical criteria of "theoretic reason" in a practical subject-matter, the context of action and its moral requirements. In this respect, then, there is no difference between the theoretic and the practical uses of reason. The rational agent, using the canons of reason, can ascertain that he and all other actual or prospective agents have the generic rights as well as the correlative duties. The rational agent is partly motivated to accept these rights because they are logically derived from the necessary goods of action to whose pursuit he, as a self-interested person, is rationally motivated.

Besides these rights of universalist morality, it is also by reason, in both its canonic and its operational aspects, that the contents of personalist and particularist morality are elicited. Having found freedom and well-being to be the necessary goods of action, reason also ascertains that these necessary goods are the central components of a good life as upheld by personalist morality. And it is by reason in a related way that the contents of particularist morality are ascertained, by seeing how the freedom and the well-being components of the principle of human rights serve to justify the loyalties to family, country, and other restricted objects of one's preferential affection.

In all these contexts reason is put to practical use to set forth the contents of various parts of self-fulfillment construed as a final end of aspirations and capacities. Even if the attainment of self-fulfillment is best assured when it is a "by-product" of other goals to which one is directly committed (2.4), it is still valued for itself, because it consists in carrying to fruition, by a self-knowing, self-reflective process, one's worthiest capacities. To fulfill oneself is not only to know the truth about oneself but also to control and value what this truth will be by adhering to the highest standards both of universalist morality and of the good life as developed in personalist and particularist moralities.

The argument I have presented here for the contents of self-fulfillment as such a final end belongs in important part to what may be called the "Kantian" tradition. The salient aspect of this tradition is that it undertakes to establish what is morally right on the basis of apodictic rationality, that is, the appeal to contradiction as a way of validating some moral judgments and invalidating others. To this extent the tradition fits into the dialectical part of what I have called the dialectically necessary method. Other philosophers, including Aristotle, have also sought to establish the rationality of final ends, but their rationality has not been apodictic in the way previously indicated.[86]

It will be helpful if we confront this Kantian thesis about the rationality of final ends with the classic objections forcefully presented by David Hume against the very possibility of such rationality. I shall here briefly consider two of Hume's arguments, together with my Kantian replies.

One argument is that because a final or ultimate end is desired for its own sake or "on its own account," no further reason can be given for desiring it, so that "ultimate ends . . . can never, in any case, be accounted for by reason."[87] The "reason" that is here in question is probabilistic or inductive (because a form of means-end and hence cause-effect reasoning), and the "end" is desiderative, not subsistent. The Kantian reply is that an ultimate end can be accounted for by reason because the principle that human beings ought to be treated as ends in themselves, as having the generic rights, can be given a stringently necessary or apodictic proof, since its denial involves self-contradiction.

A second, closely related argument of Hume is that desired ends move persons to action, but "reason, being cool and disengaged, is no motive to action"; "reason alone can never be a motive to any action of the will."[88]

There is a striking contrast here to Kant, who frequently emphasizes the motivative, practically efficacious power of reason: "Reason is given to us as a practical faculty, i.e., one which is to have an influence on the will"; "reason's proper function must be to produce a will good in itself"; "reason issues inexorable commands without promising anything to the inclinations"; "reason of itself and independently of all appearances commands what ought to be done"; "the conception of an objective principle, so far as it constrains a will, is a command (of reason)"; "an end . . . is given by reason alone"; "reason of itself alone determines conduct."[89]

To deal with this contrast, three main points are especially important. First, Hume puts his thesis about motivation in such terms as these:

[86] For fuller development of this point, see my essay, "Can Any Final Ends Be Rational?," *Ethics* 102 (October 1991): 66–95.

[87] Hume, *Enquiry concerning the Principles of Morals*, app. 1 (ed. L. A. Selby-Bigge [Oxford: Clarendon Press, 1962]), p. 293.

[88] Ibid., p. 294; and *Treatise of Human Nature*, 2.3.3, p. 413, ed. L. A. Selby-Bigge (Oxford: Clarendon Press, 1928).

[89] Kant, *Foundations*, secs. 1, 2, trans. Beck, pp. 12, 21, 24, 30, 45; Akad. ed., p. 396, 405, 408, 413, 427.

"*Reason alone* can never be a motive to any action of the will"; "*reason of itself* is utterly impotent" to "produce or prevent actions."[90] Even if we recognize that the "reason" here in question is not an entity by itself but a certain power of human beings, the crucial point is that when Hume talks of "reason alone" or "reason of itself" he is making a kind of abstraction that guarantees the practical impotence of the reasoning power. For even in such an elementary act of reason as that 2 added to 3 equals 5, the inference is not done by "reason alone" or "of itself"; on the contrary, some sort of conative or volitional operation is required whereby the inferring person wants or chooses to perform this reasoning operation and to accept its result.[91] Hence, Hume's reference to "reason of itself," in seeming to contrast a purely cognitive or intellectual faculty with a practical or action-producing one, serves to falsify even acts of reasoning themselves.

It must be noted that in the passages quoted above from Kant, he too refers to "reason of itself" and "reason alone." But in so doing he is not, like Hume, contrasting reason with will or desire; instead, he, is contrasting reason with "inclinations" and "appearances," as operating in the phenomenal sphere to set criteria for action that are different from rational criteria. Hence, Kant does not, like Hume, abstract from the volitional operations that are intrinsic parts of the reasoning process itself. A parallel consideration applies to the argument for the PGC, except that the relevant contrast is between rationally necessary and contingent contents.

A second point is that for Kant, as for Hume, reason is a second-order power in that it takes over contents gotten from other sources, including human desires, choices, or actions, and it then critically evaluates or develops these contents on the basis of rational criteria. But Hume confines this rationality to *inductive* reason, including its beginning point in empirical facts. He holds that inductive reason can influence passions and actions by examining their assumptions about what objects exist or what means will be causally efficacious to desired ends. Thus he says, "The moment we perceive the falsehood of any supposition or the insufficiency of any means, our passions yield to our reason without any opposition."[92] On this view, even an ultimate end could be irrational if the person who wanted it was making a factual mistake about its constituents or its possibility. But none of this would affect the question of the moral quality of the end; it would not serve to establish what ends morally ought to be desired.

[90] Hume, *Treatise*, 2.3.3; 3.1.1, pp. 413, 457 (emphases added).

[91] Compare the doctrine of Descartes (*Meditations*, 4) that every judgment involves a volitional as well as an intellectual component.

[92] Hume, *Treatise*, 2.3.3, p. 416.

Kant's important addition in this context is to show that *deductive* rationality can also provide criteria for evaluating the rightness of actions, and that these criteria apply to ultimate moral ends as well as means. Reason can "command" the will by setting rational requirements of logical consistency for the universalized maxims of actions; to say that reason "commands" that these requirements be fulfilled is to say that reason provides the criteria for the rational justificatory adequacy of the maxims. A parallel consideration applies to the PGC.

A third point, which follows from the first two, is that rational persons are motivated to act as reason requires. This is the "internalist" point that motivation is internal to reason. Hume himself would have to admit that when acts of deductive mathematical reasoning eventuate in contradictions, the reasoners are motivated to reject such conclusions. Since, for the Kantian doctrine, deductive rational criteria apply to the practical ends that persons set for themselves, their wills can be similarly motivated. This is not to deny that there are also other, more specifically moral motivations for acting in accordance with, and even for the sake of, moral requirements. These derive in important part from their initial basis in the necessary goods toward whose fulfillment all agents are necessarily motivated.[93]

It is through the practical use of reason that in self-fulfillment reason organizes and coordinates the other parts of the total self, as we also saw above in one of the models of duties to oneself (4.6). The emotional and conative elements, while making their own contribution to self-fulfillment, are subjected to the truth-ascertaining power of reason to determine how they should contribute, in a sound, justified way, to the self's pursuits of its purposes and its whole way of life. Self-fulfillment intrinsically includes and requires this coordinating, integrative operation of reason within the self as a whole. As a long tradition from Plato to Freud has emphasized, mental, including emotional, health is dependent on such rationality. This contributes strongly to one's making the best of oneself.

What has emerged from the considerations in this book is that although in important respects self-fulfillment is never completely attainable, it can be approximated in a social context that makes adequate provision for one's efforts as guided by reason. Just as operational reason is confronted by uncharted gulfs in its quest for knowledge of one's aspirations and capacities, so the capacities that figure in making the best of oneself always have further reaches that are never exhausted. In this respect, then, self-fulfillment is far more a process than a finished product. Nevertheless it need not be, as in the myth of Sisyphus, an unending

---

[93] See the section "Motivation and Rationality" in *Reason and Morality*, pp. 190–98.

series of fruitless behaviors; it can use its freedom and well-being in ways that positively develop both its capacities to achieve desirable purposes and its actual achievement of these purposes. There is no climactic nirvana, but there can be sequences of self-improvement that overcome the effects of alienation and achieve cherished values. One's best is never finalized, but it can be more fully approached.